The Legitimacy of the European Union after Enlargement

The Legitimacy of the European Union after Enlargement

Edited by
Jacques Thomassen

UNIVERSITY PRESS

OXFORD
UNIVERSITY PRESS

Great Clarendon Street, Oxford OX2 6DP
Oxford University Press is a department of the University of Oxford.
It furthers the University's objective of excellence in research, scholarship,
and education by publishing worldwide in

Oxford New York

Auckland Cape Town Dar es Salaam Hong Kong Karachi
Kuala Lumpur Madrid Melbourne Mexico City Nairobi
New Delhi Shanghai Taipei Toronto

With offices in

Argentina Austria Brazil Chile Czech Republic France Greece
Guatemala Hungary Italy Japan Poland Portugal Singapore
South Korea Switzerland Thailand Turkey Ukraine Vietnam

Oxford is a registered trade mark of Oxford University Press
in the UK and in certain other countries

Published in the United States
by Oxford University Press Inc., New York

© The several contributors 2009

The moral rights of the authors have been asserted
Database right Oxford University Press (maker)

First published 2009

All rights reserved. No part of this publication may be reproduced,
stored in a retrieval system, or transmitted, in any form or by any means,
without the prior permission in writing of Oxford University Press,
or as expressly permitted by law, or under terms agreed with the appropriate
reprographics rights organization. Enquiries concerning reproduction
outside the scope of the above should be sent to the Rights Department,
Oxford University Press, at the address above

You must not circulate this book in any other binding or cover
and you must impose the same condition on any acquirer

British Library Cataloguing in Publication Data
Data available

Library of Congress Cataloging in Publication Data
Data available

Typeset by SPI Publisher Services, Pondicherry, India
Printed in Great Britain
on acid-free paper by the
MPG Books Group, Bodmin and King's Lynn

ISBN 978–0–19–954899–6

Contents

List of Figures ix
List of Tables xi
Preface xiii
Contributors xv
Abbreviations xx

1. The Legitimacy of the European Union after Enlargement 1
   Jacques Thomassen
   1.1. Introduction 1
   1.2. The legitimacy of the European Union: A Union of, by, and for the people? 4
   1.3. Political representation in the European Union 9
   1.4. The legitimacy of the European Union: The support of the people 17
   1.5. The European Election Studies project 19

Part I: Political Representation in the European Union 21

2. The European Party System after Enlargement 23
   Hermann Schmitt and Jacques Thomassen
   2.1. Introduction 23
   2.2. The development of the EU party system 25
   2.3. The party systems of Central and Eastern Europe: Do they fit in? 27
   2.4. Dimensions of party competition in the European Union before enlargement 29
   2.5. Dimensions of party competition in the European Union after enlargement 33

Contents

2.6. The competitiveness and cohesion of the European party system after enlargement	35
2.7. Conclusion	39
Appendix	42

3. Light at the End of the Tunnel: Towards a European Public Sphere?   44
Claes de Vreese, Hajo Boomgaarden, Susan Banducci, and Holli Semetko

3.1. Introduction	44
3.2. A European public sphere?	45
3.3. European elections: The emergence of Europeanized national public spheres?	50
3.4. Data: The 2004 European election media study	53
3.5. Results	54
3.6. Conclusions	62

4. Towards a European Electorate: One Electorate or Many?   65
Wouter van der Brug, Mark Franklin, Marina Popescu, and Gábor Tóka

4.1. Introduction	65
4.2. Theoretical expectations	66
4.3. Differences in value orientations	69
4.4. Determinants of party choice	78
4.5. Conclusion: One electorate or many?	86
Appendix	89

5. Enlargement and the 'Normal' European Parliament   93
Erik Voeten

5.1. Introduction	93
5.2. The effects of enlargement on politics in the European Parliament	95
5.3. Partisan and national divisions in the European Parliament	99
5.4. Ideological structures	103
5.5. Conclusion	110
Appendix	112

Part II: Political Support for the European Union — 115

6. The Level of Decision Making: The Preferences of the
   Citizens after Enlargement — 117
   Lieven De Winter, Marc Swyngedouw, and Bart Goeminne
   6.1. Introduction — 117
   6.2. The debate on the level of decision making in the EU — 118
   6.3. Citizens' level of governance preferences over time,
        policy sector, and space — 122
   6.4. Hypotheses on citizens' preferences for level of
        government — 131
   6.5. The level of decision making: Explaining the
        preferences of citizens — 135
   6.6. Conclusion — 137

7. Policy Performance and Support for European Integration — 142
   Slava Mikhaylov and Michael Marsh
   7.1. Introduction — 142
   7.2. Previous research — 143
   7.3. Public perceptions of benefits — 146
   7.4. Explaining diversity and change — 153
   7.5. Analysis — 154
   7.6. Conclusions — 158
   Appendix 1 — 161
   Appendix 2 — 162

8. Trust in Political Institutions — 165
   Bernhard Wessels
   8.1. Introduction — 165
   8.2. Trust in institutions: Concept, hypotheses, and prior
        research findings — 167
   8.3. The development of trust in national and European
        political institutions — 169
   8.4. Trust in national and European political institutions after
        Eastern enlargement — 175
   8.5. Discussion — 182

9. European Citizenship and Identity after Enlargement — 184
   Jacques Thomassen and Hanna Bäck
   9.1. Introduction — 184
   9.2. European identity and European citizenship — 185
   9.3. Conceptualizations, operationalizations, and
        methods — 187

Contents

9.4. An empirical analysis of citizenship and trust	191
9.5. In conclusion	203

10. Legitimacy and Electoral Abstention in European
    Parliament Elections   208
    Cees van der Eijk and Hermann Schmitt

10.1. Introduction	208
10.2. Previous research	209
10.3. Abstentions and orientations to the EU: A first look	213
10.4. EU legitimacy beliefs amidst other factors	216
10.5. If not legitimacy beliefs, what then causes low turnout in EP elections?	219
10.6. Conclusions and reflections	220

11. In Conclusion: The Legitimacy of the European Union after
    Enlargement   225
    Jacques Thomassen

11.1. Introduction	225
11.2. The European Union and representative democracy	226
11.3. The legitimacy of the European Union: The support of the people	229
11.4. The effects of enlargement on the legitimacy of the European Union	232
11.5. The quality of political representation in the European Union	234
11.6. Party government as a cure for the democratic deficit of the EU?	236
11.7. In conclusion	241

References	245
Index	263

List of Figures

1.1.	Basic elements in the process of linkage	11
2.1.	Party positions in Eastern Europe and party positions in Western Europe	34
2.2.	Voter perceptions of party positions	36
2.3.	Party positions as estimated from expert codings of manifestos	36
2.4.	Party positions from expert surveys	36
2.5.	Voter perceptions of party positions	38
2.6.	Party positions as estimated from expert codings of manifestos	38
2.7.	Party positions from expert surveys	38
3.1.	Visibility of EU news in television newscasts, 1999 and 2004	55
3.2.	Visibility of EU news on newspaper front pages, 1999 and 2004	56
3.3.	Actors in EU stories, by country	58
3.4.	Actors in EU stories in old and new member states	59
3.5.	Location of EU news (television and newspapers), by country	60
3.6.	Explicit references to the European election campaign in the news, by country	61
3.7.	Explicit turnout prediction in the news, by country	62
5.1.	Proportion of variation in roll-call voting explained by nationality and party group	100
5.2.	Percentage of RCVs on which MEPs vote against party group but with national delegation plurality	102
5.3.	Distribution of MEP ideal points in the sixth parliament (based on optimal classification)	104
5.4.	APRE of one-, two-, and three-dimensional spatial models to roll-call voting in the five EPs (based on non-parametric model)	105
5.5.	Within-party scalings of Eastern European and EU15 MEPs	109

List of Figures

7.1.	Time-series cross-section plot for average benefit perception in EU member states (in a year with standard errors shown by vertical bars)	147
7.2.	Perceptions of benefit from EU membership in the founding six members and average perception in the EU25	148
7.3.	Perceptions of benefit from EU membership in the countries of the first-, second-, and third-accession waves and average perception in the EU25	149
7.4.	Perceptions of benefit from EU membership in the countries of the fourth accession wave and average perception in the EU25	150
7.5.	Average perceptions of benefit from EU membership in the founding six members and in countries of subsequent accession waves	151
7.6.	Standard deviation in perceptions of benefit from EU membership within founding six members, within subsequent accession waves, and overall in the EU25	152
7.7.	Estimation results of the utilitarian model after each accession wave	156
8.1.	Trust in national and European political institutions	171
8.2.	Trust in institutions in the old and new member states, 2004	176
8.3.	Difference in support for national and EU institutions – parliament and 'government'	177
8.4.	Differences in trust in national and European institutions between old (EU15) and new member states (NMS)	181
9.1.	Successive enlargements and feelings of European citizenship	194
9.2.	Trust in other peoples	197

List of Tables

1.1.	Three dimensions of democratic legitimacy and objects of support	3
2.1.	Enlargement and EP group membership	28
2.2.	Ideological positions of political parties represented in the 2004 European Parliament as predicted by group affiliation (analyses of variance – figures are R squares)	37
3.1.	Top five issues within EU news stories (both television and newspapers)	57
4.1.	Regression models for the explanation of left–right self-placement with interaction terms	71
4.2.	Political attitudes in established and consolidating democracies among the supporters of the three main EP party groups	76
4.3.	Regression models for the explanation of party preference without interaction terms	82
4.4.	Regression models for the explanation of party preference with interactions (all countries)	84
5.1.	Regression of expert judgments of national party positions on MEP ideal points (robust standard errors clustered on national party membership)	107
6.1.	Perceived and preferred levels of decision making for most important problem per country and country groups in 2004 (22 countries)	124
6.2.	Most important problem and perceived and preferred levels of decision making per policy sector in 2004 (18 countries)	127
6.3.	Perceived and preferred levels of decision making for most important issue in 1994, 1999, and 2004 (11 countries)	129
6.4.	Degree of endogeneity of most important problems in 1994 and 2004 in percentages (11 countries)	130
6.5.	Preferred level of government (European, national, regional) for solving most important problem (multinomial logistic model; all 18 countries combined)	136
7.1.	Utilitarian model of EU support	155

List of Tables

8.1.	Questions on trust in institutions in the Eurobarometer (EB) surveys	170
8.2.	Expectation regarding the correlates of the development of trust in longitudinal perspective	173
8.3.	Regression of trust in representative institutions on economic performance and length of EU membership, 1993–2006	174
8.4.	A utilitarian model of trust in institutions	180
9.1.	Correlations between items on citizenship	191
9.2.	Attitudes on European citizenship (per cent pro-European)	192
9.3.	Regression analysis with European identity as dependent variable	196
9.4.	Levels of trust by admission year	199
9.5.	Levels of trust by geographic location	200
9.6.	Regression analysis with trust as dependent variable, 474 country-dyads	202
10.1.	Turnout at elections for the European Parliament, 1979–2004	210
10.2.	Difference in the proportion of abstentions between those who consider the EU a 'bad' thing and those who consider it a 'good' thing (in percentage points)	214
10.3.	Explanatory power of EU legitimacy beliefs for analysing electoral abstention in 2004 EP election	215
10.4.	Proportion correct predictions of electoral participation versus abstention	218

Preface

This book is the major publication of the European Elections Studies Group on the 2004 European elections. The 2004 study is the latest in a long line of European Election Studies stretching back to 1979. Each of these studies led to a great number of publications, including a main book publication. Previous volumes in this series are *Choosing Europe?*, edited by Van der Eijk and Franklin (1996); *Political Representation and Legitimacy in the European Union*, edited by Schmitt and Thomassen (1999); and *European Elections and Domestic Politics*, edited by Van der Brug and Van der Eijk (2007). Each of these volumes has a specific focus and together they reflect the evolution of the European Elections Studies from 'just' an election study project to an extensive research programme on the functioning of democracy in the European Union.

The objective of this book is to assess the legitimacy of the European Union after the 2004 enlargement. The legitimacy of the Union is often said to be failing for two major reasons: first, because the political institutions of the Union hardly meet well-established criteria of democratic governance, and second, because of a lack of support of the mass public for the European project. In 2004, the Union was enlarged with an unprecedented number of new member states. According to many observers this operation would undermine the legitimacy of the Union even further, not only because the integration of ten new member states with the peculiarities of their political systems would be a major challenge for the incipient system of representative democracy in the European Union, but also because of a lack of support for this major operation among the mass public.

In this volume, we try to assess the effect of the 2004 enlargement on the legitimacy of the Union, taking into account both the democratic quality of its institutions and the political support of the European people.

As in previous studies, one major component of the 2004 European Election Study is a post-election survey among a random sample from the electorate. Such a survey was funded and conducted by national

Preface

study directors in twenty-four of the twenty-five member states. Their contribution is gratefully acknowledged (for a full list of principal investigators, national study directors, and further details of the study design, see http://www.ees-homepage.net). In addition to these surveys, the 2004 study also included a study of party manifestos and a media study.

The 2004 study was supported by CONNEX, a Network of Excellence for Research into EU governance funded under the 6th Framework Programme (see http://www.connex-network.org). CONNEX facilitated data integration and supported several of our authors' meetings. Additional funding for our meetings in Enschede and Dublin was provided by the University of Twente and the Institute for International Integration Studies at Trinity College, respectively. The valuable comments by the participants in these meetings are gratefully acknowledged.

I did much of the editorial work when I was a Fernard Braudel fellow at the European University Institute in Florence in the fall of 2007. Regina List did a fine job as a language editor. Willeke Keijsers meticulously double-checked and corrected all references. Last but not least, Janine van der Woude, my secretary, needed all her patience to convert all draft chapters, tables, and figures into a consistent format.

Jacques Thomassen
September 2008

Contributors

Hanna Bäck is a Junior Professor at the Mannheim Centre for European Social Research (MZES), University of Mannheim. Her previous work has mainly focused on parties and coalition formation in West European parliamentary democracies, political participation, and voting behaviour. She is the author of articles such as 'Making the First Move. A Two-Stage Analysis of the Role of Formateurs in Parliamentary Government Formation' in *Public Choice*; 'Combining Large-n and Small-n Strategies: The Way Forward in Coalition Research' in *West European Politics*; and 'Explaining and Predicting Coalition Outcomes' in *European Journal of Political Research*.

Susan Banducci is an Associate Professor in Political Science at the University of Exeter. She specializes in comparative electoral behaviour and public opinion. She has published in international journals such as the *European Journal of Political Research*, *Journal of Politics*, and the *British Journal of Political Science* on turnout, campaigns, media, and political parties. Her publications include *Proportional Representation on Trial: The 1999 New Zealand General Election and the Fate of MMP* (2002, with Jack Vowles, Peter Aimer, Jeffrey Karp, Raymond Miller, and Ann Sullivan, Auckland University Press); 'Political Efficacy and Participation in Twenty Seven Democracies: How Electoral Systems Shape Political Behavior' in *British Journal of Political Science* 38 (2): 311–34 (2008, with Jeffrey A. Karp); 'Ballot Photographs as Cues in Low Information Elections' in *Political Psychology* 29 (6): 903–17 (2008 with Jeffrey A. Karp, Michael Thrasher, and Colin Rallings).

Hajo Boomgaarden is an Assistant Professor for Political Communication at The Amsterdam School of Communications Research (ASCoR) at the University of Amsterdam. His research interests include media and European integration, media effect on political attitudes, and election campaigns. His work was published in *European Union Politics*, *Journal of Common Market Studies*, and *Electoral Studies*.

Contributors

Wouter van der Brug holds a Chair in Political Science in the Department of Political Science at the University of Amsterdam. His research interests focus on comparative research in collective political behaviour, in particular electoral behaviour, right-wing populism, political communication, political trust and support, and political parties. He publishes regularly in international political science journals. His most recent book publications are *The Economy and the Vote* (2007, Cambridge University Press, co-authored by Cees van der Eijk and Mark Franklin) and *European Elections and Domestic Politics* (2007, University of Notre Dame Press, co-edited by Cees van der Eijk).

Cees van der Eijk is a Professor of Social Science Research Methods and Director of the Methods and Data Institute at the University of Nottingham. He has long-standing interests in research on comparative political behaviour and European integration. Some of his books in this area include *European Elections and Domestic Politics* (2007, Notre Dame: University of Notre Dame Press, with Wouter van der Brug), *The Economy and the Vote* (2007, Cambridge: Cambridge University Press, with Wouter van der Brug and Mark Franklin); and *Choosing Europe?* (1996, Ann Arbor: University of Michigan Press, with Mark Franklin).

Mark Franklin is the Stein Rokkan Professor of Comparative Politics at the European University Institute, Florence and Senior Research Fellow at Nuffield College, Oxford. He studies the behavior and opinions of elites and mass publics in Europe and elsewhere. He has published twelve books, including *The Economy and the Vote* (2007, Cambridge University Press, with Wouter van der Brug and Cees van der Eijk); *Voter Turnouts and the Dynamics of Electoral Competition in Established Democracies since 1945* (2004, Cambridge University Press); and *Choosing Europe?* (1996, University of Michigan Press, with Cees van der Eijk et al.).

Bart Goeminne is Master in the Quantitative Analysis in the Social Sciences (KU Brussels – KU Leuven) and has been working for the Institute for Social and Political Research (ISPO) at the KU Leuven. He is now working for SAS computing as a consultant.

Michael Marsh is Professor of Comparative Political Behaviour and Dean of the Faculty of Arts, Humanities and Social Sciences at Trinity College, University of Dublin. His main research interests are electoral behaviour and public opinion in Ireland and the EU. His publications include *The Irish voter: the nature of electoral competition in the Republic of Ireland*, Manchester: Manchester University Press (2008, ed. with R. Sinnott, J. Garry and F. Kennedy), *How Ireland Voted 2007: The Full Story of Ireland's General Election*, Basingstoke: Palgrave Macmillan: 259 pp (2008, ed. with M. Gallagher); *European Elections after Eastern Enlargement: Preliminary Results of the European Election Study 2004*, Connex report Series No 1, Mannheim: Mannheimer Zentrum für Europäische Sozialforschung (2007, ed. with S. Mikhaylov and H. Schmitt).

Slava Mikhaylov is a Lecturer in Political Science at Trinity College, University of Dublin. His main research interests are political economy, comparative politics, methodology.

Marina Popescu is a British Academy Postdoctoral Fellow at the Department of Government, University of Essex, and Research Director at the Median Research Centre, Bucharest, Romania. Her research interests are comparative politics and comparative voting behaviour, especially macro–micro interactions and the role of mass media, cross-national analyses of media effects and political communication. Her publications include 'Inequalities of Political Influence in New Democracies' in *International Journal of Sociology* 37 (4): 69–95 (co-authored with Gábor Tóka); 'Districting and Redistricting in Eastern and Central Europe: Regulations and Practices' (2008, co-authored with Gábor Tóka) in *Redistricting in Comparative Perspective* (ed. by Bernard Grofman and Lisa Handley, Oxford: Oxford University Press); 'Towards What Reign of Civil Society? Understanding NGOs in Romanian Electoral Politics' (2007, co-authored with Vlad Hatieganu) in *Non-Party Actors in Electoral Politics* (ed. by David Farrell and Rüdiger Schmitt-Beck, Bremen: Nomos Verlag).

Hermann Schmitt is a research fellow of the MZES at the University of Mannheim. His main research interests are in political linkage and representation, and in multi-level electoral systems. Among his publications are 'Meaningful Choices, Political Supply, and Institutional Effectiveness' in *Electoral Studies* 27: 19–30 (2008, with B. Wessels); 'Political Parties in Decline?' (1995, with S. Holmberg) in *Citizens and the State*, Beliefs in Government Series Vol. 1; Oxford: Oxford University Press: 95–133 (eds. H.-D. Klingemann and D. Fuchs); 'Nine Second-Order National Elections: A Systematic Framework for the Analysis of European Elections Results' in *European Journal of Political Research* 8: 3–44 (1980, with K. Reif).

Holli Semetko is Vice Provost for International Affairs, Director of the Claus M. Halle Institute for Global Learning, and Professor of Political Science at Emory University in the US. Her research focuses on political communication, public opinion, and elections. She is currently editor of the forthcoming *Sage Handbook of Political Communication* and her recent articles have appeared in *Political Behavior*; *European Union Politics*; *The Journal of Politics*; *British Journal of Political Science*; and *American Behavioral Scientist*.

Marc Swyngedouw is a Professor of Political Sociology at the Centre for Sociological Research (CeSO) at the KU Leuven, Belgium. He is the Founder and Principal Investigator of the Belgian National Election Studies. He is also the Director of the Institute for Social and Political Opinion Research (ISPO-KU Leuven). His research focus is on comparative politics, voting behaviour (national, regional and European), extreme right, ethnic minorities, identity, and comparative and longitudinal research methodology.

Jacques Thomassen is a Professor of Political Science at the University of Twente in the Netherlands. His main research interests are democratic theory, political representation and political behaviour. His publications include *Political Representation and Legitimacy in the European Union* (1999, Oxford: Oxford University Press, ed. with Hermann Schmitt); *The European Voter* (2005, Oxford: Oxford University Press); 'Democratic Values' in *Oxford Handbook of Political Behavior* (2007, Oxford: Oxford University Press, eds. R. Dalton and H.-D. Klingemann).

Gábor Tóka is an Associate Professor at the Department of Political Science, Central European University, Budapest, Hungary. His main interests are voting behaviour, democratic institutions, the impact of political knowledge on citizen behaviour. His publications include 'Citizen Information, Election Outcomes and Good Governance' in *Electoral Studies* 27 (1): 31–44 (2008), 'Can Voters be Equal? A Cross-National Analysis. Parts 1 and 2' in *The Review of Sociology* Vol. 9 (2): 51–72 (2003) and Vol. 10 (1): 47–65 (2004); 'Party Appeals and Voter Loyalty in New Democracies' in *Political Studies* 46 (4): 589–610 (1998).

Erik Voeten is Peter F. Krogh Assistant Professor of Global Justice and Geopolitics, Edmund A. Walsh School of Foreign Service and Government Department, Georgetown University. He studies politics in the United Nations, the European Union, and the European Court of Human Rights and broader issues of international cooperation. Representative publications include 'The Politics of International Judicial Appointments: Evidence from the European Court of Human Rights' in *International Organization*; 61 (4): 669–701 (2007); 'The Political Origins of the Legitimacy of the United Nations Security Council' in *International Organization* 59 (3): 527–57 (2005);

'Outside Options and the Logic of Security Council Action' in *The American Political Science Review* 95 (4): 845–58 (2001).

Claes de Vreese is Professor and Chair of Political Communication and Director of The Amsterdam School of Communications Research (ASCoR) at the University of Amsterdam. He has published more than 40 journal articles on media effects, public opinion, election campaigns, and European integration. For more information: www.claesdevreese.com.

Bernhard Wessels is Senior Researcher at the Wissenschaftszentrum Berlin für Sozialforschung and Deputy Director of the research unit 'Democracy'. His major research fields are political behaviour, political interest intermediation, and political representation in comparative perspective. Recent publications include 'Representation and Democracy' in the *Oxford Handbook of Political Behavior* (2007, Oxford: Oxford University Press), 'Die Bundestagswahl 2005. Analysen des Wahlkampfes und der Wahlergebnisse' in *VS Verlag* (2007, co-editor); 'Meaningful Choices, Political Supply, and Institutional Effectiveness' in *Electoral Studies* 27 (2008, together with Hermann Schmitt).

Lieven De Winter is a Professor at the Université Catholique de Louvain and Chair of the Centre de Politique Comparée. His main interests are comparative elections, parties, parliaments, cabinets, clientelism, regional political systems, and actors (especially regionalist parties). His publications include *Elections: le reflux ? Comportements et attitudes lors des élections en Belgique* (2007, Bruxelles: De Boeck, ed. with A-P. Frognier and P. Baudewyns); *Autonomist Parties in Europe: Identity Politics and the Revival of the Territorial Cleavage* (2006, Barcelona: ICPS, volume I, 283p and II, 274p, ed. with M. Gomez and P. Lynch); 'The Politics of Belgium' in *West-European Politics* 29 (5): 863–1092 (special issue) (2006, ed. with M. Brans and W. Swenden).

Abbreviations

EP	European Parliament
EPP	European People's Party
EPP–ED	European People's Party–European Democrats
EU	European Union
GAL	green/alternative/libertarian
PES	Party of European Socialists
TAN	traditional/authoritarian/nationalist
UEN	Union for Europe of the Nations
ASCoR	The Amsterdam School of Communications Research
EPG	European party group
EES	European Election Studies
EB	Eurobarometer
WWII	World War II
GDP	Gross Domestic Product
Gini	Gini coefficient
ICRG	International Country Risk Guide
WVS	World Values Survey
MEPs	Members of European Parliament

1

The Legitimacy of the European Union after Enlargement

Jacques Thomassen

1.1. Introduction

Throughout its history the European Union's (EU) legitimacy has been a matter of concern. A major challenge to its legitimacy was the 2004 enlargement with ten new member states, eight of them previously communist states in Central and Eastern Europe. This enlargement was without precedent in the history of the Union and its earlier incarnations. It is still to be seen how well the institutions as well as the citizens of the Union will be able to cope with the consequences of this operation. The institutions of the Union were never designed for such a large number of members. As a consequence, the Union is going through a laborious process of adapting its institutions to the changing circumstances. The referendums on the draft constitutional treaty in France and the Netherlands in 2005 and the Irish referendum on its successor, the Lisbon treaty, suggest that people across Europe are having misgivings, not only about an ever-closer Union but equally about an ever-larger Union.

In this volume, we try to assess the effect of the 2004 enlargement of the Union on its legitimacy. In order to do so, we first need to develop a method of assessing the legitimacy of the Union. Essentially, there are two main methods for assessing the legitimacy of any political system. The first one is by evaluating the political system against criteria derived from normative theory. The second one is by determining empirically the degree to which the political system is 'right' in the eyes of the beholders – the members of the polity. In this study we do both.

In order to apply the first method, we need to elaborate a normative theory and to develop more specific criteria against which political reality can be evaluated. In order to determine these criteria we rely on the work of Beetham and Lord (1998*a*; see also Lord 2004). They distinguish two key normative principles of liberal democracy, *popular sovereignty* and *the proper ends and standards of government*. The first principle refers to the main components of the concept of democracy, *demos* and *kratos* (literally, rule by the people). It assumes that the only source of political authority lies with the people. This belief that the people constitute the ultimate source of political authority makes the question 'who constitutes the people' one of the most fundamental aspects or dimensions of legitimacy, and makes issues of political identity equally crucial for political legitimacy (Beetham and Lord 1998*a*: 6). Therefore, any conceptualization of democracy in the EU must start with a description of the European *demos*. This is the first dimension of legitimacy we distinguish in our study.

In addition to the demos, the principle of popular sovereignty also refers to the question of what it means for the people to rule. Because modern democracy is nearly identical with representative democracy, this aspect of popular sovereignty refers to the electoral authorization of government and stipulates the requirements of *representation and accountability* (Beetham and Lord 1998*a*: 6). In order to understand what democracy in a specific context means, we need to specify the mechanisms of representation and accountability that are needed within a given polity with a given *demos*. This is the second dimension of legitimacy we distinguish.

The second principle of liberal democracy, 'the proper ends and standards of government', can be summarized in its most classic form as the protection of the Lockean rights (life, liberty, and property), complemented more recently with welfare rights and securing the conditions for economic growth (Beetham and Lord 1998*a*: 4–6). This principle yields criteria to judge the *performance* of government, the third dimension of legitimacy we distinguish.

Summarizing, from the main principles of liberal democracy, three dimensions of legitimacy can be deduced – *identity, representation and accountability*, and *performance*. These three dimensions are reflected in most normative theories of democracy. The most concise summary is Abraham Lincoln's famous triad requiring government *of, by,* and *for* the people.

The second method for assessing the legitimacy of a political system, by determining the degree to which the political system is right in the eyes of the people, requires an analogous approach. In order to apply this method, we should first determine which aspects of the political system people's feelings are relevant for the legitimacy of the political system. Aspects considered relevant can only be based on normative criteria. Most empirical research using this method to assess the legitimacy of a political system is based on the theoretical framework originally developed by David Easton. He distinguishes three objects of support: the *political community*, the *political regime* and (the performance of) the *authorities* (Easton 1965*a*). Although Easton's original framework is more encompassing and refined, for the purposes of this project we interpret the political regime in terms of its political institutions. As shown in Table 1.1, the three objects of support are referring to the same normative dimensions of democratic legitimacy distinguished in the first column. The Eastonian framework will help us to assess to what extent the system is supported by the people.

The conceptual triad shown in Table 1.1 helps us to develop and apply both methods of assessing the democratic legitimacy of any political system. However, the EU is not just like any political system. It is a matter of dispute to what extent criteria of democratic legitimacy developed in the context of the nation state can be applied to the EU. The distinction between the three dimensions of democratic legitimacy is helpful in understanding this debate. In the next section, we summarize this debate and define our own position in it.

In Section 1.3, we derive a number of criteria from normative democratic theory that enable us to evaluate the democratic performance of the Union. We follow most modern theories of democracy by defining democracy in terms of the institutions of representative democracy and the processes of representation and accountability. Therefore, we limit our evaluation to the dimension of representation and accountability (cf. Lord 2004). In the first part of the book (Chapters 2 through 5) we then systematically test to what degree the political reality of the EU meets

Table 1.1. Three dimensions of democratic legitimacy and objects of support

Dimensions of Democratic Legitimacy	Objects of Support
Identity	Political community
Representation and accountability	Regime-political institutions
Performance	Performance of authorities

these criteria and how much the 2004 enlargement affected the extent to which it does. In Section 1.4, we explain how Easton's conceptual framework can help us assess how strongly the political system of the EU is supported by the people of Europe. In Chapters 6 through 9 we explore the development of support over time and the effect of the 2004 enlargement on the level of support for the Union.

1.2. The legitimacy of the European Union: A Union of, by, and for the people?

In most contemporary theories of democracy, democracy is tantamount to *representative democracy*, and more specifically, to *electoral democracy*. Ever since Schumpeter defined 'the democratic method' as 'that institutional arrangement for arriving at political decisions in which individuals acquire the power to decide by means of a competitive struggle for the people's vote' (Schumpeter 1976), there is a broad consensus that 'the competitive electoral context, with several political parties organizing the alternatives that face the voters, is the identifying property of the contemporary democratic process' (Powell 1983: 3). This means that democracy is primarily defined as 'government by the people'. In the context of the nation state this is hardly a matter of dispute anymore, but in discussions about the democratic legitimacy of the EU, it is. The feasibility of a full-blown system of representative democracy, understood as electoral democracy, *at the level of the EU*, is disputed on several grounds. A first argument is based on the 'no *demos* thesis', which declares that there is no European *demos* (Weiler, Haltern, and Mayer 1995). And if there is no European *demos*, there cannot be a European democracy either.

This, in a nutshell, is the argument Scharpf makes in his famous plea for an *output-oriented* rather than an *input-oriented* legitimization of EU policies. In terms of Lincoln's distinction between the main elements of democracy, input-oriented legitimization refers to government *by the people*, whereas output-oriented legitimization refers to government *for the people*. According to Scharpf the basis of legitimacy of these different kinds, or rather different aspects of democracy, is different. From the perspective of input-oriented legitimacy, political choices are legitimate if and because they reflect the 'will of the people', that is, if they can be derived from the authentic preferences of the members of a community. From the perspective of output-oriented legitimacy, political choices are legitimate if and because they effectively promote the common welfare of the constituency in question (Scharpf 1999: 6). Scharpf argues that the plausibility of what he calls the participatory rhetoric suffers as the distance between the persons directly affected and their representatives increases. Although the rhetoric of input-oriented democracy is in terms of the will of the people, for most practical purposes, decisions are taken by majority rule. The justification of majority rule must be considered as the crucial problem of input-oriented theories of democratic legitimization. Majority rule will only be accepted in polities with a 'thick' collective identity, that is, in polities based on pre-existing commonalities of history, language, culture, and ethnicity. This is not the case with regard to the Union:

Given the historical, linguistic, cultural, ethnic, and institutional diversity of its member states, there is no question that the Union is very far from having achieved the 'thick' collective identity that we have come to take for granted in national democracies – and in its absence, institutional reforms will not greatly increase the input-oriented legitimacy of decisions taken by majority rule. (Scharpf 1999: 9)

According to this view, the input perspective derives its democratic legitimacy from a pre-existing collective identity. Because such a collective identity does not exist at the level of the Union, input-oriented legitimacy is out of reach for the EU for the foreseeable future. Therefore, a more modest form of legitimization must have to uphold the Union, that is, an output-oriented legitimization brought about by *government for the people* (Scharpf 1999).

Undoubtedly, Scharpf touches upon an important problem. Still, there are at least two arguments with which one can counter his. First, as we will more extensively argue in Chapter 9, the argument that a *demos* and *citizenship* require the pre-existence of a community with a collective or national identity is anything but generally accepted. An alternative view allows for the possibility that European citizenship need not be the political projection of a collective European identity, but can essentially be regarded as a purely legal construct. In this view 'a demos is understood as in non-organic civic terms, a coming together on the basis not of shared ethnos and/or organic culture, but a coming together on the basis of shared values, a shared understanding of rights and societal duties and shared rational, intellectual culture which transcends ethno-national differences' (Weiler, Haltern, and Mayer 1995: 19). Also, the argument that a shared common identity, a *demos* in the ethno-cultural sense, should precede the constitution of a *demos*, in the sense of a community of citizens sharing the rights and duties of citizenship, has little ground in history.

In many European countries, the formation of the state preceded the development of the nation.

Second, if we take the idea of output-oriented legitimization or government for the people literally, in the sense of effectively taking care of the wants, needs, and interests of the people, it is hard to avoid thinking of Schumpeter's famous Philippic against the classic theory of democracy with its ideas of a common good and a will of the people (Thomassen and Schmitt 2004). One of Schumpeter's objections to the classic theory is that it hardly offers a criterion to distinguish democratic from non-democratic governments:

> ...the classical theory meets with difficulties on that score because both the will and the good of the people may be, and in many historical instances have been, served just as well or better by governments that cannot be described as democratic according to any accepted usage of the term. (Schumpeter 1976: 269–70)

Schumpeter convincingly argues that democracy should therefore be defined primarily as a *modus procedendi* and defines democracy as 'that institutional arrangement for arriving at political decisions in which individuals acquire the power to decide by means of a competitive struggle for the people's vote' (Schumpeter 1976: 269).

It would be incorrect though to put Scharpf's concept of an output-oriented system of government on a par with a simplistic idea of government *for* the people. His concept is far more refined and can better be classified as another version of the *liberal* or *Madisonian theory of democracy*, to be distinguished from the *populist theory of democracy* (Dahl 1956; Riker 1982). It focuses on the prevention of the abuse of power by a system of checks and balances rather than on giving a say to the people. But for that very reason, Dahl, after a thorough analysis of the Madisonian concept of democracy, concludes that it can hardly be characterized as being democratic at all because it compromises a fundamental principle of democracy: *popular sovereignty* (Dahl 1956). Popular sovereignty refers to the question of what it means for the people to rule. In modern democracy, it means the electoral authorization of government (Beetham and Lord 1998*a*: 6).

The main representative of a second kind of argument against the need for electoral democracy at EU level is Majone. His starting point is that the EU is basically a 'regulatory state' (Majone 1994, 1996). Its main task is economic, social, and legal regulation. In his view, such regulation can best be undertaken by independent bodies – central banks, administrative tribunals, executive agencies, courts of law – staffed by the relevant experts, whose judgments are more effective precisely because they are not subject to the sway of electoral or majoritarian pressure (Majone 1996). Majone then argues that EU policy making should not be 'democratic' in the usual meaning of the term. If EU policies were made by what Majone calls 'majoritarian' institutions, EU policies would cease to be Pareto-efficient, insofar as the political majority would select EU policy outcomes closer to their ideal short-term policy preferences and counter to the preferences of the political minority and against the majority's own long-term interests (Majone 1994, 1996; Follesdal and Hix 2005).

However, it can be argued that regulatory frameworks always have implicit if not explicit policy choices built into them, which carry distributional consequences. And if this is the case, who is to determine what these essentially political choices are to be (Beetham and Lord 1998*a*: 20)? Also, Majone's starting point that the EU is mainly a regulatory state responsible for purely Pareto-improving policies with no redistributive effects is more and more disputable. Many EU regulatory policies have significant redistributive consequences, and, as Follesdal and Hix (2005: 10–11) argue:

His arguments do not apply to policies which allow choices with distributive or even redistributive effects. He offers no reason why they should be isolated from democratic contestation. Where there are short- and long-term winners and losers, Majone's argument does not diminish the need for democratic, responsive and accountable decision-makers.

This again pushes us towards the conclusion that democratic decision making at the EU begs for a form of electoral democracy. Without being subject to electoral control, European decision-making fits in the category of regimes about which one might wonder 'qui custodiet ipsos custodes?' It then belongs to the category of enlightened technocracy that has no real safeguard against a less enlightened and benevolent use of non-majoritarian institutions.

An important representative of a third argument against the need for an electoral democracy at the European level is Moravcsik (2002). In his view the EU remains a largely intergovernmental organization, a cooperation between sovereign states. Therefore, by far the most important channel of political representation and accountability is at the national level. In his perception, the effectiveness of this channel tends to increase rather than to decrease because national parliaments and the national media increasingly scrutinize national government ministers' actions in Brussels. Hence, while the EU remains a largely intergovernmental organization, decisions in the

European Council and the Council of Ministers are as accountable to national citizens as decisions of national cabinets (Moravcsik 2002).

In our view, this argument can hardly be maintained. Ever since the Single European Act opened the possibility for the Council of Ministers to decide by a qualified majority instead of unanimity, national parliaments have lost part of their power to scrutinize and control the positions taken by their national governments in the European arena. Also, the EU is the source of authoritative rules and allocations that impinge directly on citizens and that require *their* acknowledgment of them as authoritative and binding (Beetham and Lord 1998a).

According to the basic principles of democracy, the democratic process should occur at the same level as that where decisions are taken. If decisions are taken at the European level according to a supranational regime, the *demos* should be defined at the level of the European people as well. Once one accepts this argument, it is only a matter of consistency to apply the same normative democratic principles to the EU as to the nation state. It is hard to meet two of the most essential requirements of democracy – political equality and popular sovereignty – without a form of electoral democracy. Therefore, it is our contention that in order to deserve the predicate 'democratic', the EU cannot do without electoral democracy at the European level.

This principle is clearly recognized in the constitutional framework of the Union and embodied in its institutions. The *Treaty establishing a Constitution for Europe* in article I-46 clearly recognized the principle of representative democracy at the European level, with a key role for European political parties:

46.1 The functioning of the Union shall be founded on representative democracy.
46.2 Citizens are directly represented at Union level in the European Parliament (EP). Member states are represented in the European Council by their Heads of State or Government and in the Council by their governments, themselves democratically accountable either to their national Parliaments, or to their citizens.
46.4 Political parties at European level contribute to forming European political awareness and to expressing the will of citizens of the Union.

In this article, two different channels of political representation are recognized. First, European citizens, that is, the *European people* or the *European demos*, are represented in the EP, the members of which are directly elected by the European voters. Secondly, the *peoples of Europe* are represented by their governments in the European Council and in the Council of Ministers by their governments, which themselves are accountable to national parliaments, which in turn are elected by a national electorate.

Of course, the Constitutional Treaty was never ratified. This article, however, was fully maintained in the new Treaty on European Union (article 10) the member states agreed upon in Lisbon in 2007. And even if the Lisbon treaty after the Irish referendum will share the fate of the Constitutional Treaty, one should realize that the principle of electoral democracy has already been embodied in the institutions of the Union. The article referred to above is no more than the codification of the practice established since 1979, when for the first time the members of the EP were directly elected by the European voters. Without the recognition of the need for a system of representative democracy at the European level, the EP and its direct election would be a strange anomaly.

Once representative democracy as a principle of government at the European level is recognized, it is difficult to see why representative democracy or the process of political representation at the European level should not meet the same criteria that were developed in the context of the nation state. It is to these criteria that we now turn.

1.3. Political representation in the European Union

Political representation is the process by which citizens' preferences are linked to government policy. How precisely this process should work is a matter of debate. According to a dominant school of thought, the idea of popular sovereignty in a representative democracy can only be realized *by party democracy* or *party government*. According to the model of party government, elections can function as an instrument of linkage when the following requirements are met (Thomassen 1994; Thomassen and Schmitt 1999*a*):

1. Voters do have a choice, that is, they can choose between at least two parties with different policy proposals.
2. Voters do vote according to their policy preferences, that is, they choose the party that represents their policy preferences best.
3. The internal cohesion of parliamentary parties is sufficient to enable them to implement their policies.
4. The party or coalition of parties winning the elections takes over the government.

5. Both the policy programs of political parties and the policy preferences of voters are constrained by a single ideological dimension.

These requirements are mostly self-evident. Elections hardly make sense if there are no serious alternatives to choose among. Political parties can only convey a clear and unequivocal message to the voters and keep their promises after the elections if they are united and well disciplined. Still, the democratic effect of elections would be futile unless the elected (majority in) parliament has a say in the formation and the policies of the government. If the formation of the government and the policies adopted by the government were not derivative of the elected parliament, there would be no direct linkage between the will of the electorate and government policy. Also, the combination of the first and fourth requirement makes the government accountable to the electorate by enabling the voters to 'throw the rascals out'.

However, even when all these conditions are met, a single vote does not necessarily convey an electoral mandate with respect to any specific policy domain. Political parties offer a package deal to the voter. By voting for a particular party, voters are forced to vote for the whole package. The voter who is in favour of party A with respect to policy domain 1, but of party B with respect to domain 2, has no alternative but to choose either one of them on the basis of his own idiosyncratic weights given to the different policy domains. This may be an acceptable solution for the individual voter, but at the level of the political system it means that there is no logical relationship between the electoral majority and the policy majority on any specific issue. This phenomenon is known as the Ostrogorski paradox (Ostrogorski 1902; Rae and Daudt 1976; Thomassen 1994). As a consequence, as Dahl puts it, 'all an election reveals is the first preference of some citizens among the candidates standing for office,' for 'we can rarely interpret a majority of first choices among candidates in a national election as being equivalent to a majority of first choices for a specific policy' (Dahl 1956).

The only solution to this paradox is that the parties, in the composition of their programmes, and the voters, when they decide which party they will vote for, are constrained by the same one-dimensional ideology. Only then is it absolutely clear where the electoral majority stands in policy matters (Thomassen 1994). This, of course, is a very severe requirement. In Europe, the left–right dimension is the most likely aspect to serve as the single dimension being able to connect the policy views of the electorate with public policy.

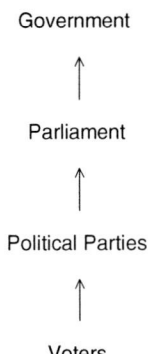

Figure 1.1. Basic elements in the process of linkage

The basic elements in the process of linkage according to the party government model are summarized in Figure 1.1.

According to the dominant political science literature none of the essential links in the chain of political representation operates effectively at the European level. First, despite the increased – and perhaps underestimated – powers of the EP, it does not form and control a European government, for the simple reason that there is no such thing as a European government – at least not in any traditional sense of the concept of a government, let alone a *responsible* government. In the institutional framework of the EU, the Commission comes closest to a kind of European government. However, there is no formal linkage between the outcome of European elections and the formation of the Commission. Therefore, '[t]he party or coalition of parties winning the elections' does not take over the government. Also, because there is no government to form or to support at the European level, the concept of government vs. opposition parties, so essential in any parliamentary democracy and a defining characteristic of the party government model, has no meaning at the European level.

Therefore, it hardly needs to be argued that at least one requirement of the system of party government, formation and control of the government by a majority in parliament, is not met. As a consequence, the European political system does not offer the voters the possibility to 'throw the rascals out'. In this sense, the democratic deficit is obvious: European elections are not translated into executive power; the commission is not accountable, directly or indirectly via the EP, to the European people.

This conclusion refers primarily to the legislative–executive relationship at the European level. In this book, we will not discuss this relationship any further. Instead, we will focus on how well the remaining requirements of the model of party government are met, that is, the requirements referring to political parties and voters. The traditional verdict with regard to these requirements is hardly less negative. According to the party government model, political parties are supposed to supply different policy platforms for the voters to choose from. At the European level they do not. European political parties as such do not compete for the votes of a European electorate. European elections are still the arena of national political parties; they are fought by national political parties and mainly on national issues. Also, voters make their choice on the basis of their opinions on national issues and their perception of the position of national political parties on these issues. As a consequence, European elections fail as an instrument of democracy at the European level, that is, they fail to express the will of the European people on European issues.

The remedy for this failure, according to some observers, is for political parties to organize themselves at the European level and fight elections on European rather than national issues. Perhaps even a reshuffle of political parties is needed according to their position with regard to European unification, on the dimension of pro- vs. anti- further European integration. Then, elections would finally be able to serve as a linkage between the policy views of the European electorate and European politics (Bogdanor 1989; Andeweg 1995). However, as we argued before (Thomassen and Schmitt 1999*b*), this position is disputable. The very idea that elections for the EP should be fought on so-called European issues, that is, on the dimension of pro- vs. anti- further European integration, is based on a fundamental misunderstanding. It makes little sense to base a system of representation, and therefore a party system, on issues that are decided at a different level. Formal decisions on essential so-called European issues, like a further transfer of sovereignty from the national to the European level or further enlargement, are mainly subject to the intergovernmental regime of European decision making. They need the consent of national governments and are, at least in principle, under the control of national parliaments and national electorates. Therefore, the interesting paradox is that what usually are called *European* issues are basically *national* issues. As far as the existing party system fails to offer a meaningful choice to the voters on these issues, it paradoxically is a problem at the national rather than the European level.

In a healthy and stable democracy, the political debate and political conflict will usually refer to substantive policy issues within the constraints of a constitutional order. The constitutional order itself should not be a matter of permanent dispute. If the unification of Europe is at all viable, major political disputes must gradually shift from constitutional to substantive policy issues. The relative consensus among political elites across Europe about the future of Europe is not a *problem* but rather a *condition* for further development of the EU as a democratic political system. The crucial test for the effectiveness of the European system of political representation is therefore the extent to which it is effective with regard to more substantive policy issues. However, this conclusion can hardly change the verdict on the European system of political representation. It is still true that European political parties as such do not compete for the votes of a European electorate, that European elections are fought by national political parties and mainly on national issues, that voters make their choice on the basis of their opinions on national issues and their perception of national political parties on these issues, and that as a consequence, European elections fail as an instrument of democracy at the European level, that is, they fail to express the will of the European people.

Most of this is supported by hard empirical evidence. However, the one disputable part of this argument is whether all this necessarily means that European elections fail to express the will of the European people. This is still to be seen. Once we accept the argument that the European level of governance is mainly responsible for substantive rather than constitutional issues, there is no reason to assume that the issues on the European agenda are very different from the policy agendas at the national level. The allocation of the main responsibility for particular issue dimensions to a particular level of government is only partly a matter of principle and more often a consequence of the economy of scale and boundary effects. If the relevant issue dimensions at the European level are not really different than at the national level, one might expect the same dimensions of contestation to be relevant at both levels. This means that there is no reason why the basic structure of the party system at the European level should differ from that at the national level. Quite the contrary, as the effectiveness of a European system of political representation does not depend on its ability to politicize the issue of European integration, but rather on its ability to aggregate and integrate national political agendas and the national cleavage structures at the European level. The major challenge for an effective democratic political system at the European level is to overcome the traditional dividing lines in Europe, i.e. the national borders. The more political differences coincide with national borders, the more disruptive the politicization of these differences will be. But the more political parties base their policy appeals on cross-national cleavages rather than on national interests, the better they can serve their function of 'expressing the will of citizens of the Union'.

A truly European system of political representation requires cross-cutting cleavages not only at the level of political parties, but also at each of the levels distinguished in Figure 1.1. If political parties from the same party family across member states develop widely different party manifestos and profiles during their election campaigns, if the political discourse totally differs from country to country, if voters across Europe voting for parties belonging to the same party group in the EP have widely different policy priorities and vote according to different considerations, or if being a member of a particular party group has no consequences for the political views and the roll-call behaviour of members of the EP, then a truly European system of political representation is certainly out of reach. On the other hand, the more similarity we discover at each level within each party group and across member states, the more likely it is that European elections are effective as an instrument of linking the will of the European people to the process of decision making in the EP, and the more justified we are in concluding that a truly European system of political representation is at least feasible.

Previous research has shown that the compatibility of national systems of political representation at all levels of Figure 1.1 is surprisingly high due to a roughly similar cleavage structure across Western Europe. However, it is yet to be seen to what extent this is still the case after the 2004 enlargement.

Therefore, it is one of the core objectives of this study to see the degree to which the requirements of the party government model at each level are met and how this is affected by the recent enlargement. These are the questions we try to answer in the first part of the book.

In the next chapter we explore to what extent the first requirement of the model of party government is met at the European level: do European voters actually have a choice between at least two parties with different policy proposals? Of course, we already know that in a formal sense this requirement is not met at all; there are no European political parties competing for the votes of a European electorate. However, if we try to assess the *feasibility* of an effective model of party government as we just argued, the relevant question is to what extent national party systems can be aggregated into distinct and cohesive European party groups. This can only be the case if the policy proposals of national political parties, which belong to the same party federation or 'family', are compatible and if they compete on the same policy dimensions. Previous research has shown that the compatibility of national party systems is surprisingly high due to a roughly similar cleavage structure across Western Europe and the dominance of the left–right dimension as the main dimension of contestation between political parties. The main question we pursue in this chapter is whether the party systems in the new member states are sufficiently similar to their Western European counterparts to fit into the existing party system. Are their policy programmes compatible and do they compete on the same policy dimension(s)? More particularly, we try to assess whether and how the eastward enlargement might have weakened the existing EU party system in terms of its distinctiveness and the cohesion of party groups.

An additional requirement for the development of a truly European system of political representation is the development of a European public sphere. So far, we have not discussed this as it usually is not included as a requirement of the model of party government. However, the development of a European public sphere is essential for the development of a truly European system of political representation. Even if the policy programmes of political parties of the same party family are compatible, this still does not mean that the political messages reaching the voters across Europe are compatible. Very few voters read what political parties have on offer in official documents like party manifestos. What reaches them and in particular what is emphasized as being more or less important is filtered by the media. Therefore, compatible policy views of political parties can only reach the European electorate if there is a certain compatibility of the public discourse in the different sub-segments of a potential European public sphere. As originally defined by Habermas (2001), a public sphere refers to 'the perception, identification, and treatment of problems affecting the whole society'. Habermas considers the development of a European public sphere, conceptualized as a singular, supra-national, pan-European public sphere, implying a common language, a shared identity, and a transnational media system as a condition sine qua non for the development of a European democracy (Habermas 2001). In the literature, we can observe a development from focusing on this 'public sphere heavy' notion of a singular, pan-European public sphere to focusing on a 'public sphere light' notion of coexisting national public spheres in regard to European politics. This is the approach that serves our purposes, since assessing the compatibility of national systems of political representation across member states is exactly what we are trying to do. Therefore, in Chapter 3 we try to assess to what extent the media coverage of the European elections in 2004 revealed the emergence of a European public sphere in the sense of compatible national public spheres. Given that a European public sphere was not well established prior to enlargement, we expect that the addition of ten new members and media systems is not conducive to the emergence of a European public sphere.

In Chapter 4, we focus on the requirements that need to be met on the voters' side. According to the model of party government, voters should base their vote choice on policy considerations. If they do not, elections can hardly be an instrument for connecting the policy views of the voters to political decision making. Also, effective political representation is unlikely to materialize if voters have idiosyncratic sets of policy preferences motivating their decisions. Therefore, a small number of ideological dimensions – preferably only one – should structure the behaviour of voters as well as that of political parties. Prior research has established that the left–right dimension structures the behaviour of parties and voters in most Western European countries. Therefore, this dimension functions as an important link in the chain of democratic representation both at the national and European level. However, we cannot know *a priori* whether the left–right dimension structures the behaviour of voters in the new member states equally well. Also, even if voters in the separate member states of the EU vote largely on the basis of the same ideological dimension – left–right – the substantive meaning of left–right may be different in different countries. Therefore, in order to assess whether the twenty-five separate national electorates operate as a single European electorate in European elections, we focus on these two aspects.

In Chapter 5, we turn to the questions whether and how enlargement affects politics in the EP and in particular Parliament's role in the development of a truly European system of political representation. According to the model of party government, such a system requires the development of cohesive supranational parties competing in a common low-dimensional ideological space. Previous research found the party groups operative in the EP to be surprisingly cohesive. Members of European Parliament (MEPs) are organized in political groups rather than in national delegations. Supranational partisan politics along left–right ideological lines rather than national divisions have become dominant in the EP. Therefore, two important requirements for the development of a truly European system of political representation seem to be met. However, there are, at least, two reasons to suspect that enlargement may affect both the cohesiveness and the dominance of ideology-based competition between supranational parties in EP politics. First, it is unclear to what extent the (MEPs) from the new member states fit in the existing ideological and partisan structure of the EP and thus, whether 'old' and 'new' EU members share a 'common political space'.

Second, the new members may share a set of common interests that go across party lines, which may lead to increased contestation along national lines in the EP. Against this background we evaluate whether there are early indications that expansion has affected the partisan nature of EP politics, the overall ideological structure of the Parliament, and whether national divisions have become a more prominent explanatory source for variation in roll-call vote choices. Finally, we examine whether individual MEPs from the new member states fit as comfortably within the EP's ideological and partisan structure as their counterparts from the EU15.

1.4. The legitimacy of the European Union: The support of the people

In the second part of the book, we try to assess the degree to which the EU is legitimate in the eyes of the beholders, that is, the European citizens. Again our main question is to what extent the legitimacy of the Union has been affected by the 2004 enlargement? Following Easton we make a distinction between people's support for the *performance* or the policy *output* of (the authorities of) the Union, for its political *institutions*, and for the EU as a *political community*. The general level of support for each of these aspects of support can have been affected by the enlargement in two different ways. First, enlargement might have affected the level of support in the older member states. Second, enlargement might have brought in new member states whose citizens support the Union to a lesser degree than the people from the older member states.

We start with people's perception of the performance of the EU. First we must query how much European citizens across the EU really want, that is, in which policy fields they want the Union to take responsibility. The question as to which decision-making level is most appropriate to deal with different policy problems is a central aspect of the legitimacy of a political system. With regard to the level of governance in the EU, the discussion is structured around the meaning and application of the principle of subsidiarity, permitting EU action when member states or regions cannot sufficiently act to solve a problem, or when for reasons of scale or effects, actions could be better achieved by the EU.

In 2001, the European Council still believed that European citizens wanted the Union to take a greater responsibility in a large number of policy sectors:

The Legitimacy of the European Union after Enlargement

The image of a democratic and globally engaged Europe admirably matches citizens' wishes. There have been frequent public calls for a greater EU role in justice and security, action against cross-border crime, control of migration flows and reception of asylum seekers and refugees from far-flung war zones. Citizens also want results in the fields of employment and combating poverty and social exclusion, as well as in the field of economic and social cohesion. They want a common approach on environmental pollution, climate change and food safety, in short, all transnational issues that they instinctively sense can only be tackled by working together. Just as they also want to see Europe more involved in foreign affairs, security and defence, in other words, greater and better coordinated action to deal with trouble spots in and around Europe and in the rest of the world. (Laeken declaration – The future of the European Union; 15 December 2001).

In Chapter 6, we will see whether this enthusiasm is shared by the European people and which level of government they regard as the appropriate level for a number of policy sectors, how these opinions have evolved over time, and whether or not citizens from the new member states are more reluctant in transferring policy responsibilities to the European level.

The remaining chapters (7, 8, and 9) in this part of the book hardly need any further introduction as each of them focuses on one of the objects of support distinguished earlier in this chapter, *output* (*performance*), *political institutions*, and the *political community*, respectively. In Chapter 7, we explore how heavily people's support for the EU depends on their perceptions of its policy performance. Public perceptions of benefits accruing from EU membership have been explained previously in terms of broadly utilitarian considerations: national economic circumstances, subjective evaluation of economic well-being (the 'feel-good' factor), and sufficient time to allow those and other benefits to be felt (duration of membership in the EU). In this chapter, we examine to what extent utilitarian explanatory models can explain the ups and downs in people's perceptions of benefits accruing from EU membership. If they do, the effect of enlargement will depend, first, on how much the people in the new member states think they will profit from their country's membership and, second, on the effect people in the older member states think enlargement will have on how much they benefit from their country's membership.

In Chapter 8, we try to assess whether and how people's perceptions of policy performance spill over to their support for the political institutions of the EU. Following Easton, we should expect a continuously positive policy performance to lead to a gradual development of diffuse support for the political institutions of the Union. This implies that we do not expect a high level of support for these institutions in the new member states for the simple reason that their experience with EU policies is too short for the development of diffuse support.

In Chapter 9, we address the third object of support, the political community. As indicated in Table 1.1, the concept of a political community is related to the dimension of citizenship and identity. We argue that a social, cultural, or national identity should conceptually be distinguished from citizenship. The concept of European citizenship implies that European citizens are prepared to accept all citizens of the (enlarged) Union – without exceptions – as their fellow citizens and to accept that all EU citizens are therefore entitled to all rights that come with the citizenship of the Union. In this chapter, we assess whether they in fact do so. A second indicator of European citizenship is the extent to which people do *consider* themselves as citizens of the EU. Following Deutsch, the 'sense of European community' is operationalized in terms of mutual trust. We examine the degree to which both the sense of European citizenship and the sense of community are a function of socialization, that is, the length of membership of a country. If they are, enlargement is bound to have a negative effect both on the sense of citizenship and the sense of community. Finally, we address the problem of turnout in EP elections. The level of turnout in these elections has been notoriously low from the very first direct European elections. Therefore, it is no wonder that the high levels of abstention have often been interpreted as a hard indicator of low levels of support for the EP and more in general for the EU. In Chapter 10, we examine whether this interpretation is justified.

1.5. The European Election Studies project

This volume is based on the European Election Studies (EES) project (see http://www.europeanelectionstudies.net), in particular the 2004 election study, and succeeds previous main publications (Van der Eijk and Franklin 1996; Katz and Wessels 1999; Schmitt and Thomassen 1999; Van der Brug and Van der Eijk 2007). The EES project started on the occasion of the first direct elections of the EP in 1979 and has continued ever since. The 2004 study is the only available data source for a systematic study of the consequences of the 2004 enlargement at the level of the electorate. However, as this volume shows, the EES has evolved into a much broader project than just an election study. It now encompasses not only a survey among the electorate in each member state but also a study of the party manifestos of all political parties taking part in the European Elections (www.europeanelectionstudies.net/euromanifestos). Also, the project is strongly connected to another ongoing project, investigating the role of the media in framing issues of enlargement and the impact media coverage has on public opinion (See chapter 3 of this book De Vreese, Semetko et al.) and studies of roll-call behaviour in the EP. Some of the activities of the EES 2004 were supported by CONNEX, a network of excellence funded by the European Commission under the 6th framework programme.

Part I

Political Representation in the European Union

2

The European Party System after Enlargement

Hermann Schmitt and Jacques Thomassen

2.1. Introduction

In the introductory chapter we argued that despite the lack of a truly *European* process of political representation, elections for the European Parliament (EP) can still serve as an instrument of linkage between the will of the European people and the political decision making at the European level if a number of conditions are met.

The first condition is that European party groups are competitive, i.e., distinct, and internally cohesive with regard to major policy dimensions. This condition will only be met if national political parties belonging to the same party group in the EP present compatible policy programmes to their national electorates. In this chapter we try to assess to what extent this first condition is met: are the grand policy directions of national political parties that belong to the same party group similar enough to constitute and represent distinct and cohesive European party groups?

From previous research we already know that up to 2004 this condition was remarkably well met. As long as the EU still consisted of fifteen member states, European party groups were as distinct and cohesive on the main dimension of contestation as most national political parties (Schmitt and Thomassen 1999). This successful formation of European party groups is mainly due to the similarity of political cleavages in most European countries at the time of the gradual introduction of general suffrage and the emergence of mass political parties at the end of the nineteenth and the early twentieth centuries, that is the time when social cleavages were first translated into electoral alliances. At the time, the basic and most salient socio-political conflict was between industrial labour and capital. This led almost everywhere to the formation of labour unions and, in the political and parliamentary sphere, of a labour party (or a socialist or social democratic party) opposing the liberal and conservative forces that were more or less closely allied with entrepreneurial interests. Other, older socio-political conflicts – between the primary and secondary sector, between church and state, and between centre and periphery – have also contributed to the characteristic form of Western European party systems (Lipset and Rokkan 1967).

In modern politics, these additional cleavages have contributed to and shaped a more 'virtual' or ideological representation of them. Over the years several authors have 'asserted that the left–right dimension obtains a superior all-inclusive status within the hierarchy of cleavages' (Sani and Sartori 1983). In this interpretation the left–right dimension not only reflects the ideological component of the class cleavage but also is a kind of 'super issue' encompassing various issue domains. Sani and Sartori argue that, although electorates can be distributed into multiple dimensions of identification, this does not necessarily entail that parties also compete along the same dimensions. They maintain that, even if some European countries can better be understood as having a two-dimensional competitive space, these dimensions are of unequal rank, the left–right dimension being by far the most important dimension of conflict. Therefore, as has been confirmed by many studies, the electoral competition in most modern Western democracies can to a large extent be reduced to a single ideological dimension: the left–right dimension.

These commonalities in the national cleavage structures upon which Western European party systems are based were strong enough to support an EU-wide 'super structure' that successfully aggregates, in a few EU-wide parties, almost every national party gaining representation in the elections to the EP.

In Central and Eastern Europe, party systems only emerged in the early 1990s as part of the process of democratization. Therefore, it is still to be seen to what extent they rest upon socio-political cleavages compatible with those in Western Europe, or on less stable pillars like specific issue alliances or the personal charisma of political elites that predominated during regime change.

Against this background we try to assess to what extent the 2004 Eastern enlargement had an effect on the characteristics of the European party system, in particular on the distinctiveness and cohesion of European

The European Party System after Enlargement

party groups. In other words, do the parties from these new member states fit in the European party system existing before enlargement?[1]

In pursuing this research question, we first recapitulate the major developments of the EU party system prior to Eastern enlargement and review what is known about the evolution of Eastern European party systems after the collapse of communism. In Section 2.3, we describe to what extent the members of the EP from the new member states have joined the party groups already existing in the Parliament. In Sections 2.4 and 2.5, we discuss the effect of enlargement on the dimensionality of party competition in the EU. Finally, in Section 2.6, we assess the effect of the 2004 enlargement on the distinctiveness and cohesion of the European party system.

2.2. The development of the EU party system

During its first five decades, the EU party system was a remarkably efficient device for integrating a host of new entrants into a rather 'lean' structure.[2] Its basic design was established already in 1953 when, in the Common Assembly of the European Coal and Steel Community, Christian-democrats, socialists, and liberals established the first trans-national parliamentary groups. From the very beginning of the European project, just eight years after the end of World War II, national political parties organized their European co-operation on the basis of common socio-political roots and ideological proximity rather than nationality.

New entrants to be integrated in the already defined European party system came from altogether nine additional member countries that joined the original six between 1973 and 1996.[3] But also 'really new' parties emerging in the existing member countries eventually entered Parliament.[4]

For what is now called the EU party system, 1973 was a turbulent year: three new political groups emerged. A communist group was formed out of French (PCF) and Italian (PCI) deputies. Later, in 1989, with the breakdown of communism and some time ahead of the collapse of the post-World War II party system of Italy in 1992, this group lost the main successor-party of the PCI (the Italian PDS) to the Socialist Group, leaving the French communists with some new 'far-left' acquisitions (the German PDS, among others) in a severely diminished far-left group.

Still in 1973, British Conservatives (and allies) and French Gaullists (and allies) formed a new political group each. Due to their different social roots and political perspectives (not least on matters of European integration), both did not easily fit into the Christian-democratic European People's Party (EPP). Yet the gravitation force of this powerful agglomeration of EP members eventually overcame these socio-political obstacles: The British and Danish conservatives associated themselves with the EPP in 1992 (following the Spanish conservatives who already had joined the EPP in 1989), and the Gaullist RPR joined after the 1994 EP election.

All of these parties institutionalize socio-political conflicts that originate in the more or less distant past. But EP elections also helped the new party family[5] of the Greens to establish itself. The first Green deputies entered Parliament after the EP election of 1984 and settled with a rather heterogeneous 'Rainbow Group'. One election later, in 1989, the Greens became numerous enough to build a readily identifiable ecologist group which gained representation in every Parliament since.

Christian-democrats and conservatives, socialists, liberals, the far-left and the Greens – together they define the basic structure of the EU party system. There are two additional groups right-of-centre that aggregate Euro-critical views of different rigour: the Europe of Democracies and Diversities (EDD), which became the Independence and Democracy Group after the 2004 election, and the Union for a Europe of Nations (UEN). Both groups are of about equal size; they compete with one another for members of the same ideological background, and one might assume that in the long run only one of them will prevail. Finally there is the group of the 'Non Inscrits', which traditionally has been dominated by extreme-right members.[6]

Just before Eastern enlargement, the EU party system integrated about 130 national parties in not more than five consolidated party groups, and in two less consolidated but minor 'ideological areas' – the Eurosceptic right-of-centre and the far-right. These numbers, as small as they are, still give a false impression of the format of the EU party system, which is essentially characterized by two predominant political groups – the Socialists on the left, and the Christian Democrats on the right. It is therefore certainly right to say that the European party system has been extraordinarily successful in integrating an ever increasing number of national political parties in not more than a handful of relevant party groups at the European level.

The EP election of June 2004 added about 40 Central and Eastern European parties to the EU system, thus increasing the overall number to some 170 national parties sending delegations to the EP. Obviously, this enormous influx presented a serious challenge for the distinctiveness and cohesion of EU-wide parties. As argued above, the successful formation of European party groups is mainly due to a similar development of political cleavages at the time of the emergence of mass political parties at the end of the nineteenth and the early twentieth centuries. In Central and Eastern Europe, political party systems only emerged in the early 1990s as part of the process of democratization, and might be based on less stable pillars like specific issue alliances or the personal charisma of political elites that predominated during regime change. The latter supposition, sometimes referred to as the *tabula rasa* theory, has received little empirical support (Kitschelt et al. 1999). Actually, there seems to be a stable structure of social divisions (Evans and Whitefield 2000), although the political sphere is still characterized by substantial levels of volatility both on the voters' and the parties' side (e.g., Birch 2001; Tavits 2008).

This reminds us of the fact that social divisions are necessary but not sufficient conditions for socio-political cleavages. Social divisions only become cleavages when they are organized as such (Bartolini and Mair 1990: 216). Organization requires time, resources and opportunities, all of which might not yet have been sufficiently available in post-communist democracies. In addition, the formation of cleavages also requires political elites actively promoting the partisan organization of social divisions. Under present-day conditions of mass political communication, however, this is not necessarily always in their own best interest.[7] Therefore, it is still an open question to what extent social conflicts in Central and Eastern Europe are translated into ideological divisions between political parties compatible with those in Western Europe.

2.3. The party systems of Central and Eastern Europe: Do they fit in?

A first simple test of the effect of the 2004 enlargement on the EU party system is the extent to which the elected Members of the European Parliament (MEPs) from these countries have joined the existing party groups in the EP after the 2004 elections. Table 2.1 clearly shows that most MEPs from the accession countries have done so. While MEPs from Central and Eastern Europe are slightly more likely to be unaffiliated with any party group than MEPs from the original fifteen, the overwhelming majority of Eastern European MEPs (82 per cent) formally joined a supranational group.[8] Over sixty percent of them are members of the two major party groups, the Party of European Socialists (PES) (Socialists) and the European People's Party–European Democrats (EPP–ED) (Christian Democrats and Conservatives).

Comparing the vote shares that the different groups of the EP received in 'old' and 'new' Europe, we find that EPP–ED support was somewhat stronger in the East, while PES and far-left support were considerably weaker there. Support for liberal parties was almost identical. The same holds for EU-sceptical parties (taking UEN and IND/DEM members together): vote shares are limited in the West and in the East, and certainly much less dramatic than some authors suggested ahead of the election (e.g. Beichelt 2004). So enlargement did have some effect on the mutual strength of the major party groups, but the important thing here is that in general MEPs from the new member states found a place in the existing party system. Therefore, on the surface, at least, the 2004 enlargement has hardly affected the EU party system. However, for our purposes we should scratch below the surface. The major research question to be answered in this chapter is to what degree the 2004 enlargement has affected the distinctiveness and cohesion of the party groups. Since distinctiveness and cohesion can only be assessed with regard to particular policy dimensions, we start by assessing the effect of enlargement on the dimensionality of the party system.

Table 2.1. Enlargement and EP group membership

EP Group	EP15	Central-Eastern Europe	Other New Members	Total
EPP–ED (European People's Party–European Democrats)	213	62	4	279
	35.7%	49.2%	36.4%	38.1%
PES (Party of European Socialists)	168	28	3	199
	28.1%	17.7%	28.9%	27.2%
ALDE (Alliance of Liberals and Democrats for Europe)	52	14	1	67
	11.5%	8.9%	9.1%	9.2%
Greens–EFA (European Greens–European Free Alliance)	39	1	0	40
	6.5%	0.6%	0.0%	5.5%
EUL/NGL (European United Left/Nordic Green Left)	31	6	2	39
	5.2%	3.8%	18.2%	5.3%
UEN (Union for Europe of the Nations)	16	11	0	27
	2.7%	7.0%	0.0%	3.7%
IND/DEM (Independence and Democracy)	15	0	0	15
	2.5%	0.0%	0.0%	2.0%
Other (No Affiliation)	36	29	1	66
	6.0%	18.4%	9.1%	9.0%
Total	596	158	11	732
	100.0%	100.0%	100.0%	100.0%

Note: Entries are numbers of seats and column percentages.
Source: European Parliament at http://www.europarl.europa.eu.
Results as of 30 June, 2004.

2.4. Dimensions of party competition in the European Union before enlargement

It is hardly a matter of dispute that the left–right dimension and the integration–independence dimension are the two major dimensions of political contestation in EU politics, but there is an ongoing debate on the relative importance of these two dimensions and their mutual relationship. Steenbergen and Marks (2004) distinguish four logical possibilities, each of which has its proponents in the literature. According to the *international relations model*, contestation about European integration is independent from the left–right dimension of domestic contestation, and the latter dimension is irrelevant for understanding contestation on European integration.

Just like the international relations model, the *Hix–Lord model* claims that the two dimensions are independent. The two dimensions cannot be collapsed into a single dimension because they mobilize cross-cutting political coalitions. The left–right dimension involves the allocation of resources and values between *functional* groups, whereas the integration–independence dimension involves the issue of national sovereignty and therefore the allocation of resources and values between *territorial* groups. Since the major political parties compete on social and economic policies and not on the question of the institutional design of the emerging supranational political system in Europe, they leave opposition to minor parties at the ideological extremes. This implies that the dimension of integration–independence is of minor importance only and the distribution of political parties on the two orthogonal dimensions follows a horseshoe pattern.

The *regulation model*, just like the international relations model, conceives of a single dimension of contestation for European issues, but in contrast to its rival model it assumes that EU politics is fused to domestic competition between the left, which pushes for common economic regulation across Europe, and the right, which favours less EU regulation.

Finally, the *Hooghe–Marks* or *'regulated capitalism' vs. 'neoliberalism' model* distinguishes a left–right dimension ranging from social democracy to market liberalism and a European integration dimension from nationalism to supranationalism. According to the model these dimensions are neither fused nor orthogonal to each other. Certain aspects of European integration are likely to be absorbed into the left–right dimension. To the extent that this is the case, integration and independence and left and right become indistinguishable. However, not all aspects of integration are easily incorporated into the left–right dimension and to the extent that they cannot be, a distinct integration–independence dimension emerges.

There is no simple way of telling which of these models is empirically more valid than the other. To some extent these models and the empirical evidence supporting them are based on different conceptualizations of what in particular the dimension of European integration stands for, in addition to differences in methods and data. Also, they sometimes refer to different political arenas or regimes of decision making. The traditional international-relations perspective strongly focuses on the *process* of European integration rather than on the EU as a polity of its own. As we explained in the introductory chapter, the *process* of European integration mainly refers to issues on the integration–independence dimension, which are subject to the intergovernmental regime. If one focuses on these kind of issues, it would be surprising *not* to find a dominant integration–independence dimension. Equally, if one focuses on issues of economic regulation by the EU one can hardly be surprised to find that political parties and party groups can be found on the same side of the divide as they are at the national level, depending on their position on the left–right continuum. Therefore, depending on one's perspective, one can find supportive evidence both for the international relations model and the regulation model. This is essentially what the Hooghe and Marks model claims.

In this book, we are interested in the process of political representation at the European level, i.e., the process connecting the policy preferences of the European people to decision making in the EP. The main question in this chapter is to what extent the choices political parties offer the voters are connected to the dimensions of contestation in the EP. In other words, what is relevant here is to what extent political parties at the supply side of politics are distinct and cohesive with regard to the policy dimensions dividing the party groups in the EP.

The empirical evidence on what these dimensions were until the 2004 enlargement is unequivocal. Analyses of roll-call behaviour in the EP prove that the left–right dimension is by far the most important dimension of contestation, classifying about 90 per cent of legislators' votes correctly (Thomassen, Noury, and Voeten 2004; Hix et al. 2006*b*; McElroy and Benoit 2007; see also Chapter 5 of this book), just as it is the dominant constraint underlying attitudes of individual members of Parliament. Also, on this dimension European party groups were distinct and cohesive (Schmitt and Thomassen 1999; Thomassen and Schmitt 1999*c*). This applies not only to the party groups in the EP but also to the party manifestos the national political parties composing the European party groups present to their voters (Thomassen and Schmitt 2004; Wüst and Schmitt 2007).

The second, but far less important, dimension is the European integration dimension, defined in terms of integration vs. independence. On this dimension the major party groups were hardly distinct. From the beginning, European integration has been built on a basic consensus among the member states and among the major political parties. As a consequence, these parties do not compete on this dimension but on the left–right dimension. Competition on the integration–independence dimension is mostly left to the smaller parties at the left and the right. As a consequence, political parties in this two-dimensional space are distributed in the form of a horseshoe, with centrist parties being located in the Euro-positive quadrants, while extreme left *and* extreme right parties position themselves in the Euro-sceptical quadrants. Therefore, the empirical evidence on the dimensionality of the European party system strongly supports the Hix–Lord model.

More recently the two-dimensionality of the European party system has become a matter of dispute. According to several scholars, the libertarian–authoritarian dimension should be taken into account as well. Although the relevance of this dimension has been known for quite some time (Hix and Lord 1997; Thomassen and Schmitt 1999c), only recently has it been recognized as a potentially powerful dimension of contestation.

To some extent this debate is a reflection of a current debate on the number and content of the relevant dimensions of political contestation at the national level, a debate which in turn is strongly related to the rise of populist parties both at the left and right. The success of these parties can hardly be understood in the framework of either the traditional cleavage structure or the simple left–right framework. Kriesi et al. (2006), for example, argue that the antagonism between winners and losers of the contemporary process of 'globalization' leads to a conflict between *integration* and *demarcation*. This new conflict is partly embedded into the existing socio-economic conflict dimension as it can be expected to reinforce the classic opposition between a pro-state and a pro-market position, while giving it a new meaning. The pro-state position is likely to become more defensive and of a more protectionist nature, while the pro-market position is likely to become more assertive in favour of the enhancement of national competitiveness on world markets.

However, the new conflict has a cultural dimension as well. This dimension is expected to increasingly take on an ethnic or nationalist character. Also, related issues like European integration and immigration are expected to be integrated into this cultural dimension. The demarcation pole of this new cultural conflict should be characterized by opposition to the process of European integration and by restrictive positions with regard to immigration.

Kriesi et al. (2006) suggest that established parties are repositioning and realigning themselves as a result of the rising new conflict. A spatial analysis of the media coverage of the electoral campaigns of political parties in six European countries confirmed the existence of a two-dimensional party space. The positions of parties were found to vary as strongly with respect to the cultural issues as with respect to the economic ones. Both dimensions are polarizing. Furthermore, Kriesi et al. claim that the cultural dimension has been gaining in importance as it has become the primary basis on which new parties or responsive established parties seek to mobilize their electorate.

If European politics is domestic politics by other means as we essentially argued in the introductory chapter, this development should be reflected in the European party system as well. This is exactly what Hooghe, Marks, and Wilson (2004) argue. They investigate the influence of what they call *a new politics dimension*, which they conceive as ranging from GAL (green/alternative/libertarian) to TAN (traditional/authoritarian/nationalist).[9] They do not provide any hard evidence proving the increasing importance of this dimension. Their primary purpose in introducing this dimension is to explain political parties' stances on European integration. They find strong correlations between the GAL/TAN dimension, overall support for European integration, and support for particular aspects of European integration, including environmental policy, asylum policy, and strengthening the EP. Parties near the TAN pole, that is, radical right and right-populist parties, are, without exception, highly Eurosceptical. Hooghe et al. expect that the GAL/TAN dimension might increase in importance because the relative electoral weight of these parties has grown considerably over the past two decades.

Summarizing, there is strong empirical evidence for the following characteristics of the EU party space up to the 2004 enlargement:

- The EU party space is dominated by two issue dimensions, the left–right and the integration–independence dimension. The relevance of a third dimension, the libertarian–authoritarian dimension might be increasing;
- The left–right dimension is by far the most important dimension of contestation;

- There is no linear, but rather a curvilinear relationship between positions of political parties on the left–right dimension and the dimension of European integration, i.e., party groups in a two-dimensional space form a horseshoe pattern, and;
- European party groups are distinct and cohesive and therefore potentially competitive on the left–right dimension; on the integration–independence dimension the major party groups hardly differ, but as a group they are distinct from the smaller party groups at the left and the right.

2.5. Dimensions of party competition in the European Union after enlargement

Still, the empirical evidence for these characteristics of the EU party space is based on analyses of the EU party system before the 2004 enlargement. The question that concerns us here is to what extent the 2004 enlargement affected these characteristics. Or, to phrase it differently, to what extent do the party systems from the new member states from Central and Eastern Europe fit in this pre-existing party space?

There is no reason to take this for granted. First, as observed above, the surprisingly successful formation of European party groups is based on the commonalities in the cleavage structure of the countries in Western Europe. It is still to be seen whether and how the new party systems in the accession countries that are not necessarily based on these common cleavages easily fit in the existing European party system.

Second, the dominance of the left–right dimension over the European integration dimension does not necessarily apply to the new member states. Since the issue of joining the EU came up almost simultaneously with the democratization process in most of these countries, it has been a matter of debate to what extent the issue of EU membership would develop into a major political issue. On the one hand, it has been argued that the issue of EU membership was highly politicized in these countries making integration a major issue of contestation. To the extent that this was the case, we might expect to find more competitive and therefore distinct positions of the major political parties than in the older member states. On the other hand, it also has been argued that there is a long-standing broad policy consensus on the 'return to Europe'. As a result, '... the integration question has remained largely a second-order political concern rather than a primary contestation issue in the charged competitive dimension of the former communist states' (Bielasiak 2004: 22). Whether the former or the latter argument is correct might make quite a difference for how easily the parties from the accession countries fit in the pre-2004 EU party system.

For obvious reasons the empirical evidence with regard to these questions is limited so far. Our own data suggest that the EU dimension is of greater behavioural relevance in the enlargement countries (Schmitt et al. 2008). As far as the evidence from other research projects goes, it seems to confirm the major importance of the left–right dimension in these countries. On the basis of an expert survey, Rohrschneider and Whitefield (2008) find that the left–right dimension, understood as a socio-economic issue dimension, is predominant across Central and Eastern Europe: '..... just as in Western Europe, where social class is a common denominator whereas religious and ethnic conflicts introduce diversity across nations, economic issues constitute the common basis for party competition in the region and other conflicts add a country-specific flavour' (Rohrschneider and Whitefield 2008: 14).

Our own data enable us to assess the relationship between the left–right dimension and the European integration dimension, both in the old member states and the accession countries. Figure 2.1 graphically display the outcome of a regression analysis, regressing the positions of (national) political parties on the pro-/anti-integration dimension on their positions on the left–right dimension. These positions are derived from popular perceptions (arithmetic means) of the location of nationally relevant parties on the left–right dimension[10] and the integration–independence dimension[11] as measured in the European Elections Study 2004.[12]

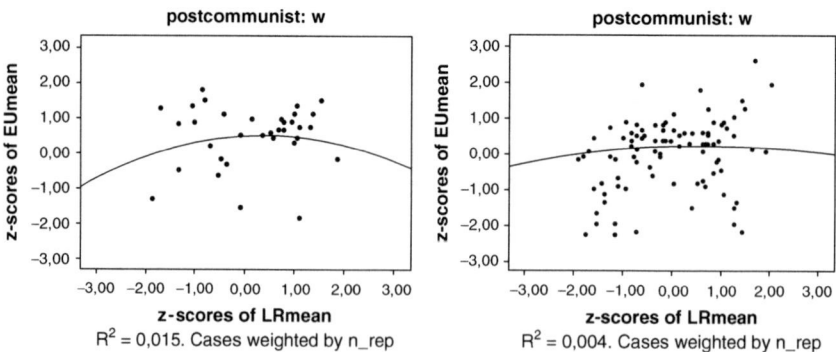

Figure 2.1. Party positions in Eastern Europe and party positions in Western Europe

The interpretation of these two figures is straightforward: there is hardly a linear relationship between left–right position of political parties and their position with regard to European integration, neither in the West nor in the East. Although in both regions the relationship between the two dimensions is significant, suggesting that political parties have a somewhat higher chance for Euro-positive orientations the more to the right they are, the model fit in both cases is very poor. In this respect there is no difference between East and West. This suggests that in both regions the EU political space can better be described as two-dimensional, with left–right orientations and pro-/anti-EU attitudes independently structuring it.

In fact, as Figures 2.2 through 2.4 demonstrate, there is not a linear but a curvilinear relationship between the two dimensions—at least if we look at EP groups. These figures are based on three different data sources measuring the position of political parties on the two dimensions. In addition to popular perceptions of party locations as established by the European Election Study these sources are a content analysis of the 2004 EP election programmes of the parties (Euromanifestos)[13] and the Chapel Hill expert survey.[14] The figures display the familiar 'horseshoe', the pattern of party competition consistent with the Hix and Lord model described above. While there is a considerable spread of EP group positions along the left–right dimension in both regions, variation along the pro-/anti-EU dimension is less pronounced. Nevertheless, far-left and far-right parties tend to be somewhat more sceptical about the EU than centre-left and centre-right parties. The latter also tend to be the larger ones, which might have nurtured the familiar view that there is hardly any choice offered to the voter in EP elections. So again the most important conclusion is that the pictures of East and West are very much the same.

2.6. The competitiveness and cohesion of the European party system after enlargement

The final and most essential question to be addressed in this chapter refers to the effect of enlargement on the competitiveness and cohesion of the European party system. Our first approach to answering this question is an effort to predict the positions of political parties on the two main policy dimensions on the basis of their party group membership, both in the East and the West. Once again we use the three different data sources introduced in the previous section. Table 2.2 shows the results of this analysis.

The Legitimacy of the European Union after Enlargement

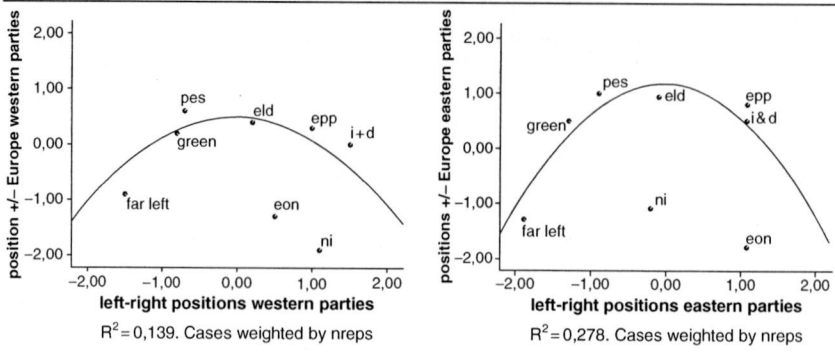

Figure 2.2. Voter perceptions of party positions

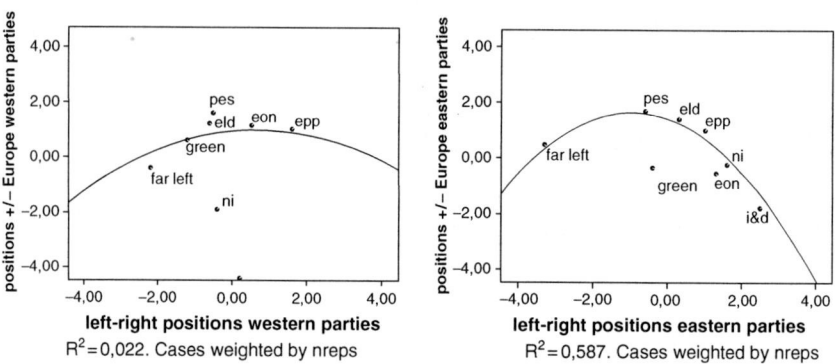

Figure 2.3. Party positions as estimated from expert codings of manifestos

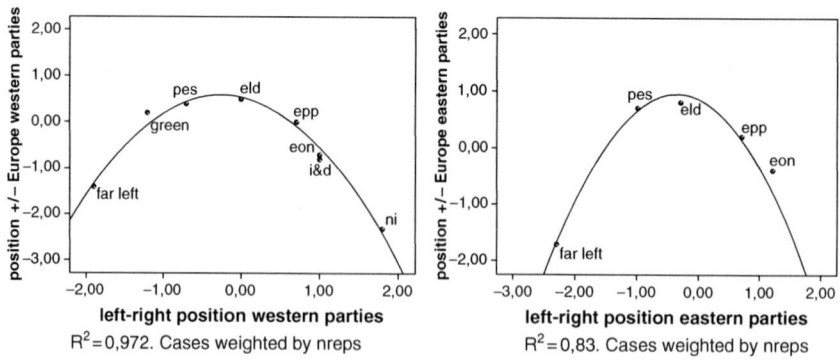

Figure 2.4. Party positions from expert surveys

The European Party System after Enlargement

Table 2.2. Ideological positions of political parties represented in the 2004 European Parliament as predicted by group affiliation (analyses of variance – figures are R squares)

	Left–Right			Pro/Anti-Europe		
	W	E	All	W	E	All
Voter perceptions	.81	.80	.79	.49	.77	.53
Manifestos	.42	.59	.41	.56	.46	.50
Experts	.84	.71	.79	.47	.64	.53

Note: Party positions are weighted with (multiplied by) the number of EP representatives of the respective parties.

At least three observations are worth mentioning. First, and most importantly in our context: EP group membership is a strong predictor of the policy positions of political parties, both in the East and the West. The relationship between party group membership and left–right is very similar in the two regions, although the relationship between membership and the European integration dimension is a bit stronger in the East than in the West. This seems to support the view of some observers that the issue of European integration is more politicized in the East than in the West. Second: left–right positions are better explained by party group membership than integration–independence positions. Third: all three data sources tell the same story, with almost identical results from the voter and expert surveys and similar but weaker coefficients from the analysis of Euromanifestos data.[15]

This first and somewhat global test suggests that an Eastern or Western background does not affect the position that political parties take on the left–right and the integration–independence dimension. As these are the two major issue dimensions structuring the EU political space, this can only mean that Eastern enlargement has done surprisingly little to the EU party system. With or without the new members – the party groups look very much the same, both with regard to their left–right and their pro-/anti-Europe positions. The new parties seem to fit very well in the existing structure.

A more telling test of the effect of enlargement on the competitiveness and cohesion of the European party system is to compare the average policy positions of old and new members. Figures 2.6 through 2.8 summarize the results of this comparison. They present six scatterplots that confront the mean left–right and pro-/anti-Europe positions of new and old members, for each of our three data sources. The degree of distinctiveness is indicated by the range of positions that is found in the (z-transformed) data; the relative cohesion of new and old members is indicated by the

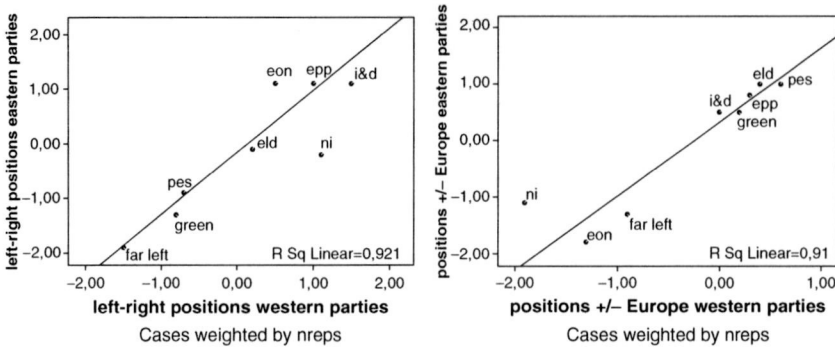

Figure 2.5. Voter perceptions of party positions

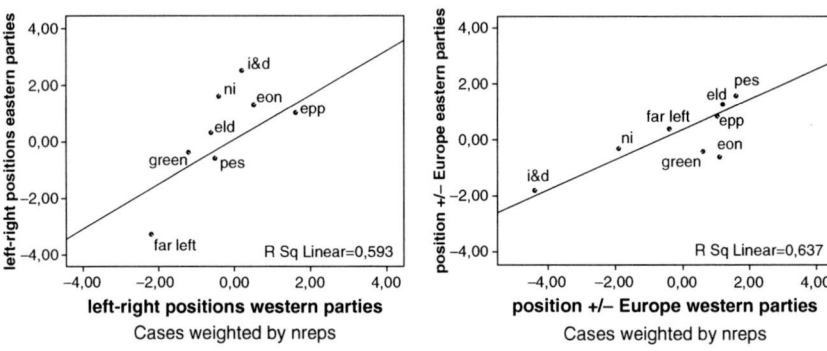

Figure 2.6. Party positions as estimated from expert codings of manifestos

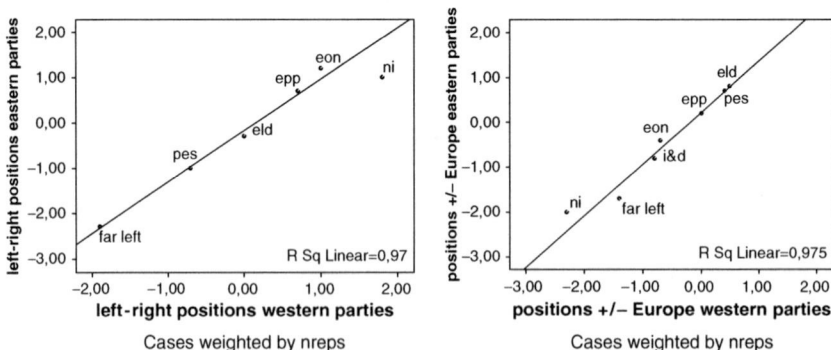

Figure 2.7. Party positions from expert surveys

concentration of party (EP group) positions around the regression slope and the resulting R square.

The general impression one gets from these six scatterplots is that the EU party system is still remarkably distinctive and cohesive. The spread of party positions is enormous, on both dimensions. PES and EPP, the two hegemonic parties of the system, offer clearly different left–right policies while they are comparatively close with regard to the integration–independence dimension. This confirms the findings of previous studies.

But the most astonishing finding from this analysis is that the 2004 enlargement hardly had an effect on the competitiveness and the cohesion of the party system. Both in the graph based on voters' perceptions and the one based on expert views, most party positions are almost perfectly located on the regression line, meaning that there is a perfect match between the Eastern and Western components of these party groups. The manifesto data suggest a somewhat weaker fit. The same observation holds for the positioning of EP groups relative to one another: voter and expert surveys by and large reveal the same configuration, while the manifesto data suggest a somewhat different structure.[16]

2.7. Conclusion

In this chapter we tried to assess the effect of the 2004 Eastern enlargement on the characteristics of the European party system, in particular its competitiveness and cohesion. Surprisingly enough, the EU party system has not changed much as a result of Eastern enlargement. The EPP–ED has gained additional strength, both PES and the Far Left suffered, and the proportion of unaffiliated members has increased due to the fact that a good number of Eastern members did not join one of the traditional political groups.

Also, the enlargement had hardly any effect on the characteristics of the party system studied in this chapter. The party space is still dominated by two dimensions, the left–right dimension and the integration–independence dimension. Party competition in the EU on these two dimensions can still be characterized by a horseshoe pattern, with centre-left and centre-right groups more in favour of further integration than far-left and far-right groups. The competitiveness and cohesiveness of the party system was hardly affected by enlargement. The party groups by and large still are as competitive and cohesive as they were before enlargement.

Notes

1. Of course, the 2004 enlargement included Cyprus and Malta as well, but in this chapter we limit ourselves to the effects of the Eastern enlargement. We use accession countries, Eastern Europe, Central and Eastern Europe and the East interchangeably.
2. See for the following Henig (1979); Hix and Lord (1997); and the web pages of the political groups of the EP.
3. The parties of Ireland, Britain, and Denmark entered the EP in 1973; those of Greece in 1981; Spanish and Portuguese parties entered in 1983; Austrian, Finnish, and Swedish parties in 1996.
4. Examples are the green parties that emerged in many European countries in the 1980s (e.g., Müller-Rommel 1989); or the parties of the second Italian republic from 1992 on (e.g., Mershon and Pasquino 1995).
5. See Mair and Mudde (1998) for a useful discussion of the somewhat unwieldy concept of 'party family'.
6. With the accession of Romania and Bulgaria to the EU on 1 January 2007, extreme-right representatives in the EP became numerous enough to form their own parliamentary group.
7. See here also Sitter (2002) and Enyedi (2005) who highlight the impact of party (leader) strategy on East European party system stability and change.
8. Once Parliament was in session this percentage went up to 94 per cent.
9. In the operationalization of this dimension these three aspects do not appear though. In fact, experts are asked to position political parties on a classic libertarian–authoritarian dimension (Hooghe et al. 2004: 122).
10. The question wording goes as follows: 'In political matters people talk of "the left" and "the right". What is your position? Please indicate your views using any number on a 10-point scale. On this scale, where 1 means "left" and 10 means "right", which number best describes your position?... And about where would you place the following parties on this scale? How about the Labour Party? And...' The Swedish study used an 11-point scale, which we tried to adjust as described in the next footnote.
11. The question wording is: 'Some say European unification should be pushed further. Others say it already has gone too far. What is your opinion? Please indicate your views using any number on a 10-point scale. On this scale, 1 means unification "has already gone too far" and 10 means it "should be pushed further". What number on this scale best describes your position?... And about where would you place the following parties on this scale? How about the Labour Party? And...' Note that in the Swedish study an 11-point scale (from 0 to 10) was used and that respondents were asked whether they agree with or oppose Sweden's EU membership, and where they locate the Swedish parties on this scale. We tried to adjust the different scale format by collapsing scale categories '0' and '1' into scale category '1'. The Belgian survey

did not ask this question which is why Belgian parties cannot be considered in this analysis.
12. Van der Brug and Van der Eijk (1999) have shown that voters' perceptions of party locations (the latter being operationalized by party elite perceptions of where the party is) are relatively accurate as long as general policy and, in particular, ideological dimensions are concerned. We believe that both the EU dimension and the left–right dimension that are analysed here are of such a general nature and that party positions can be reliably estimated on the basis of representative mass surveys.
13. For more detailed information on this data source see appendix to this chapter.
14. The Chapel Hill 2002 expert survey dataset provides data on party positions on European integration for 171 parties in 23 of the 25 current EU member states (not Luxembourg and Estonia) as well as in Bulgaria and Romania. The survey was administered between September 2002 and April 2003 to 636 academics specializing in parties, European integration, or closely related topics in one of the countries considered. 238 surveys were completed, which amounts to a 37 per cent response rate. We again use the general left–right placement of parties and their positioning on European integration. The expert survey used the following questions: 'First, we would like you to classify the parties in terms of their broad ideology. On the scale below, 0 indicates that a party is at the extreme left of the ideological spectrum, 10 indicates that it is at the extreme right, and 5 means that it is at the center. For each party, please circle the ideological position that best describes a party's overall ideology'.

And for the measurement of parties' positions on the European integration dimension: 'First, how would you describe the general position on European integration that the party's leadership has taken over the course of 2002? For each party row, please circle the number that corresponds best to your view. Circle only one number'. A 7-point answering scale was provided, with the categories strongly opposed, opposed, somewhat opposed, neutral, somewhat in favour, in favour, and strongly in favour.
15. Note that these findings are largely independent of the weighting decision: whether we count each party observation only once, or as many times as its delegation size suggests, hardly affects the results.
16. Note that some of the variation in EP group positions is certainly caused by the fact that the three methods analyse not fully identical samples of EP member parties, that is to say that some parties that are covered by the voter survey could not be studied in the Euromanifesto analysis, etc.

APPENDIX: CHAPTER 2

A.2.1. Euromanifesto content

The party manifestos issued on the occasions of elections to the European Parliament (EP) have been collected and analysed for all parties ever represented in the EP. Euromanifestos have been collected for the period from 1979 to 2004, and preparations are currently under way to collect them also for the 2009 elections. Analyses presented in this book exclusively rely on the 2004 Euromanifestos. In general, national political parties issue their own Euromanifestos, but in some cases the national parties adopted their European party federation's Euromanifesto completely, so these documents have also been collected and coded.

A.2.2. Project information

The Euromanifestos Project has been funded by two grants of the German Research Foundation (DFG, Germany) and by the European Commission under the 7th Framework Programme as a part of the Design Infrastructure Project PIREDEU. PDF copies of all collected Euromanifestos are being archived at the MZES (QUIA archive), and an integrated dataset of the expert coding of the manifestos from 1979 to 2004 are publicly available at Gesis-Zentralarchiv für Empirische Sozialforschung in Cologne. An internet page on the Euromanifestos project provides background and up-to-date information on the project: www.europeanelectionstudies.net/euromanifestos.

A.2.3. Coding

For the expert coding of the Euromanifestos, a Euromanifesto Coding Scheme (EMCS) has been developed (Wüst and Volkens 2003).[1] The EMCS is a modified and 'mirrored' coding scheme compatible to and based on the classical coding frame used for the Comparative Manifesto Project (CMP) (Budge et al. 2001; Volkens 2002). The EMCS provides the fifty-six original content categories in seven policy domains, but to include EU-specific issues, one domain ('political system') has been split into the classical political system domain and a new EU political system domain, which includes thirteen new EU-specific categories. In total, the

EMCS thus provides sixty-nine content categories and various new sub-categories. Further, the mirroring technique enables us to simultaneously identify the governmental frame a party uses when it refers to any of the sixty-nine issues covered by the EMCS: national, European, worldwide, and unspecific. Consequently, the Euromanifesto expert coding results in empirical information on the content of the Euromanifestos (like the CMP does for the national party manifestos) combined with data on the political arena in which each of these issues is discussed.

A.2.4. Weighting

The Euromanifesto data presented here are weighted in such a way that a manifesto is weighted by the number of representatives the respective party is sending to the EP. In that way, the content of big parties' manifestos becomes more important than the manifesto content of small parties. Parties that failed to gain representation are weighted by '0' and thereby deleted from the analyses.

Note

1. Also available online: <http://www.mzes.uni-mannheim.de/publications/wp/wp-64.pdf>.

3

Light at the End of the Tunnel: Towards a European Public Sphere?

Claes de Vreese, Hajo Boomgaarden, Susan Banducci, and Holli Semetko

3.1. Introduction

Questions about the democratic legitimacy of the EU, as suggested in the introductory chapter to this volume, have focused on both normative and empirical considerations both in terms of the political system itself and how its citizens view the EU. Evaluations of the democratic legitimacy of the EU as a political system tend to posit and compare descriptions of the exercise of EU power to normative ideals either in terms of accountability and representation (e.g. see Beetham and Lord 1998*b*), technocratic efficiency (Majone 1993), or indirect legitimacy through the authorization of member states (Moravscik 1998). Most of the work focusing on how citizens view the institutions and processes of the EU rely on an Eastonian framework (Easton 1965*a*) of the different objects of political support: community, regime, and the performance of authorities. In both the discussion of the legitimacy of the political system as compared to a normative standard and whether citizens view the political system as legitimate, there is the notion that a community or *demos* exists. For notions of accountability and representation to have meaning a citizenry with popular sovereignty is assumed. Likewise, identity with and attachment to the community demonstrate a degree of system legitimacy.

From both perspectives, the existence of a public sphere is an essential requirement. For those working from the tradition of the EU as a political system, a common identity has emerged as one of the prerequisites for legitimacy and feasible representation. A shared identity is also viewed as necessary for legitimacy measured from the bottom up (see Chapters 1 and 9). Whether it is necessary that this identity is based on the cultural or political community is a matter of debate, but some have suggested that a shared communication space, a public sphere, is necessary for the development of a common identity (Habermas 1996). Therefore, communication about European integration and EU institutions plays a potentially important role in the development of a shared identity and the related system legitimacy. Finding this shared space has been the focus of much academic work.

We will argue in the next section that the development of a European public sphere is necessary for a feasible European system of political representation. As elections to the European parliament represent a collective European event where political and media attention is likely to be focused, we examine the question whether these elections represent an occasion in which a (shared) European public space emerges. We will see that the ingredients for a European public sphere are contested in the normative literature. We then turn to an empirical examination of the evidence for a European public sphere, taking into account the 2004 enlargement.

We will also argue that the public sphere, in particular news media coverage of the EU, plays a role in influencing the legitimacy of the EU. It is then important to consider not just whether the issue of Europe is on the agenda but how the EU is covered. More critical coverage may dampen enthusiasm for the EU. While the availability of information, cross-references to other countries, and presence of European actors can contribute to legitimacy in an indirect sense, the media can also matter for legitimacy in a more direct sense. Media coverage of politics can contribute to the perceived legitimacy of political institutions (Nye et al. 1997). In the case of elections, the coverage of the campaign can influence perceptions of both the elections and the institutions. It is therefore important to assess the degree to which the media portray the elections as containing a political choice and as important to European citizens (Van der Eijk and Franklin 1996). Valentino et al. (2001) and De Vreese and Semetko (2002) have shown that evaluations of the campaign in the media can affect voters' satisfaction with the campaign. Valentino et al. (2001) also found dissatisfaction to diminish turnout, while De Vreese and Semetko (2002) did not find support for a negative impact on turnout.

3.2. A European public sphere?

It can be argued that a vibrant and healthy European public sphere has existed since the late seventeenth century when ideas of European enlightenment and civilization were the subjects of deliberations across Europe that involved the development of transnational networks in academia, churches, and courts (e.g. Schulz-Forberg 2007). Following the creation of and developments in the European Community, however, research on the European public sphere has generally acknowledged that a single, monolingual, identity-forming European public sphere – resembling that of the nation state – has never existed. Instead, developments towards a degree of Europeanization of and compatibility between national public spheres have been observed.

In this chapter a public sphere is referred to as a space or arena for (broad, public) deliberation, discussion, and engagement in societal issues. The term public sphere is often related to Jürgen Habermas' work and in particular to *The Structural Transformation of the Public Sphere* (Habermas 1962). The original Habermasian notion of a public sphere conceives it as an arena for 'the perception, identification, and treatment of problems affecting the whole society' (Habermas 1962, 1996). It is here that 'new problem situations can be perceived, discourses aimed at achieving self-understanding can be conducted and collective identities and need interpretations can be circulated'. There is a strong body of scholarship in Europe sparked and inspired by Habermas's work. Many of these ideas have resonated over the past two decades in the English language literature, in particular following the translation of some of Habermas's key pieces. Shortcomings, limitations or differences in conceptualization of the public sphere notwithstanding, the public sphere can be defined as *an arena which enables citizens to interact and talk about political issues*.

Many see a European public sphere as an important condition for the development of a European system of political representation, though there is some disagreement on how 'heavy' or 'light' this public sphere should be (see De Vreese (2007), for an overview). From a normative perspective, why is a *European* public sphere necessary and what does it entail? Needless to say, the European Union today has only some similarities to a nation state but many more differences, including behind-closed-doors decision making, a weak parliament, and a fragmented media system (Kleinsteuber 2001). In later work, Habermas (1996: 365) has pointed out that the EU is challenged to be related to a meaningful public sphere: 'The political public sphere can fulfill its function of perceiving and thematizing encompassing social problems only insofar as it develops out of the communication taking place among *those who are politically affected*. It is carried by a public recruitment from the entire citizenry'. Habermas (2001: 65) is very explicit about the necessity for the emergence of a European public sphere: 'The deficit in democracy can only be eliminated if a European public sphere comes into existence in which the democratic process is incorporated. [...] [T]he pan-European political public sphere is the solution to the problem of insufficient social integration in the processes of Europeanization'. In this vein Habermas is thus advocating a European political public space much akin to the national public sphere. Such a sphere would imply spanning sovereign states within a common system and with shared messages and meanings occupying this space.

The notion of a singular, supranational, pan-European public sphere was conceptualized as a communicative space requiring a common language, a shared identity, and a transnational media system (Kielmansegg 1996; Habermas 2001; Grimm 2004). Theorists were quick to acknowledge that a European public sphere is close to impossible due to communication barriers imposed by, for example, the different languages. However, as later acknowledged by critics of this notion of a European public sphere (e.g. Schlesinger 1999; De Vreese 2002), the European Union 'is not a community of communication, hardly a community of shared memories; it is merely, and in a limited sense, a community of shared experiences'. The notion of a monolithic, singular, and pan-European public sphere has also been largely discarded in the light of the failure of attempts to create pan-European media (including, e.g., the newspaper *The European* and the heavily subsidized *Euronews*) (De Vreese 2002). In the literature over the past two decades we can observe a development from focusing on a 'public-sphere heavy' notion of a singular, pan-European public sphere to focusing on a 'public-sphere light' notion of coexisting national public spheres in regard to European politics.

In considering the scope and quality of the public sphere as an arena or 'a system of communication where issues and opinions are being gathered (input), processed (throughput) and passed on (output)' (Neidhardt 1994: 8), most scholars have – rightfully – turned to the media, as is evidenced by a review of the normative debates surrounding the European public sphere. The media and communication play a key role in the interplay between a polity's institutions, civil society, and citizens' attitudes and behavior and are therefore taken as the best 'proxy' and expression of the public sphere. There are indeed good (and practical) reasons to almost equate the media and their contents with the public sphere; mass media enables public communication as speakers are unable to reach their audience, and democratic political entities need mechanisms to link the political arenas. The media functions as 'glue' for the segmented public spheres (Erbe 2005). Indeed most of what citizens experience about politics involves media to some extent, and the media represents an organized and confined space where speakers and actors can provide input for public discussions. News media are an arena in which political actors, civil society and (even) citizens can express views and make announcements. In the European case, the media is an important location for manifestations of the public sphere. Very few people have direct experiences with EU politics, and many policy competences of the EU do not spark interpersonal discussions without being prompted by the media. In sum, when studying the public sphere, the media is an inevitable component as it can be seen as a marketplace of ideas, statements and images of Europe, nations in Europe, and the process of European integration.

Outside the debate on the necessity for a European public sphere, there is a discussion about what this public space could possibly look like. One version of the public sphere has distinguished *segmented transnational public spheres*, which have been conceptualized as issue-specific communicative spaces, largely dominated by political and economic elites (Eder 2000). Novy (2003), for example, emphasizes that a constructive examination of the EU's communicative spaces has to happen at the level of national media, but he emphasizes that the communication will center on specific topics and in specific segments, defined as 'elite quality newspapers'. However, at the end of the day, elitist national newspapers and a handful of commercial news outlets with a global outreach and a significant European audience, such as the *Financial Times*, have a limited, elite readership that makes it hard to speak of a *public* sphere (De Vreese 2002, 2003; Koopmans 2007).

Another version of the public sphere focuses on one or another version of Europeanized public spheres. Different distinctions in Europeanization can be made. One important difference is between news about the EU, its policies and institutions on the one hand, and news about events and issues from other European countries. This distinction has been coined *vertical* and *horizontal Europeanization* (Koopmans and Erbe 2004). Vertical Europeanization refers to national actors addressing European actors, national actors addressing European issues, or European actors partaking in national debates on European issues. Horizontal Europeanization is referred to as national media covering issues in other EU member states and national actors addressing issues or actors in another EU member state.

In addition to the above versions of a European public sphere, several scholars have formulated minimal criteria for a European public sphere. The criteria indeed include corresponding media coverage in different countries with shared points of reference in which 'speakers and listeners recognize each other as legitimate participants in a common discourse that frames the particular issues as common European problems' (Risse and Van de Steeg 2003: 22). From the normative debate and conceptualization of a European public sphere, it is possible to then identify several factors that are necessary in order to claim that a public sphere exists. The discussion of *segmented national spheres* suggests that the outlets and level of actors involved are important. Networks of elites may emerge that address a particular issue area. These debates are likely to take place in quality newspapers and global broadcast outlets. From the *vertical and horizontal Europeanization model* the location or origin of actors involved in the debate is important. Therefore, at the very least, a European public sphere should reflect national media reporting on the same topic using common sources, including EU sources and sources from other EU countries.

3.2.1. *Empirical evidence for a European public sphere?*

Although there is no consensus about the extent to which Europeanized national public spheres exist, it is possible to sketch the contours of a European public sphere. This emergent sphere is perhaps due to the growing contestation over the shaping of the EU polity (as evidenced in the constitutional process) and its growing policy reach and scope (as evidenced by the proportion of EU law that is ratified by national legislatures). Koopmans and colleagues, investigating print news in 1990, 1995, and 2000 to 2002 found strong Europeanization in the Swiss public sphere, and public spheres in Italy and the Netherlands to be 'less European' because discussions about European issues take place among national actors. Issues such as monetary politics and immigration show signs of vertical Europeanization, while horizontal Europeanization is virtually absent (Koopmans 2004). Trenz (2004), in an analysis of broadsheet newspapers in 2000 in Germany, France, Britain, Italy, and Spain, concluded that cross-national differences notwithstanding, there are positive indicators of an absolute degree of European public sphere. Peters et al. (2007), focusing on the quality press in Germany, Great Britain, France, Austria, and Denmark, also distinguish different types of transnationalization. In terms of what they label 'monitoring governance', that is, reporting about the EU and its institutions, they find a clear process of Europeanization between 1982 and 2003. In terms of horizontal integration, however, they found that European countries are not reporting more about each other today than twenty years ago. In terms of referring to discussions and topics of European speakers, they report a relative stability over the past two decades. Finally, this team reports that references to 'Europeans' as a collective or 'we' are rare, albeit marginally increasing over time.

By and large, studies that rely on analyses of broadsheet, quality newspapers tend to find some evidence of Europeanized news coverage (e.g. Eder and Kantner 2002; Trenz and Eder 2004; Peters et al. 2007). Quite to the contrary, research that has focused on (national) television news, which is the most widely cited source of information about the EU for citizens in Europe (Eurobarometer), has concluded that there is no trace of a European public sphere and only occasional, and brief, indications of Europeanization (Peter and De Vreese 2004).

The notion of Europeanized national public spheres has found most resonance in large-scale comparative studies of the media's coverage of European integration. The media coverage of European affairs does not entail a constant flow of news and is best described as cyclical, with occasional peaks and long periods of little news (De Vreese et al. 2001; De Vreese 2002; Peter and De Vreese 2004). Key events, such as national referendums and EU summits, can take up a substantial part of the news (Semetko et al. 2003; De Vreese and Semetko 2004; De Vreese and Boomgaarden 2006), but most of the news is seen through the prism of the nation state.

Taking stock of our current knowledge leads to diverging conclusions with respect to the extent, scope, nature and consolidation of Europeanization of national public spheres. Much of the difference in conclusions can be traced back to different criteria, operationalizations, and foci of the studies. Based on our discussion of the normative debate and a review of the empirical findings, our key empirical indicators for assessing the Europeanness of public spheres include the visibility of European topics (and issues with a European perspective) and some degree of mutual observation and quotation, typically in the form of inclusion of EU actors and actors from other EU countries (see De Vreese 2002; De Vreese et al. 2006). These are operationalized in the section below where we report findings from our study of the 2004 European parliamentary election media coverage.

3.3. European elections: The emergence of Europeanized national public spheres?

To adequately answer the question of a European public sphere we need to turn to one of the most important links between the political arena and citizens: the media. Assessing the degree to which the media contributes to or inhibits the emergence of a European public space is closely connected to the question whether the media contributes to the legitimacy of the European polity, its institutions, and policies. Democratic legitimacy is contingent upon the approval of the governed, and the media provides the arena in which debates and discourse take place that can contribute to or decrease the legitimacy of a system. In the context of European integration the underlying assumption is that a shared European space, a European public sphere, may contribute to the (public) legitimacy of the EU polity, in much the same ways as has been suggested for national public spheres.

In this chapter, we assess the degree to which European elections in a post-enlargement EU constitute a moment of a common European public space. Given that the existence of a European public sphere, as discussed above, was not well established prior to enlargement, we may expect that the addition of ten new members and media systems is not conducive to the emergence of a European public sphere and legitimacy of the elections. Yet, there are signs of emerging Europeanization of national debates. Most importantly, however, claims about the extent of a European public sphere and its link to the legitimacy of European elections remain in lieu of appropriate data. To better understand the relationship between a shared public sphere and democratic legitimacy in the EU, we draw on a content analysis of television news and newspapers in the twenty-five EU member states. We use several indicators to address this: (*a*) the *visibility* of the elections in the news, (*b*) the *contents* and *compatibility* of the debate and the campaign coverage, and (*c*) reference to EU countries and the EU and the visibility of key EU political *actors* and *institutions*. In addition to these indicators, which reflect the degree to which the media portrayed the 2004 elections for the European parliament as part of a legitimate system of governance, we include two other indicators that also contribute to or discuss the legitimacy of the system: (*d*) portraying the elections as containing a *political choice* and (*e*) portraying the elections as intrinsically *important*.

We assess how the news media in the EU performed on each of these dimensions. We make comparisons between the 'old' EU-15 and the 'new' EU-25, between types of media (newspapers and television), between outlet types (public broadcasters versus commercial broadcasters, broadsheets versus tabloid newspapers) and – in the 'old' EU-15 – over time (between 1999 and 2004). We then outline the different relevant indicators to assess a European public space and discuss how these relate to more general indicators of the legitimacy of a political system. In the final part of the chapter we provide evidence from our cross-national analyses of the media.

Elections for the European Parliament (EP) arguably constitute an opportunity for the emergence of a European public space or compatibility between national spheres. The first elections in 1979 were virtually absent from the European media agendas until the final week before the elections (Siune 1983). Twenty years later, when a comparative study of the news coverage of the campaign in the two weeks prior to the EP elections in the then-fifteen countries of the EU was conducted at The Amsterdam School of Communications Research (ASCoR), it was found that the elections received about 7 per cent of the time in national television news programs. Belgium, Germany, Ireland, the Netherlands, Spain and the United Kingdom devoted less than 5 per cent of news to the elections. Austria, Denmark, Finland, France, Greece, Italy, and Sweden were somewhat above average, with 8–13 per cent of news time devoted to the European elections (De Vreese et al. 2007). There was a low visibility of European actors in the news, and there were few references to either the debates in other countries or the European character of the election. As summarized elsewhere (De Vreese et al. 2007: 129), in many countries 'the European elections were given low priority in the news, they rarely made the opening of the news bulletins, the coverage was domestic in nature with most stories taking place in the home country and addressing issues with implications for the home country. Only few representatives of EU institutions made it into the news and these EU actors were rarely quoted and they were evaluated less favorably than other actors'. On the basis of these results we might have low expectations about the potential for Europeanized public spheres to emerge during the campaign for the 2004 elections. By 2004, however, the EP had gained in competences, the euro had become the currency in twelve states, important European issues such as the admission of Turkey and the EU Constitution were on the agenda, and euroskepticism was emerging in several countries. These factors might impact upon the degree to which the elections constitute a moment of European and/or compatible debates.

With the inclusion of ten new member states in 2004, most post-Communist societies that present different and economic backgrounds, there was little reason to assume that the Europeanization trend found in the old EU-15 would also be found in the new countries. After all, in specific relation to the European elections, it took several elections for Europeanization to be a visible feature of national news in the old member states. Moreover, with language and cultural barriers being the most often cited obstacles inhibiting the emergence of European public sphere, the inclusion of ten new countries and several languages and cultures could hardly be expected to be conducive to developments towards Europeanization.

3.4. Data: The 2004 European election media study

The chapter relies on a study of the news coverage of the 2004 EP elections (see De Vreese et al. [2006] for details).[1] Two television news programs and three national newspapers from each EU member state were included.[2] We analysed the main national evening news broadcasts of the most widely watched public and private television stations, two 'quality' (broadsheet), and one tabloid newspaper from each country. These outlets were selected to provide a general and broad picture of the news coverage in each country and in order to ensure comparability with a study of the 1999 elections (De Vreese et al. 2007).

For television, our sample consists of forty-nine television networks, and the newspaper sample consists of seventy-four different newspapers.[3] For television, we coded the entire news program of each station. Our unit of coding and of analysis is the individual news story, defined as a change of topic, typically introduced by the anchorperson or a new headline in newspapers. For television we based all analyses on the length of the individual news story as part of the total length of each news program. In total, 9,339 television news stories were analysed. For newspapers, we also used the individual news story as the unit of analysis. We coded all stories on the front page of the newspaper as well as a random page inside the main section of the newspaper and all news stories about the EP elections throughout the newspaper. In the analyses presented here, we use the analysis of the front pages as the base, for reasons of comparability with the study from 1999. The *n* for this analysis is 8,280.

Measures: Our first measure used here is *visibility of the EP elections*. Each news story was coded for *topic*. News about European elections was designated a range of codes that enabled us to identify when a story was about the elections. In addition, stories about the EU were identified by a topic code for each news story. Topics were coded rather narrowly and were recoded into broader, consistent categories that included, for instance, finance and budget, social and employment policies, or the European constitution. We assessed the visibility of different topics with respect to the EU and could compare the presence of these topics across countries.

To tap the *domestic versus European* nature of the story, we relied on the coding of actors in the news. An actor is defined as a person (e.g. MEP candidate), group of persons (e.g. political party), institution (e.g. national parliament), or other organization (e.g. Red Cross) that is featured in the story. Coders first identified the main actor (in terms of importance) and then other actors in order of appearance. Actors have been classified as EU actors, domestic political actors, or other actors. EU actors include EP candidates as well as the EU president and EU commission members. Domestic political actors are members of the government, spokespersons for government agencies, or members of opposition parties. This includes all members of the national parliaments. The category of other actors includes journalists, celebrities, ordinary citizens, and other actors that do not fall into the EU or domestic political actor categories.[4] Across all news stories a total of 19,851 actors were coded. In addition we used a measure of the *location* of the news to assess the degree of vertical and horizontal Europeanization.

Furthermore, a number of variables relate to the theoretical considerations introduced above and were only coded if the elections or the campaign were specifically mentioned in a news story. First, it was assessed whether the election campaign and the election were portrayed as being *exciting versus boring*. Second, we coded explicit projections of the *turnout* (as being either high or low).

3.5. Results

3.5.1. *The visibility of the EP elections*

The visibility of EU election coverage is of central concern when it comes to assessing the emergence of a European public sphere. Overall, the 2004 EP elections were more visible in the news media in Europe than the 1999 elections. As shown in Figure 3.1, the share of television news coverage was 9.8 per cent on average in 2004, with a somewhat higher visibility in the ten new member states (10.4 per cent) than in the old fifteen (9.2 per cent). Arguably this is due to some kind of novelty effect in the new member states that contributed to more interest from television news. Comparing the visibility of campaign coverage in 1999 and 2004 in the old member states, we find an overall increase of the television news devoted to the EP elections from 6.6 to 9.2 per cent. In ten of the fifteen old member states the visibility of EP elections news increased.

In terms of the old versus new member state comparison, the coverage in newspapers shows a picture similar to the television coverage (see Figure 3.2). Overall in all twenty-five member states 5.9 per cent of the newspaper front-page stories were devoted to EU news. In the old member states we find 5.6 per cent of all front-page stories dealing with the elections, whereas this was 6.1 per cent in the ten new member states. For the old members, we see a

Light at the End of the Tunnel: Towards a European Public Sphere?

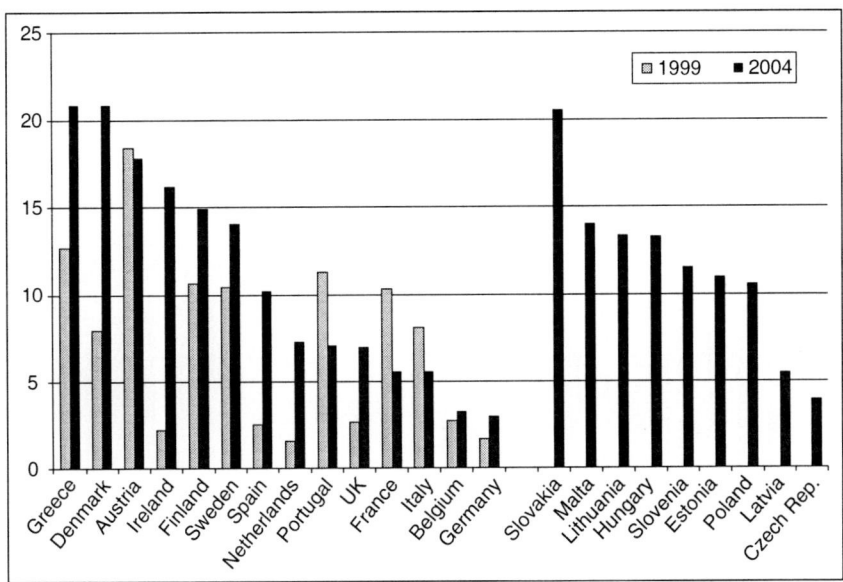

Figure 3.1. Visibility of EU news in television newscasts, 1999 and 2004

Note: Values are length-based percentages within the countries and election periods. All stories in television newscasts were included. Values display the proportion of news stories about the EP election and about other EU news. 1999 $n = 4,781$; 2004 $n = 9,339$.

Source: De Vreese et al. 2006.

decrease in coverage from 6.2 per cent in 1999. So overall visibility of the 2004 election campaign was higher in the new member states, and the old member states on average saw a small decrease in visibility from 1999.

3.5.2. *The national debates*

The second indicator looks at the national debates of different topics with regard to the EU. Table 3.1 displays – by country – the top five issues dealt with in EU news stories (i.e. stories mentioning the EU). By and large we see that in all countries most of the news stories mentioning the EU related to the campaign. Thus, EU news during the campaign was dominated by considerations related to the elections and the campaigns rather than policy issues. The visibility of the campaign as a topic, however, varied considerably across countries, with the lowest visibility in Luxembourg (40 per cent) and the highest in the UK (94 per cent).[5] Besides the campaign, the most visible topics dealt with European integration, economic policies of the Union, and the EU constitution, but there was also

The Legitimacy of the European Union after Enlargement

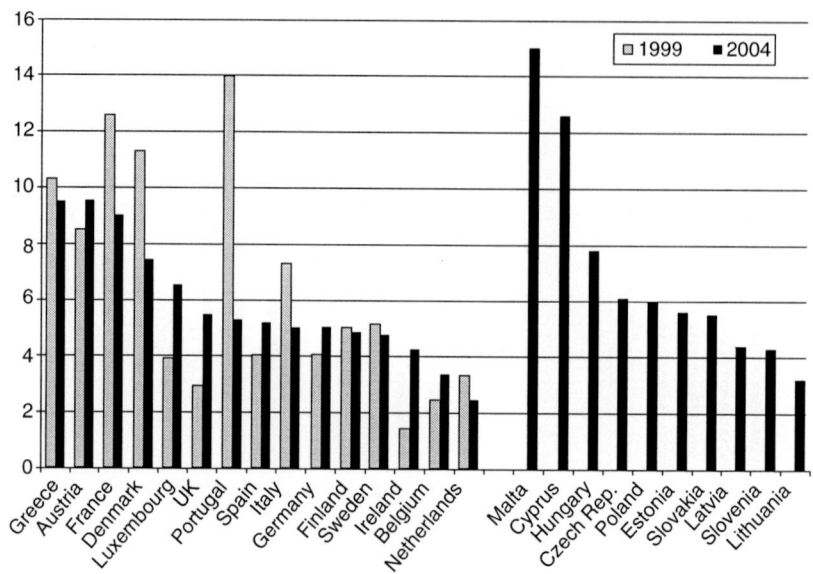

Figure 3.2. Visibility of EU news on newspaper front pages, 1999 and 2004

Note: Values are story-based percentages within the countries and election periods. All stories on newspaper front pages were included. Values display the proportion of news stories about the EP election and about other EU news. 1999 $n = 2,224$; 2004 $n = 8,280$.

Source: De Vreese et al. 2006.

variation across countries. EU integration as a topic was most visible in Cypriote news media (14 per cent) and not mentioned at all in Germany, Ireland, Latvia, and the UK. Economic policy issues were highly visible in Poland (15 per cent) but invisible in Latvia, Lithuania, Slovakia, and the UK. Last, the constitution was most visible in Germany (7 per cent) and not discussed at all in Hungary and Latvia. In conclusion, most of the EU news pertained to the campaigns as such, and policy issues were mostly less dominant than the campaigns itself. Moreover, there is only limited evidence of the same policy issues being addressed in different countries but ample evidence to suggest that the issues are mostly idiosyncratic to the individual country.

3.5.3. *Europe is getting a face*

Our third indicator of a possibly evolving Europeanization of national public spheres involves the presence of political personalities and actors

Light at the End of the Tunnel: Towards a European Public Sphere?

Table 3.1. Top five issues within EU news stories (both television and newspapers)

	Top issue	2nd issue	3rd issue	4th issue	5th issue
AT	EPE campaign	Domestic EU politics	EU integration	EU parliament	EU enlargement, EU institutions
BE	EPE campaign	EU parliament	Economic policy	EU integration	EU institutions
CZ	EPE campaign	Economic policy	Finances/Budget	EU integration	All others
CY	EPE campaign	EU integration	Economic policy	EU constitution	Other EU issue
DK	EPE campaign	Agriculture/consumer protect. policy	EU parliament	EU constitution	EU integration
EE	EPE campaign	Domestic EU policies	EU integration	EU constitution	Other EU issues
FI	EPE campaign	EU institutions	EU constitution	Economic policy	EU parliament
FR	EPE campaign	Economic policy	Domestic EU policy	EU enlargement	EU integration
GE	EPE campaign	EU constitution	Finances/budget	EU institutions	Economic policy, EU parliament
GR	EPE campaign	EU constitution	Domestic EU policy	EU enlargement	Finances/budget, economic policy, EU integration
HU	EPE campaign	EU integration	all others		
IR	EPE campaign	Economic policy	EU constitution	Social/employment policy	EU (policies) in general
IT	EPE campaign	EU institutions	EU parliament	Finances/ budget	EU (policies) in general
LV	EPE campaign	Other EU issue			
LI	EPE campaign	EU integration	Domestic EU policy	Social/employment policy	All others
LX	EPE campaign	EU integration	Finances/budget	Social/employment policy	Energy/science/environmental policy
MA	EPE campaign	Economic policy	EU constitution	Domestic EU policy	EU integration, EU enlargement
NL	EPE campaign	EU parliament	EU integration	Other EU issue	EU enlargement/EU institutions
PL	EPE campaign	Economic policy	EU constitution	EU enlargement	EU integration
PT	EPE campaign	EU constitution	EU institutions	Economic policy	Other EU issues
SK	EPE campaign	Domestic EU policies	Social/employment policy	Economic policy	EU integration
SI	EPE campaign	Other EU issues	EU integration	EU enlargement	EU institutions

(Continued)

Table 3.1. (Continued)

	Top issue	2nd issue	3rd issue	4th issue	5th issue
SP	EPE campaign	EU constitution	EU parliament	EU integration	EU enlargement, EU (policies) general
SW	EPE campaign	Domestic EU policy	EU integration	Agriculture/consumer protection policy	EU constitution, EU institutions, economic policy
UK	EPE campaign	EU constitution	EU parliament		
EU 25	EPE campaign	EU integration	Economic policy	EU constitution	EU parliament

at the EU level (such as candidates for the EP and members of EU institutions) in the news. This can be considered a necessary condition for the functioning of political representation in a democracy (De Vreese 2002).

Figures 3.3 and 3.4 look at the presence of different EU-level actors in EU news stories. It is shown that the news coverage was still clearly dominated by non-EU actors (which tend to be national political actors), as indicated by the overall rather low percentages for visibility of EU actors. The share of EU actors in news about the EU ranged from around 5 per cent in Portugal,

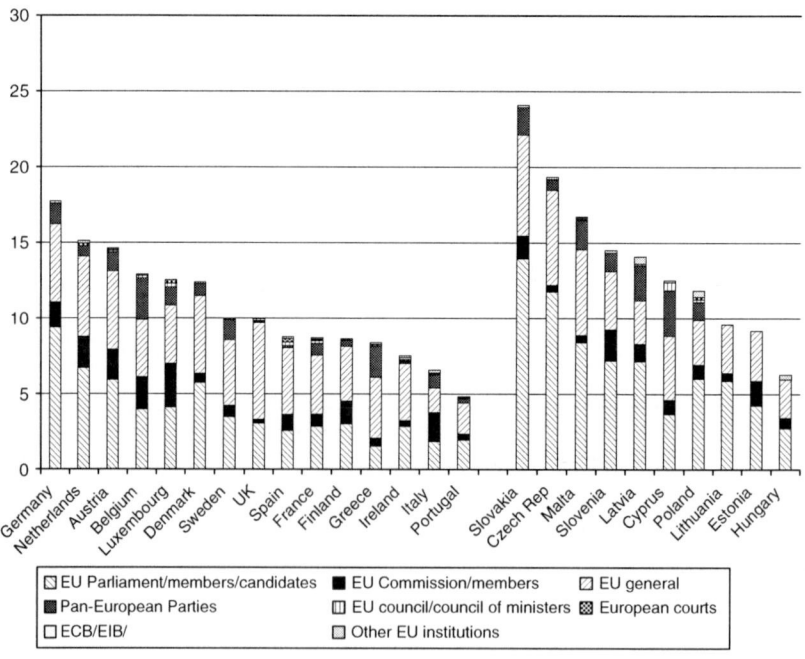

Figure 3.3. Actors in EU stories, by country

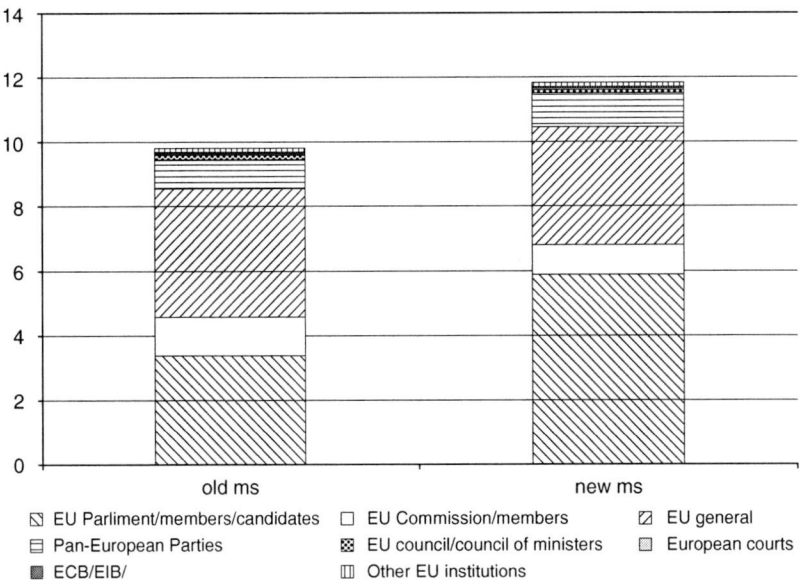

Figure 3.4. Actors in EU stories in old and new member states

Hungary, and Italy to more than 15 per cent in Malta, Germany, the Czech Republic, and Slovakia. The two most commonly shown groups of EU actors in the news were members of or candidates for the Parliament (i.e. the actors these elections are actually about) and the EU in general. The EU Commission also featured somewhat prominently in most member states. Other actors classified as EU actors were almost invisible in EU news.

Overall, and as shown in Figure 3.4, there were considerably more EU actors in the news in the new member states compared to the old member states. Whereas the EU in general was about equally visible in the old and new member states, in particular the members of and candidates for parliament were almost twice as visible in the new member states. The Commission and its members also featured more prominently in the news in the new member states. Compared to 1999, there were some changes evident in 2004 (for more information, see De Vreese et al. 2006). While the coverage was still focused on domestic actors, there was an overall increase in the proportion of EU actors in the fifteen old member states. That EP election news is dominated by national political actors suggests that if Europeanization is taking place it is vertical integration with national political actors taking part in the debate over EU level issues. However, we might also take this to mean that the discourse on European-level issues is dominated by domestic

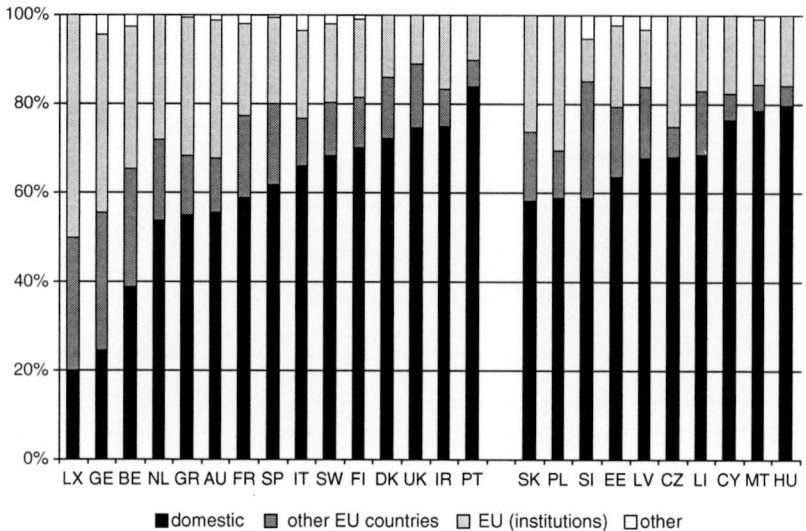

Figure 3.5. Location of EU news (television and newspapers), by country

concerns. As far as giving a face to the EU in national news programs, though, we see a definite increase between 1999 and 2004. Furthermore, as national news media adjusts to the changing nature of EU membership, we would expect a greater face to the EU to emerge in these countries.

The geographical focus of election news is used to indicate the degree of horizontal integration where national news media addresses EU issues in other EU member states or covers EU news in other member states. Figure 3.5 shows that news in Luxemburg, Germany, Belgium, and the Netherlands showed a fair degree of horizontal Europeanization of the EU stories. In Luxemburg, 30 per cent of the EU news stories focused on another EU country, while 45 per cent of the news came from Brussels and the EU institutions. This is in contrast to, for example, Portugal, where more than 80 per cent of the EU news took place in Portugal. We see a somewhat stronger focus on other European countries and the EU in news stories in a few old member states – basically the BeNeLux and Germany. Overall, however, the old and new member states did not differ systematically in their degree of vertical or horizontal Europeanization of the news.

3.5.4. *Boring campaign, low turnout: A self-fulfilling prophecy?*

We finally turn to the explicit evaluations of the campaign in the news. In particular, we consider whether the campaign was evaluated as rather boring or exciting, and whether turnout was predicted to be high or rather low. Overall, most news stories did not contain an explicit evaluation of the campaign, a pattern which is common to the news genre in general. When evaluations were present, however, they were largely negative – labeling the campaign 'boring' – as shown in Figure 3.6. The degree to which that was the case differs again across countries, with some news in particular in Lithuania, Slovakia, and Poland strongly emphasizing the 'boringness' of the campaign. By contrast, in Denmark, the Netherlands, and Slovenia the campaign was more often assessed as exciting than boring in the news. In others, such as Luxembourg, Austria, or Hungary no positive or mixed assessment was found. We did not find a convincing pattern that the news in the new member states was more negative. Beyond country differences, we found that commercial television news carried more evaluations than public television and also more negative evaluations. In the newspapers, there were more (and more negative) evaluations in broadsheets than in tabloids (both not shown here).

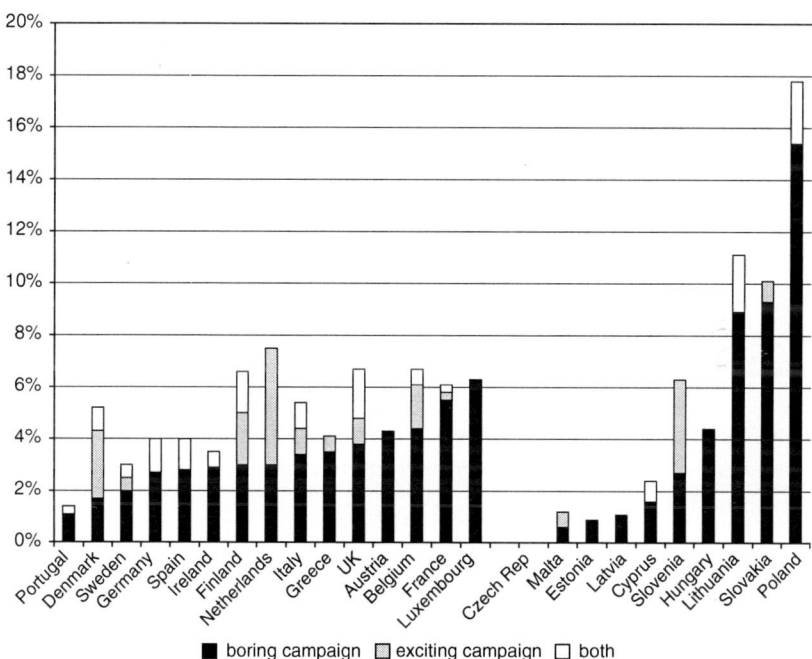

Figure 3.6. Explicit references to the European election campaign in the news, by country

The Legitimacy of the European Union after Enlargement

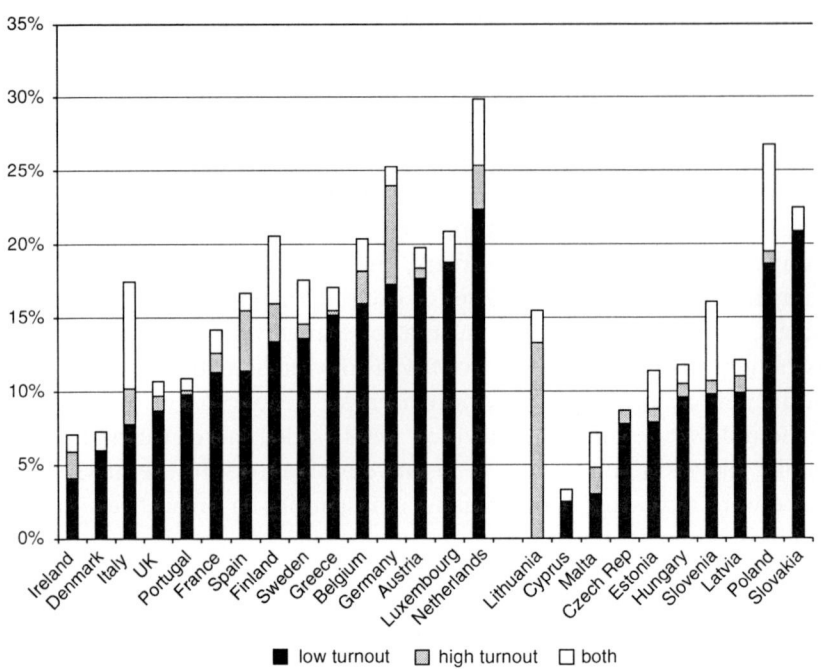

Figure 3.7. Explicit turnout prediction in the news, by country

With respect to turnout predictions, we found that about 15 per cent of all news stories contained explicit mention of the expected turnout level (see Figure 3.7). In some countries, this was one in four stories, such as in Germany, the Netherlands and Poland. When turnout was mentioned, it was by and large predicted to be low. This was particularly the case in Poland and Slovakia, and in the BeNeLux, Germany, and Austria. In general, low turnout predictions were more common in the news in the old fifteen member states. Overall these last results indicate that the media – *ceteris paribus* – did not contribute to a picture of exciting elections with something at stake.

3.6. Conclusions

This chapter set out to answer the questions of (*a*) whether the European elections represent a moment in which a European public space emerges and (*b*) what the consequences of the 2004 enlargement are for the emergence of such a space. The chapter is based on a systematic analysis of the news media coverage in the Union's member states, which is taken as the most appropriate indication of a public sphere. In short, the 2004 European Parliamentary elections – like the previous elections – did not represent a *single* European public sphere, in the sense of a pan-European debate taking place in pan-European media. However, there were signs of a substantial degree of Europeanization of national debates that suggest that a European public sphere 'light' in the form of Europeanized national debates is gaining ground and seems feasible.

For a convincing case of Europeanization of national public spheres we would need to see highly visible elections, references to European countries and to European and EU actors, news coverage addressing a common agenda, and news depicting the elections as important and with real choices. Our only real benchmark is 1999 (for the 'old' EU 15), and we found greater visibility of the elections in 2004 than in 1999, more vertical Europeanization, and a higher presence of EU actors. We can therefore conclude that a shared sense of importance is emerging, with visibility on the rise (see also De Vreese et al. 2006). That said, the debate is hardly an aggregation of similar debates, and the national debates are still largely represented by national actors. Nonetheless, there can be said to be 'light at the end of the tunnel'.

The 2004 enlargement of the EU does not seem to reduce the emergence of Europeanization. The elections were slightly more visible and the news contained more EU actors in the new member states than it did in the old member states. This conclusion, however, should be seen in the light of the modest presence of EU news overall. This reservation notwithstanding, the news coverage in the new countries and the degree of Europeanization of the national debates suggest that it will not take five rounds of European elections for the newest members of the Union to become part of the development towards Europeanized political space. The new EU members are as Europeanized as their old counterparts – or as little Europeanized as the old EU 15, depending on the perspective. Moreover, it cannot be neglected that the elections are – despite some signs of change – generally depicted as boring and likely to draw only small parts of the electorate to the polls.

Looking into the future, it seems that the large expansion of the Union in 2004 has not decreased the potential for legitimizing the EU through processes of Europeanized national debates. However, the only viable strategy in this enterprise appears to be in the form of a European public sphere 'light', which is de facto a Europeanization of national public spheres. The prospect of a single European space, as represented through the media, remains a dream of the elite and is sustained empirically neither in the 2004 elections nor in a longitudinal perspective. However, with the growing importance of the European institutions, including the Parliament, but more importantly, increasing political contestation over European issues (e.g., the constitution) by political actors, the news media is likely to follow and devote more attention to Europe in the form of synchronized national EU debates. In this vein, the emergence and consolidation of euroskeptic parties might turn out to be conducive to the legitimacy of the EU.

Notes

1. The study was coordinated by Susan Banducci, Claes de Vreese, and Holli Semetko. Coding was organized by *Media Tenor* and conducted by trained and supervised coders, largely native speakers of the languages involved. Coders were monitored and intra- and intercoder-reliability tests showed between 80 and 100 per cent agreement for the measures reported below.
2. The study was funded by research grants from the Dutch National Science Foundation [NWO], The Halle Foundation, the EU CIVICACTIVE Research Program, Emory University, and The Amsterdam School of Communications Research/University of Amsterdam to the principal investigators.
3. Television: in Belgium two French and two Flemish stations were included; in Finland and Germany four newscasts; in Spain and Poland three newscasts; in Austria, Greece, and Ireland one newscast. We had to exclude Cyprus (for technical reasons) and Luxembourg (for linguistic reasons). Newspapers: in Belgium, three French and three Flemish newspapers were included; in Luxembourg, Malta, Lithuania, and Cyprus, only two newspapers were included because of availability. For more technical details concerning the media sample and coding procedure, see de Vreese et al. (2006).
4. It should be noted that a difference in coding during the 2004 study necessitates classifying actors into main protagonists (those actors that were the primary focus of the news story) and other actors (actors that were mentioned in the news story but were not the main focus).
5. The percentages are within-country percentages of the total amount of EU news coverage.

4

Towards a European Electorate: One Electorate or Many?

Wouter van der Brug, Mark Franklin, Marina Popescu, and Gábor Tóka[1]

4.1. Introduction

The previous two chapters focused on the practice of political representation in the European Union (EU) from the perspective of the 'supply side' of the electoral market: parties and their political programmes and how the media communicate what is at stake at the elections. In this chapter we focus on the 'demand side': the electorates of the different European countries. Thomassen argued in the introductory chapter that the behaviour of voters should meet a number of requirements for them to be represented meaningfully. In the first place, voters should base their choice on policy considerations. It is very unlikely that political parties represent the opinions of their voters if these opinions do not guide electoral choice. Secondly, political representation is unlikely to materialize if voters have idiosyncratic sets of policy preferences that motivate their decisions. The responsible party model requires that a small number of ideological dimensions – preferably only one – structure(s) the behaviour of parties and voters (e.g. Thomassen 1994).

Prior research has established that the left–right dimension structures the behaviour of voters and parties in most Western European countries (e.g. Fuchs and Klingemann 1990; Klingemann et al. 1994; Van der Eijk and Franklin 1996; Hix 1999; Van der Eijk et al. 1999; Van der Brug et al. 2007). Left–right positions of parties and voters reflect their positions on the most salient issues in each of the countries, so that the left–right dimension functions as an important link in the chain of democratic representation.

However, these results do not warrant the conclusion that opinions of voters will also be represented at the European level after the 2004 enlargement. In the first place, we cannot know a priori whether the left–right dimension structures the behaviour of voters and parties in the ten new member states. Moreover, even if voters in the separate member states of the EU vote largely on the basis of the same ideological dimension – left–right – the substantive meaning of left–right may be very different in different countries. So, in order to assess whether the twenty-five separate national electorates operate as a single European electorate in European elections, we will focus on these two aspects.

Our main focus will be on similarities and differences between voters in different countries in the determinants of party choice at the 2004 European Parliament (EP) elections. At those elections, do we find cleavage voting more prevalent in some countries than in others? Are the effects of ideology and policy considerations different? However, in order to be able to conduct meaningful analyses of voting behaviour across old and new member states, we first need to be sure that the variables we analyse have largely the same meanings in the two parts of Europe. In order to address this question we will first investigate similarities and differences among the opinions of voters of parties of the same family. Are there big differences between voters for Christian Democratic parties in different countries? What about voters for liberal or socialist parties? Since we wish to assess the consequences of the 2004 enlargement for democratic representation, we are primarily interested in the differences between the new accession countries and the 'old' member states. Theoretically, we have no reason to expect that length of membership of the EU would affect patterns of voting behaviour. However, as we will outline below, there are theoretical reasons to expect such differences to exist between established democracies and democracies with a recent history of communist rule, where party systems are being consolidated. Therefore, our main focus in this chapter is on the distinction between established and consolidating democracies.

4.2. Theoretical expectations

What differences do we expect to find in voting behaviour between established and consolidating democracies? In the first place we may expect to find differences in political orientations and underlying social values between the two sets of countries. The consolidating democracies in Central

Europe have lower levels of economic development than even the poorest of the fifteen pre-2004 member states. Nearly all went through a very deep and painful recession in the early 1990s, while the rest of Europe – with the initial exception of Finland, which, like Central Europe, was hard hit by the collapse of the Soviet economy – reached previously unprecedented levels of affluence. Moreover, the consolidating democracies share the legacy of a unique social, economic, and political experiment with communism that lasted for more than four decades in all of these countries. Since most generations in these countries were politically socialized under communist rule, the citizens of these countries can be expected to hold different social and political attitudes than the citizens of the other EU member states.

Regional differences in social and political opinions are not necessarily problematic from the point of view of political representation. Within each of the European member states there are regional differences in political opinions, which translate into support for different kinds of parties. In some parts of Britain the Conservatives will almost always get a majority of the votes, and in other parts Labour is more popular. As long as these differences in party support reflect differences in public opinions, there is no problem. So, differences in value orientations between different countries are not problematic, as long as these translate into aggregate-level differences in support for party families in the EP. This, in turn, requires that votes for a socialist party in Poland or in Hungary are guided by the same considerations as votes for the socialists in France or Germany. Are there reasons to expect these considerations to be different?

The differences that are relevant to vote choice concern the sources from which voters get their cues. Prior research shows that voters in established democracies take their cues from reference groups, locate themselves and the policy alternatives in left–right terms, and take account of strategic considerations. How might these cues be different in a consolidating democracy? Will all these forces have the same relative strength there as in established democracies?

Until the 1960s and in some countries also in the 1970s, voters in established democracies were guided by strong group loyalties, which boosted the effects of social structure and limited the effects of policy positions (and presumably also of strategic considerations). There is some controversy in the scholarly literature as to whether this also happened when democratic party systems developed in countries that had previously been ruled by communist parties. Some scholars have predicted that, as a result of the fact that communist parties attempted to eliminate or suppress religious and class differences, there will only be weak effects of religious and social cleavages on the vote in post-communist societies (Lindström 1991; White et al. 2000; Meulemann 2004). On the other hand, others have argued that in countries where party systems are new and especially where they are in flux, voters are in desperate need of other cues, which may be 'cheaply' provided by social and ethno-religious distinctions. This would lead us to expect a strong effect of these cleavages (Kitschelt 1992; Klingemann and Wattenberg 1992; Tóka 1992; Evans 1996*a*, 1996*b*; Mateju and Reháková 1996; Szelényi, Fodor, and Hanley 1997; Tomka and Zulehner 1999; Gijsberts and Nieuwbeerta 2000). So, we have no very clear expectations for the importance of social structure relative to other effects, or relative to their importance in established democracies. However, we do have quite strong expectations for the relative importance of policy positions compared to those in established democracies.

This is because one of the most important things that might be different in a consolidating democracy, compared to established democracies, is the clarity of the party system. Established democracies have established party systems that remain much the same over a sequence of elections. Having the same parties competing for political power from the same locations in the left–right spectrum at election after election serves an educational function. Voters learn their way around their political system over the course of their first two or three elections by experiencing it at work. In a consolidating democracy the necessary consistency may not be present. Parties do not necessarily appear fully formed on the political scene with a reasonably stable size and left–right location. In a newly democratizing country, parties are more likely to repeatedly adapt their policies and ideological profiles in the face of changing opportunities for political mobilization. Frequent changes in the identity and location of political parties will be confusing to voters and prevent the sort of learning that would occur in more established systems. If the system is in sufficient flux, voters may fail to learn where parties stand in left–right terms, and may even be unsure of such fundamental facts as which parties are large and which are small (cf. Rose 1995; Rose and Mishler 1998; Miller and Klobucar 2000). Without knowledge of which parties are serious contenders for power, voters will be unable to employ the strategies that in more established systems enable them to winnow down the contenders to those with a serious chance of becoming major parties of government.

We should stress that we do not expect all consolidating democracies to have the same characteristics any more than we expect this of all established democracies. Countries differ in the speed with which their party systems consolidate and in the extent that consolidated systems present voters with clear and simple choices. Enough time may have elapsed in several of the new EU member countries for the party systems to have become quite well consolidated (Kitschelt et al. 1999).

So, there may in practice be as many differences among consolidating systems as there are between the two groups of countries. However, we would expect the effects of left–right location to be generally less in post-communist states, and effects of issues to be correspondingly greater, relative to each other. This follows findings in past research showing that in countries where ideology is less important, issues play a correspondingly greater role (Van der Eijk and Franklin 1996).

Our study involves two sets of analyses. The first set focuses on the structure of value orientations in new and old member countries, and on differences between the opinions of voters regarding parties of the same party family. These analyses serve to validate the variables employed in this chapter and to provide the basis for a second set of analyses, which focus on the determinants of party choice. To what extent are voting decisions in the different member states of the EU motivated by the same considerations? The two sets of analyses require different data sources and different methodological approaches. Therefore, the rest of this chapter is divided in two separate sections, discussing the separate sets of analyses. Each of these sections will open with a discussion of the methodology used in that section.

4.3. Differences in value orientations

When studying value orientations, a central role is played by the concepts of left and right. The left–right dimension is considered to be a summary measure of ideological allegiances on the various dimensions of party competition in each country. However, because of historical differences between the countries, the terms left and right may have very different meanings in political discourse in the different countries. Therefore, we start with an analysis of what concrete policy preferences are related to left–right self-placement and support for different European party families in the eight Eastern European new member states in comparison to the older democracies in the Union. Before we discuss our results, we will first discuss our methodology and the data employed in these analyses.

4.3.1. *Methodology to compare the determinants of left–right positions*

In order to compare across countries the relationship between left–right self-placement and party choice on the one hand, and value orientations on the other, we employ data from the European Values Study 2000. In this survey respondents were asked to place themselves on a ten-point scale of which the extremes were labelled left (at '1') and right (at '10'). This question was asked in all EU member states except Cyprus, which is therefore the only country missing in this part of the analyses. The total sample size in these countries is 31,316 respondents, ranging from 1,000 in Great Britain, Hungary, and Portugal to 2,409 in Spain. Throughout the analysis we weighted the cases with the original weighting variable provided with the European Values Study data set but only after adjusting the latter to assure that each country has an equal weighted sample size of 1,305, so that the weighted number of cases corresponds to the unweighted number of cases in the data file.

The drawback of this data set is that it was collected in 1999 and 2000, when, especially in some of the new democracies, quite a few parties that are currently represented in the EP were not even in existence, and other parties occupied their places in the party system. Moreover, electoral alignments and citizens' attitudes on various issues may have changed since then. However, in spite of this drawback, among all comparative surveys, the European Values Study offers by far the best chance to accomplish our task here. The reason for this is the richness of this study – and the deficiency of all readily available alternatives – in mapping citizens' attitudes and value orientations in a variety of policy-relevant domains. Moreover, to the extent that changes will have taken place since 2000, these will likely have reduced the differences between old and new member countries, so the differences we find with these data represent, if anything, an over-estimate of differences that will have existed in 2004. In this survey, we identified as many as thirty-one attitude items relevant for our exercise. Since presenting the analyses for so many separate items would be unwieldy, the items that tapped similar attitude dimensions were aggregated, through summing up their standardized scores, into a single attitude scale. This way we constructed a total of thirteen attitude variables, which cover most of the policy dimensions associated with left and right in common parlance. All these scales have a mean of zero and unit variance in the pooled and weighted twenty-four-country data set (see Appendix for details of scale construction).

Table 4.1. Regression models for the explanation of left–right self-placement with interaction terms

	Established democracies only			Consolidating democracies only			All countries together		
	b	SE	Beta	b	SE	Beta	b	SE	Beta
(Constant)	5.345	0.014		5.471	0.025		5.345	0.014	
Economic individualism	0.230	0.014	0.115**	0.129	0.023	0.062**	0.230	0.015	0.114**
Equality over freedom	-0.148	0.014	-0.076**	-0.141	0.022	-0.071**	-0.148	0.014	-0.075**
Equality over merit	-0.243	0.014	-0.127**	-0.213	0.024	-0.102**	-0.243	0.014	-0.124**
Distrust NATO	-0.199	0.015	-0.103**	-0.347	0.028	-0.172**	-0.199	0.016	-0.101**
Social liberalism	-0.071	0.016	-0.037**	-0.104	0.027	-0.047**	-0.071	0.017	-0.036**
Women's liberation	-0.040	0.015	-0.021*	-0.082	0.024	-0.037**	-0.040	0.015	-0.020*
Postmaterialist	-0.056	0.014	-0.029**	0.109	0.024	0.051**	-0.056	0.015	-0.028**
Environment	-0.039	0.014	-0.020*	0.055	0.024	0.025*	-0.039	0.014	-0.019*
Distrust EU	-0.001	0.015	-0.001	0.001	0.029	0.000	-0.001	0.015	-0.001
Anti-immigrant	0.251	0.015	0.129**	0.020	0.025	0.009	0.251	0.015	0.127**
Family values	0.016	0.014	0.008	0.027	0.027	0.011	0.016	0.015	0.008
Religiosity	0.270	0.016	0.140**	0.090	0.024	0.044**	0.270	0.016	0.137**
Clericalism	0.178	0.015	0.093**	0.334	0.025	0.157**	0.178	0.015	0.090**
Consolidating democracies							0.126	0.028	0.029**
Economic individualism* Consolidating democracies							-0.100	0.027	-0.028**
Equality over freedom* Consolidating democracies							0.007	0.025	0.002
Equality over merit* Consolidating democracies							0.030	0.027	0.008
Distrust NATO* Consolidating democracies							-0.149	0.031	-0.042**
Social liberalism* Consolidating democracies							-0.033	0.031	-0.009
Women's liberation* Consolidating democracies							-0.042	0.028	-0.011
Postmaterialist* Consolidating democracies							0.165	0.027	0.045**
Environment*							0.093	0.027	0.025**

(Continued)

Table 4.1. (Continued)

	Established democracies only			Consolidating democracies only			All countries together		
	b	SE	Beta	b	SE	Beta	b	SE	Beta
Consolidating democracies Distrust EU*							0.002	0.031	0.000
Consolidating democracies Anti-immigrant*							−0.232	0.028	−0.061**
Consolidating democracies Family values*							0.011	0.030	0.003
Consolidating democracies Religiosity*							−0.180	0.028	−0.050**
Consolidating democracies Clericalism*							0.156	0.029	0.042**
Consolidating democracies R^2-adjusted (N-weighted)	.156 (17,689)			.112 (7,842)			.143 (25,531)		

*: Significant at $p < .01$; **: significant at $p < .001$.

In order to assess whether left–right has a different meaning in the political discourse in different countries, we will estimate regressions with the ten-point left–right self-placement scale as the dependent variable. The independent variables in these analyses are the thirteen attitude scales. If these attitude scales exert a different effect on left–right positions in different countries, this would indicate that left–right has a different substantive meaning.

4.3.2. Results: How different are the determinants of left–right positions?

Table 4.1 presents three regression analyses with left–right positions as the dependent variable and the thirteen attitude scales as independent variables. It presents these analyses first for the sixteen established and for the eight consolidating democracies separately, and then for all twenty-four countries together, but adding interactions between the dummy variable identifying consolidating democracies and the thirteen attitude scales.

Three findings emerge from Table 4.1. First, when looking at the analyses for all countries, we find a small but significant positive effect of the variable 'consolidating democracies'. This shows that if we compare citizens with identical positions on the thirteen attitude scales in the two groups of countries, citizens of consolidating democracies place themselves on average one-sixth of a point to the right from their otherwise like-minded counterparts in established democracies. This difference of 0.13 on a ten-point scale is of course rather minor. We attribute it to the enduring unpopularity of the left-wing dictatorships of the recent past in Eastern Europe.

Second, if we regress left–right self-placement on the thirteen attitude variables separately for old and new democracies, it turns out that values offer a less potent explanation of the respondents' left–right position in consolidating than in old democracies. This finding is most likely explained by the fact that the determinants of political attitudes show more idiosyncratic individual variation in new than in long-established democracies.

Third, at face value we see remarkable similarities of the effects of the thirteen attitude scales on left–right positions in the two parts of Europe. These similarities overwhelmingly dominate the noteworthy but relatively minor differences. What emerges from the results is that left is associated with distrust of NATO and support for equality over both freedom and meritocratic allocation, social liberalism, and women's liberation in both old and new democracies. Likewise, right is associated with religiosity and support for economic individualism, and what we abbreviate as clericalism – that is, a strong political role of churches – in both sets of countries. Equally remarkably, trust in the EU is not significantly correlated with a left–right position in either.

Despite the large similarities in the two sets of countries, there are also some differences. The statistical significance of these is tested with the interaction terms between each of the thirteen attitude scales and the dummy variable identifying consolidating democracies on the other appearing in the last equation estimated for all twenty-four countries together. Statistically significant interaction terms suggest differences in what is associated with 'left' and 'right' in these two parts of Europe.

The most striking difference in the effects of the thirteen attitude scales in the two groups of countries emerges with respect to post-materialist values and support for stronger environment protection. These attitudes tend to be associated with the left in the established democracies but more often than not with the right in the consolidating democracies. Similarly, anti-immigrant views tend to be associated with a right-wing self-placement in older democracies, albeit only weakly so, but remain uncorrelated with left and right in the East. The most plausible explanation of these findings probably includes the association of left with the authoritarian (communist) past, and the absence of both green parties and immigration as a major social and political issue in the new member states.

Some further differences between consolidating and established democracies concern the exact degree to which various attitude scales correlate with left–right self-placement. The somewhat weaker effect of clericalism in the established democracies probably just makes up for the stronger effects of religiosity in comparison with consolidated democracies. What may be substantively more interesting is that economic individualism is less strongly, and attitudes towards NATO more strongly, associated with left and right in Eastern Europe than in the established democracies. We think that this finding can be related to post-communist transitions, which generated a great deal of policy consensus but little popular enthusiasm regarding the main direction of economic transformation in the region, and involved a major shift in the foreign policy orientation of these countries that was very popular with the bulk of the population, but created some resentment among supporters of the ex-communist left.

4.3.3. Results: Attitudinal differences among voters for the same party family

Table 4.2 concludes the first part of our empirical analysis with a look at value differences between consolidated and consolidating democracies, and at how the supporters of socialist, conservative and liberal parties differ in their attitudes in established and in consolidating democracies. It must be stressed again that our data come from 1999/2000, and in the typical European country less than half of the national sample expressed a voting preference for a party that would gain seats in the EP at the 2004 elections as a member of the European People's Party (EPP), the Party of European Socialists (PES) or the European Liberal Democrat and Reform Party (ELDR). For the other party groups in the EP we did not have a sufficiently large and cross-national pool of supporters in these data – for instance, the Union for Europe of the Nations group was overwhelmingly represented by Irish respondents. Therefore, we only present this part of the analysis for the supporters of the parties that were included in the EPP, PES, or ELDR groups in the EP following the 2004 election.

Table 4.2 displays the mean value of the same thirteen attitude scales presented in Table 4.1 for the three party groups in both established and consolidating democracies. The last three columns flag the statistical significance of the differences between citizens in these two groups of countries within each of the three main party groupings.

The most striking feature of these comparisons is that the differences between the means of voters for the same party family tend to be small. The largest differences are about half a standard deviation (i.e. 0.5 on any one of our thirteen standardized scales), but in most cases the differences are much smaller than that. Because of the large sample size, most differences are statistically significant between the two types of countries, and it is to those differences that we now turn.

The EPP supporters differ significantly between old and new democracies on ten out of the thirteen scales, and the same is the case with the ELDR supporters. The socialist party grouping is less divided in this comparison: their supporters in old and new democracies only differ in six out of the thirteen dimensions. Remarkably, the only dimension where none of the three shows such division is the one that appeared to be unrelated to the left–right self-placements in the electorate, namely trust in the EU. More generally, it seems that foreign policy, religion (i.e. the religiosity and clericalism scales), and women's liberation are least likely to create the potential for an East–West divide in the electorate of the three major

Table 4.2. Political attitudes in established and consolidating democracies among the supporters of the three main EP party groups

	Mean value in established democracies among supporters of the....			Mean value in consolidating democracies among supporters of the....		
	EPP	PES	ELDR	EPP	PES	ELDR
Economic individualism	0.30	−0.01	0.25	0.04**	−0.14**	−0.06**
Equality over freedom	−0.13	0.07	−0.25	−0.08*	0.10	−0.06**
Equality over merit	−0.29	0.05	−0.49	−0.08**	0.00	0.06**
Distrust NATO	−0.32	0.01	−0.41	−0.37	−0.01	0.07**
Social liberalism	−0.23	0.13	0.52	−0.36**	−0.17**	−0.01**
Women's liberation	−0.26	0.00	0.19	−0.16**	−0.01	0.22
Postmaterialist	0.04	0.08	0.18	−0.19**	−0.27**	−0.16**
Environment	0.03	−0.01	0.17	0.13**	0.01	−0.05**
Distrust EU	−0.28	0.00	0.03	−0.25	−0.04	0.10
Anti-immigrant	−0.02	−0.15	−0.03	0.38**	0.46**	0.05*
Family values	0.03	−0.15	−0.33	0.45**	0.37**	0.22**
Religiosity	0.40	−0.12	−0.24	0.27**	−0.16	−0.24
Clericalism	0.33	−0.15	−0.23	0.32	−0.28**	−0.03**
Weighted N (unweighted N in parentheses)	3,760 (3,944)	4236 (4,235)	1,631 (1,420)	1,806 (17,14)	904 (883)	964 (780)

*: The difference between the mean value of the supporters of member parties in the old and the new democracies is significant at $p < .01$.
**: Significant at $p < .001$.

Note: 'EPP–ED (PES, ELDR) supporters' mean respondents who declared a voting preference (if there were an election next weekend) for a party that belongs to the EPP–ED (PES, ELDR).

party groupings. In contrast, economic individualism, family values, post-materialist and anti-immigration dimensions generate particularly large attitude differences between the electorate of the party groupings in new and old democracies. Preference for egalitarianism over merit-based allocation shows a unique pattern in that it does not create an East–West divide in the PES electorate at all, but creates a particularly large one among liberals.

The apparent reason for many of these divides within party groups is that Eastern Europeans in general tend to differ greatly from the citizens of the established European democracies in a number of dimensions. As a comparison of the columns of Table 4.2 shows, they are more egalitarian, anti-immigrant and socially conservative than Westerners. Hence, even when the differences between party groupings follow the same pattern in new and old democracies, the East–West differences within the party groups are in a few cases even larger than the differences between them. Anti-immigration attitudes are probably the best example of this. In consolidating democracies, liberal supporters are the least likely to display such attitudes, but the ELDR-supporters in the East are nonetheless far more anti-immigrant than the most anti-immigrant of these groups (the EPP-supporters) in the established democracies. The same or similar pattern is repeated for family values, social liberalism, and economic individualism.

The probably most notable oddity is the different attitude profile of the liberal supporters in terms of environmentalism and egalitarianism in the two parts of Europe.[2] The PES and EPP supporters, however, show exactly the same kind of differences from each other in both old and new democracies on all dimensions except post-materialism. Hence, the pattern that seems most clearly to emerge from Table 4.2 is that the Eastern enlargement made all three party groupings internally more diverse. Yet, this happened in such a way that did not make the European party groups less meaningful agents of representation, at least with the exception of the post-materialist and possibly the environmentalist dimension. After 2004 each of the main party groups will need to aggregate a broader range of opinions, but the supporters of an EPP-member organization differ from those of a socialist party much the same way in the new as in the established democracies, and with some caveats the same can be said about the liberals too.

On the basis of these findings we are ready to move on to the second part of this chapter, which investigates the determinants of party choice in the EP elections of 2004. The study we employ for this analysis contains many fewer variables than the ESS (which is why we could not use it for the exploratory study reported above) and, in particular, does not include measures of post-materialism or environmental concerns. So the variables that might have proved problematic in a cross-national study including new and old member countries are not included in the analyses that follow. We have seen that other measures do have much the same meanings across the new-old divide.

4.4. Determinants of party choice

4.4.1. *Methodology to compare determinants of party choice across countries*

How does one compare the determinants of party choice across different countries? The most fashionable 'plug-and-play' methodologies for analysing party choice, such as multinomial logit, do not enable us to answer our research questions. In such approaches the dependent variable (party choice) is a nominal variable, which reflects a different choice set in each country. As long as we do not want to redefine this dependent variable to a dichotomy (such as a vote for the government versus a vote for the opposition), we would have to carry out twenty-five separate country studies, without straightforward means of systematically comparing the results between the countries.

Therefore, our enquiry proceeds along the same lines as in *Choosing Europe?* (Van der Eijk and Franklin 1996). In each country voters were asked, for each party in their political system,[3] how likely it was (on a scale of 1 to 10) that they would ever vote for it. These questions have been carefully designed to yield measures that can be interpreted as the propensity to vote for each of the parties (Van der Eijk and Franklin 1996; Van der Eijk 2002; Van der Eijk et al. 2006). They can be regarded for ease of exposition as preferences, and we know that voters make their choice in each election for the party they most prefer.[4] The determinants of vote propensities are therefore the same as the determinants of party choice. Employing vote propensities as the dependent variable rather than party choice itself has been shown to have many advantages (Van der Eijk 2002; Van der Eijk et al. 2006; Van der Brug et al. 2007). In this chapter the most important function is to provide us with a dependent variable that is comparable across countries.

When the data matrix is stacked so that each voter appears as many times as there are parties for which preferences have been measured, the conventional research question 'What attracts people to Party X?' can be reformulated as 'What attracts people to a party?' We already know that voters virtually always vote for the party they express the strongest preference for. Thus, an answer to the question 'What is it that attracts people to a party?' is also an answer to the question 'What determines which parties are voted for?' This way of analysing the determinants of party choice has been validated elsewhere (Tillie 1995; Van der Eijk et al. 2006).

In order to compare determinants of party choice across different countries we employ data from the European Elections Study 2004. In this survey the question about 'propensities to support parties' has been asked in thirteen established democracies (Austria, Cyprus, Denmark, Finland, France, Germany, Great Britain, Greece, Ireland, Italy, the Netherlands, Portugal, and Spain), and in seven consolidating democracies (the Czech Republic, Estonia, Hungary, Latvia, Poland, Slovakia, and Slovenia). We employ the data from the respondents in each country who answered the question whether they voted in the last European election. The total sample size in these countries is 20,497 respondents, which is 1,025 per country on average, ranging from 430 in Greece to 1,606 in Estonia.

From these data we created a stacked data matrix in which the party X respondent combination is the unit of analysis. This data set has 154,509 entries, but we weighted our stacked data to the original number of respondents ($N = 20,497$). When computing the weight variable, we first employed a weight that makes each sample representative in terms of party choice in the European Elections conducted at the time of the interview. After that we constructed a second weight, which ensures that each of the twenty contexts exerts an equal weight on the results.

Rather than having a separate dependent variable for each party, we now have a dependent variable in the stacked matrix that refers to parties in general. The problem, of course, is how to define meaningful independent variables that explain the variance in this variable. Since the unit of analysis is the party X respondent combination, it is straightforward to include party characteristics in this data matrix. We included one variable at the party level, party size, which represents a strategic consideration that voters may take into account: we hypothesize that when two or more parties are about equally attractive for some voters, then those voters tend to vote for the largest of these parties because it has the best chance of achieving its policy goals.

Adding individual characteristics to these data is less straightforward, however. For left–right location and the position regarding European unification, the surveys measured not only the self-declared positions of respondents, but also how they perceive the location of each party on the same scale. Therefore, we were able to transform these variables into the distance between each voter's own position and the position of each party. If voters preferred parties close to them in left–right terms or in terms of position regarding European unification, then the resulting measure should exert a negative effect on vote propensities: the smaller the distance between voter and party, the greater the preference for the party. For respondents who did not answer the question about the position of any particular party, we replaced their missing values with the national sample mean of the perceived position of the party in question. If, however, no answer was provided about the voter's position, the distance measure records a missing value.[5]

When party-specific information is lacking, it is more problematic to construct a meaningful independent variable. As a case in point, social class may have a positive effect on the propensity to vote for party A (meaning that this party attracts its support disproportionately from the higher classes), and a negative effect on the propensity to vote for party B. When inserting the variable social class in the stacked data matrix, these effects would cancel each other out, so that we would wrongly conclude that social class has no effect on the vote. The solution to this problem involves linear transformations of the original independent variables, party by party and country by country, into predicted scores (y-hats) of the dependent variable. The y-hats for each independent variable from the different sets of predicted scores can then be stacked and treated as a generic version of that independent variable. The procedure is explained elsewhere in detail (e.g. Van der Eijk and Franklin 1996; Van der Brug et al., 2000; Van der Brug, 2004) and will not be repeated here.

The following independent variables were transformed in this manner: 'social class', 'religion', 'gender', 'importance of issues' (what is the most important problem facing the country), 'government approval', and 'satisfaction with the functioning of democracy'. As a result of these transformations, the effects of the y-hat variables will necessarily be positive. The large benefit is that they allow us to conduct comparative research without transforming the dependent variable. This benefit does, however, come at a certain price. Because the variables are transformed party-by-party and country-by-country, after the linear transformation cross-country differences will be incorporated in these newly created variables. Although country differences will still be visible in the standardized regression coefficients (betas), it is unlikely that one will find interaction effects between these transformed variables and country dummies. Therefore, we will not focus in this chapter on differences between established and consolidating democracies in the effects of these variables. Instead, we focus on differences between countries in the effects of left–right distance, the issue of European unification, and of strategic considerations, which are captured by the variable party size.

4.4.2. Results: How different are the determinants of choice?

Table 4.3 shows the effects of the various independent variables, created as explained above, on vote propensities. The table contains three panels, of which the first pertains to all countries and the other two distinguish between established and consolidating democracies. We explain 31 per cent of the variance in party preferences for all countries taken together, using these independent variables (34 per cent among established democracies and 24 per cent among consolidating democracies). In single country studies the variance explained is normally higher than this, because such models normally include the position issues that are most relevant in each of the particular countries. In this joint data collection effort, only one position issue was included (position on European unification), but in most countries other position issues will be relevant as well. Left–right distance is probably closely correlated with the distance between parties and voters on issues everywhere, but past studies suggest that in most countries distance on a number of specific position issues would explain an additional 5 per cent to 10 per cent of the variance in party preferences after left–right distance is controlled for. Not having measured more position issues therefore lowers the explanatory power of the models.

More important than the proportion of explained variance, however, are the striking similarities in the findings for established and consolidating democracies. Because of the way we constructed the y-hat variables (from social class through satisfaction with democracy), the unstandardized regression coefficients cannot be compared in a straightforward manner. The standardized coefficients, however, indicate that the strengths of the effects are very similar in the two sets of countries. The former communist states see somewhat stronger effects of religion, satisfaction with democracy and age, and somewhat weaker effects from social class and government approval than more established democracies do. But overall the effects seem very similar.

Table 4.3. Regression models for the explanation of party preference without interaction terms

	All countries together			Established democracies only			Consolidating democracies only		
	b	SE	Beta	b	SE	Beta	b	SE	Beta
Social class	.550	.048	.077**	.573	.054	.083**	.492	.099	.064**
Religion	.652	.036	.118**	.600	.044	.107**	.762	.067	.142**
Gender	.712	.127	.037**	.698	.145	.037**	.741	.254	.036*
Education	.513	.056	.062*	.551	.065	.067**	.432	.110	.052**
Age	.341	.070	.033**	.294	.087	.027**	.452	.120	.048**
Importance of issues	.670	.052	.085**	.643	.059	.084**	.741	.106	.086**
Government approval	.634	.023	.192**	.628	.025	.204**	.649	.051	.162**
Satisfaction with democracy	.412	.042	.067**	.372	.049	.060**	.496	.078	.082**
Issue distance on European unification	−.081	.009	−.058**	−.073	.011	−.053**	−.098	.018	−.069**
Left–right distance	−.377	.009	−.292**	−.394	.011	−.304**	−.335	.017	−.262**
Consolidating democracies (dummy variable)	−.096	.042	−.015						
Party size	4.252	.126	.221**	4.325	.135	.246**	3.776	.304	.153**
R^2-adjusted (N-weighted)	.306 (16,464)			.336 (11,421)			.241 (5,043)		

*: Significant at $p < .01$; **: significant at $p < .001$.

We now turn to the variables of primary interest: left–right distance, distance on the issue of European unification, and party size. Note that these variables were deductively derived and thus the unstandardized regression coefficients are directly comparable across countries. The results show that the effects of left–right distance are particularly reduced in former communist states. Strategic considerations also play a lesser role in the former communist states, as shown by the lesser effect of party size. The issue of European unification, on the other hand, seems to play a somewhat more important role for electoral decisions in the new democracies. However, the differences are small in all three cases. Indeed, the strongest message to take from the comparison between established and consolidating democracies is how little difference we see. It is only the variance explained that is notably lower in consolidating democracies, suggesting the presence of rather more unmeasured and perhaps more idiosyncratic effects on vote choices in new than in established democracies. The fact that the effect of a dummy variable for 'formerly communist countries' fails to prove significant in the analysis when all countries are pooled together shows that after controlling for the relevant determinants of party preferences, the overall level of party support is not different in the two sets of countries. This is unexpected, given the emphasis in the extant literature on the weakness of citizens' party attachments in the former communist countries (see Rose 1995; Rose and Mishler 1998), but has no bearing on the hypotheses examined here.

The analyses of Table 4.3 did not provide a test for whether differences in the effects of party size, left–right distance and distances on the issue of European unification in established as compared to consolidating democracies are statistically significant. We now turn to this topic (Table 4.4). Model A includes three interaction terms between whether the country in question is a former communist state on the one hand, and left–right distance, party size and distances on the issue of European unification, on the other. Once again, it turns out that the effect of left–right distance on party choice is somewhat weaker (less negative) in former communist states than in the more established democracies. The differences are small however. The main effect (unstandardized) is $-.394$. In former communist states this effect is .056 weaker, that is, it is $-.338$. Even though the differences are small, they are statistically significant at $p < .01$.

An equally important finding is that the other two interaction effects are *not* statistically significant. In other words, the strategic consideration – that a larger party is more likely to have influence on government and hence should be a more attractive candidate for one's vote – applies

Table 4.4. Regression models for the explanation of party preference with interactions (all countries)

	Model A			Model B			Model C		
	b	SE	Beta	b	SE	Beta	b	SE	Beta
Social class	.551	.048	.077**	.541	.048	.076**	.542	.048	.076**
Religion	.653	.036	.118**	.656	.036	.119**	.657	.036	.119**
Gender	.713	.127	.037**	.709	.126	.036**	.710	.126	.036**
Education	.512	.056	.062**	.511	.056	.062**	.510	.056	.062**
Age	.346	.070	.033**	.334	.069	.032**	.339	.069	.033**
Importance of issues	.669	.052	.084**	.666	.052	.084**	.665	.052	.084**
Government approval	.631	.023	.191**	.624	.023	.188**	.621	.023	.188**
Satisfaction with democracy	.414	.042	.067**	.400	.042	.065**	.401	.042	.065**
Issue distance on European unification	−.072	.011	−.052**	−.082	.009	−.059**	−.073	.011	−.052**
Left–right distance	−.394	.011	−.305**	−.378	.009	−.293**	−.395	.011	−.306**
Party size	4.385	.141	.228**	4.307	.126	.224**	4.451	.141	.231**
Consolidating democracies (dummy variable)	.014	.063	.002				.030	.063	.005
Consolidating democracies* left–right distance	.056	.018	.024*				.054	.018	.023*
Consolidating democracies* issue distance	−.029	.020	−.011				−.028	.020	−.011
Consolidating democracies* party size	−.728	.312	−.024				−.779	.312	−.026
LR system agreement* LR distance				−.439	.069	−.042**	−.440	.069	−.042**
LR system agreement* issue distance				−.347	.410	−.006	−.347	.410	−.006
R^2-adjusted (N-weighted)	.307 (16,464)			.308 (16,464)			.308 (16,464)		

*: Significant at $p < .01$; **: significant at $p < .001$.

equally in the two sets of countries. Moreover, the issue of European unification is *not* more important in elections in former communist countries (which are all new member states) than in the more established democracies. So, Model A strongly supports the impression gathered from Table 4.3, which is that the determinants of party choice in the two sets of counties are very similar.

So far we distinguished between two sets of countries only. This separation of countries into two different groups is based upon the central research question, but leaves open the possibility that various other types of differences exist between voting patterns across the different countries, and these differences are not well captured by the distinction between established and consolidating democracies. Yet, we have already said that we would expect differences between countries within both groups. After all, Van der Eijk and Franklin (1996) did find differences between the then-member states that could only be accounted for by interactions defined at the country level. We would expect that this still holds, and that we can find similar idiosyncratic differences among consolidating democracies. An extensive search for interactions between country dummies and individual-level variables demonstrated that the effect of left–right on party choice was significantly different from the general pattern in Model A in four countries: Denmark, Portugal, Cyprus, and the Czech Republic. Moreover, the effect of party size turned out to be different in several countries.

The analyses in *Choosing Europe* (Van der Eijk and Franklin 1996) indicated that a systemic variable could explain differences in the effect of left–right distance on party choice. When positions in left–right terms are very clear, these left–right positions provide a good indication of parties' ideological complexions, and thus of their future actions. When, on the other hand, voters are not so aware of the positions of parties on a left–right dimension, left–right positions help voters less in learning about the political programme of the parties. Therefore, voters are most likely to rely upon left–right positions of parties when these positions are very clear, and less likely to do so when these positions are fuzzy. An indication of the extent to which voters are aware of party positions is the amount of agreement among them. The more they agree about where a party stands, the less ambiguous this position apparently is.

To test whether this is indeed the case, Model B introduces an interaction term between the amount of perceptual agreement (see Van der Eijk 2002) about the left–right positions of parties on the one hand, and left–right distances on the other hand. Model B shows that the effect of left–right distance depends indeed upon the degree of perceptual agreement. Van der Eijk and Franklin (1996) and Van der Eijk et al. (1999) report the same findings on two different sets of data, so this pattern turns out to be very robust. The question is whether the interaction between former communist states and left–right distance (see Model A) still remains significant after we control for the interaction between left–right system agreement and left–right distance. Model C shows that it does. So, even though the differences between established and consolidating democracies are small, the effects of left–right distances are significantly weaker in the latter countries, even beyond what can be explained by differences in the extent of agreement on left–right party locations.

To what extent does Model C explain the different patterns of party choice in each of the twenty countries? Only two of the interactions between individual country dummies and left–right distance are significant in Model C, those for Cyprus (where the effect of left–right distance is significantly stronger than in the other countries) and Italy (where the effect is significantly weaker). Moreover, none of the interactions between countries and the issue of European unification turned out to be significant. Significant interactions were found with party size: the effect is different from the general effect in seven countries. There are evidently idiosyncratic factors at work in these countries to account for the fact that party size has unusually small or unusually large effects there. Unfortunately, we were unable to find specific variables that explicate these differences.

4.5. Conclusion: One electorate or many?

This chapter set out to answer the question whether patterns of electoral behaviour in the EU are likely to be different as a result of the 2004 enlargement. Eight of the ten countries that joined the EU in 2004 are former communist countries, and we argued that there are some theoretical reasons to expect differences between established and consolidating democracies for this and other factors. Therefore, this chapter focused on differences in patterns of voting behaviour in the new enlargement countries and in the established democracies of the EU. We looked for differences in the major determinants of party preferences and in the socio-political attitudes associated with left–right ideology, as well as electoral support for member organizations of the three main party groupings in the EP. The underlying concern is whether the addition of new countries to the EU, which brought a change of the composition of the European electorate, also brought a change in patterns of voting behaviour leading to major differences that might hamper effective political representation through the existing party groups.

Our analyses found that nearly the same factors, and above all the same left–right dimension, structure the behaviour of voters and parties within the entire European electorate. Moreover, there is a shared basic meaning of left–right in terms of value and issue dimensions relative to egalitarianism, religion, social liberalism, foreign policy orientations, and economic individualism. So, the main conclusion from this study is that patterns of voting behaviour are not likely to change in the EU as a result of the inclusion of eight consolidating democracies after the 2004 enlargement.

This does not mean that there are no differences between established and consolidating democracies. It simply means that although there are differences both between and within the Eastern and Western electorates of the party groups, essentially the same factors determine voting behaviour in both parts of the EU. Moreover, the choice of one party group versus the other follows similar policy preferences in the Eastern member states and elsewhere in the Union.

Citizens in former communist countries in Central Europe appear to be more egalitarian and more socially conservative along a number of dimensions, but less supportive of economic individualism than citizens of Southern and Western European democracies. This is consistent with findings in previous studies and may be explained partly by differences in level of socio-economic development (Renwick and Tóka 1998). In principle, these differences need not be more consequential for political representation in values than differences between, say, the North and the South of England. In practice, however, our findings suggest that the observed value differences between the old and new member states increase value heterogeneity in the electorates of the main party groupings in the EP. Interestingly, however, they do not radically alter the meaning of the differences between vote for a conservative or a socialist or a liberal party.

The methods used in this study were perfectly able to detect genuine differences where they do exist between old and new democracies. Eastern Europeans, probably because of the novelty and volatility of their party systems, are less likely than Western Europeans to agree on the left–right placement of the parties, and their voting behaviour, at the individual level, seems more idiosyncratic than that of their counterparts in the established democracies. We also found that post-materialist and environmentalist orientations are differently related to support for the main party groups in established and consolidating democracies, and that some other attitude dimensions are not equally strongly related to left–right

The Legitimacy of the European Union after Enlargement

self-placement in these two types of countries. But the balance of the evidence suggests that similarities are far more numerous and significant than dissimilarities. Thus, this chapter suggests that the inclusion of the post-communist countries into the EU did not produce a fundamental change in the left–right structuring of mass voting behaviour and the European party system.

Notes

1. The fourth author's work on this chapter was supported by a Marie Curie Intra-European Fellowship at the University of Oxford under the TMR programme of the EU, contract no. 025384.
2. Note however that the liberal supporters in Table 4.2 are a peculiar mix in terms of their national origin, coming exclusively from the Nordic and Low Countries and the UK for the sample of established democracies, and exclusively from the Baltic States, Hungary and Slovenia among the new member states. This may have some impact on their attitude profile. For instance, their particularly irreligious outlook may have as much to do with the fact that most of these countries are particularly secularized as with the fact that these respondents support a liberal party in their home country.
3. In practice the parties asked about included only those with representation in the national parliament or those widely expected to obtain representation in the EP.
4. In practice this occurs about 93 per cent of the time in established EU member states.
5. In this way, about 80 per cent of the respondents could be included in the analyses. If we had only included the respondents who answered the questions on party positions, we would have lost an additional 25 per cent of the sample.

APPENDIX: CHAPTER 4

All thirteen attitude scales appearing in Tables 4.1 and 4.2 were created, in the 1999/2000 European Values Study data, by summing up the standardized scores of responses to the questions listed after the name of the respective scale below. Where appropriate, response scales were reversed so that they matched the direction suggested by the name given to the summary scale. For example, since on both input variables defining the Religiosity scale high values stood for the opposite of religiousness, it was actually their negative standardized values that were summed up to create the Religiosity scale. Missing values on the original variables were replaced with the weighted mean for individuals with the same voting preference and nationality. A few variables that were altogether missing for a particular party were substituted with a constant of zero for the given country. Each of the thirteen scales was standardized to have a zero mean and unit variance in the pooled and weighted twenty-four-country sample. We grouped items into scales not on the basis of their scalability but in order to simplify the presentation of the results by aggregating item-by-item results where several items refer to the same policy domain. The extent to which the items form distinct attitude dimensions varies across countries, partially as a consequence of cross-national differences in the politicization of the given policy domains. Moreover, the inter-item correlations within scales are sometimes distorted by methodological artefacts – such as ipsativity in the case of our post-materialism scale. Therefore, we do not present measures of scalability here.

A.4.1. Economic individualism

Two items were used for this scale from the same battery: 'How would you place your views on this scale? 1 means you agree completely with the statement on the left; 10 means you agree completely with the statement on the right; and if your views fall somewhere in between, you can choose any number in between. [...] The government should take more responsibility to ensure that everyone is provided for OR People should take more responsibility to provide for themselves. [...] Competition is good. It stimulates people to work hard and develop new ideas OR Competition is harmful. It brings out the worst in people.'

A.4.2. Equality over freedom

A single item was used for this scale: 'Which of these statements is the nearest to your opinion? (A) I find that both freedom and equality are important. But if I were to choose one or the other, I would consider personal freedom more important, that is, everyone can live in freedom and develop without hindrance. (B) Certainly both freedom and equality are important. But if I were to choose one or the other, I would consider equality more important, that is, that nobody is underprivileged and that social class differences are not so strong.'

A.4.3. Equality over merit

Three items were used for this scale from the same battery: 'In order to be considered 'just', what should a society provide? Please tell me for each statement if it is important or unimportant to you. 1 means very important; 5 means not important at all. The three selected items were: 'Eliminating big inequalities in income between citizens'; 'Guaranteeing that basic needs are met for all, in terms of food, housing, clothes, education, health'; and 'Recognizing people on their merits.'

A.4.4. Distrust NATO

The item on NATO was used for this scale from the following battery: 'Please look at this card and tell me, for each item listed, how much confidence you have in them, is it $1 =$ a great deal, quite a lot, not very much or $4 =$ none at all?'

A.4.5. Social liberalism

The 'homosexuality', 'abortion', 'divorce' and 'euthanasia – ending the life of the incurably sick' items were used for this scale from the same battery: 'Please tell me for each of the following statements whether you think it can always be justified, never be justified, or something in between, using this card.' The original coding of the responses ran from $1 =$ never justifiable to $10 =$ always justifiable.

A.4.6. Women's liberation

Three items were used for this scale. The first read: 'If a woman wants to have a child as a single parent, but she doesn't want to have a stable relationship with a man, do you approve or disapprove?' The second and third asked: 'For each of the following statements I read out, can you tell me how much you agree with each. [...] A working mother can establish just as warm and secure a relationship with her children as a mother who does not work. [...] Being a housewife is just as fulfilling as working for pay.'

Appendix

A.4.7. Post-materialist

The two input variables were based on responses (recoded as 2 = 'Giving people more say in important government decisions' or 'Protecting freedom of speech'; and 1 = 'Maintaining order in the nation' or 'Fighting rising prices') to the following question: 'There is a lot of talk these days about what the aims of this country should be for the next ten years. On this card are listed some of the goals which different people would give top priority. If you had to choose, which of the things on this card would you say is most important? [...] And which would be the next most important?'

A.4.8. Environment

Two items were used for this scale from the same battery: 'I am now going to read out some statements about the environment. For each one I read out, can you tell me whether you (1) agree strongly, (2) agree, (3) disagree or (4) disagree strongly?' The two items were: 'I would agree to an increase in taxes if the extra money were used to prevent environmental damage'; 'I would give part of my income if I were certain that the money would be used to prevent environmental pollution'.

A.4.9. Distrust European Union

The item on the EU was used for this scale from the following battery: 'Please look at this card and tell me, for each item listed, how much confidence you have in them, is it 1 = a great deal, quite a lot, not very much, or 4 = none at all?'

A.4.10. Anti-immigrant

Three items were used for this scale. The first asked: 'Which of these statements is the nearest to your opinion? (A) For the greater good of society it is better if immigrants maintain their distinct customs and traditions. (B) For the greater good of society it is better if immigrants do not maintain their distinct customs and traditions but take over the customs of the country.' The second response was considered less immigrant-friendly. The second item asked: 'How about people from less developed countries coming here to work. Which one of the following do you think the government should do? (1) Let anyone come who wants to. (2) Let people come as long as there are jobs available. (3) Put strict limits on the number of foreigners who can come here. (4) Prohibit people coming here from other countries.' The third item asked: 'Do you agree or disagree with the following statement: When jobs are scarce, employers should give priority to [NATIONALITY] people over immigrants.'

A.4.11. Family values

Three dichotomous items were used for this scale. The first asked: 'If someone says a child needs a home with both a father and a mother to grow up happily, would you tend to agree or disagree?' The second asked: 'Do you think that a woman has to have children in order to be fulfilled or is this not necessary?' The third asked: 'Do you agree or disagree with the following statement? [...] Marriage is an out-dated institution.'

A.4.12. Religiosity

Two items were used for this scale: 'Apart from weddings, funerals and christenings, about how often do you attend religious services these days? [CODING: (1) More than once a week, (2) once a week, (3) once a month, (4) only on special holidays, (5) once a year, (6) less often, (7) practically never.]' 'Independently of whether you go to church or not, would you say you are... (READ OUT) (1)... a religious person; (2) not a religious person; or (3) a convinced atheist?'

A.4.13. Clericalism

Four items, with the responses originally coded on a scale from 1 = strongly disagree to 5 = strongly agree, were used for this scale. The question asked: 'How much do you agree or disagree with each of the following statements?' The selected items were: 'Politicians who do not believe in God are unfit for public office'; 'Religious leaders should not influence how people vote in elections'; 'It would be better for [COUNTRY] if more people with strong religious beliefs held public office;' 'Religious leaders should not influence government decisions'.

5
Enlargement and the 'Normal' European Parliament

Erik Voeten[1]

5.1. Introduction

How does enlargement affect politics in the European Parliament (EP)? A large body of research indicates that the EP increasingly functions like a 'normal' parliament. This statement refers not only to the body's gradually expanding legislative powers but also to the observation that its politics have not become dominated by national divisions but rather by supranational partisan politics along left–right ideological lines (Attina 1990; Thomassen and Schmitt 1997; Hix 2001; Kreppel 2002; Noury 2002; Raunio 2002; Kreppel and Hix 2003; Alter 2004; Hix, Noury, and Roland 2005, 2006a, 2006b). These findings are important because competition between supranational parties in a common low-dimensional ideological space helps to establish ties between the EU policy-making process and the European public. For this reason, this development is widely viewed as an essential precondition for a truly European system of political representation (see introductory chapter).

There are at least two reasons to suspect that enlargement may affect the dominance of ideology-based competition between supranational parties in EP politics. First, it is unclear to what extent the Members of European Parliament (MEPs) from the new member states fit in the existing ideological and partisan structure of the EP and thus, whether 'old' and 'new' EU members share a 'common political space' (see Marks and Steenbergen 2002). This fear is fed primarily by the observation that the eight new

Central and Eastern European countries have experienced a rather distinct trajectory of political and cultural development from the other EU members. Second, the new members may share a set of common interests that go across party-lines, which may lead to increased contestation along national lines in the EP. This latter concern arises out of the assumption that the new countries have shared economic and security concerns, which override partisan motivations.

This chapter uses data from the first eighteen months of roll-call votes in the sixth EP to evaluate these issues. I evaluate whether there are early indications that expansion has affected the partisan nature of EP politics and the overall ideological structure of the Parliament, and whether national divisions have become a more prominent explanatory source for variation in roll-call vote choices. Finally, I examine whether individual MEPs from the new member states fit as comfortably within the EP's ideological and partisan structure as their counterparts from the EU15.

In general, I find no evidence that enlargement has affected the overall ideological structure or that it has weakened partisan divisions and sharpened national divides in the EP. This is consistent with the main finding of another study of early sixth Parliament voting (Hix and Noury 2006). This holds despite the use of a different, and I argue superior, method for assessing the relative importance of party- and nation-based voting. This method is based on non-parametric analysis of variance rather than cohesion scores. It leads to notably different insights from earlier studies about the overall trajectory of party- and nation-based voting since the first Parliament, but affirms the general preponderance of party-based voting.

Aside from the general finding of continuity, disaggregated analyses do point out some possible areas of concern. MEPs from Central and Eastern Europe appear to fit somewhat less comfortably in the EP's ideological structure. MEPs from two of the largest Eastern European new members, the Czech Republic and Poland, are much more likely than the average EU15 MEP to defect from their European party group (EPG) in order to vote with their national delegations. Yet, this tendency is not noticeably larger than amongst MEPs from Sweden and the UK. Finally, there is evidence that an East–West split has occurred within the Socialist party group (PES) on 'new politics' (values) issues.

This chapter proceeds as follows. The first section evaluates the various arguments for how enlargement might affect EP politics. The focus is on the two issues identified above: the extent to which new MEPs can be expected to fit in the pre-existing political structure of the EP, and the possibility that enlargement may lead to increased voting along national lines. The next two sections evaluate the evidence from the sixth Parliament.

5.2. The effects of enlargement on politics in the European Parliament

5.2.1. *Enlargement and the common political space*

Enlargement increased the number of MEPs from 625 to 732. Moreover, these MEPs now represent twenty-five rather than fifteen countries, many of which democratized only recently and are among the poorest of EU members, to name but two characteristics that set these countries apart. The resulting increase in heterogeneity of membership plausibly leads to less predictable and less stable voting patterns. Moreover, it may complicate coalition formation across national lines.

The concern about fit into the pre-existing cleavage structure is most apparent for the eight former Communist countries. As argued in Chapter 2, the dominance of left–right conflict in most Western European political systems is generally attributed to certain historical commonalities, in particular the industrial revolution (Lipset and Rokkan 1967). Eastern European party systems are of much more recent origin and the nature and relevance of cleavages in these systems are contested. Some scholars argue that national political parties in the East are not easily placed in party families based on durable ideological cleavages such as left–right conflict (e.g. Evans and Whitefield 1993; Commisso 1997; Lawson, Rommele, and Karasimeonov 1999). Instead, these parties are said to compete along ethnic lines or leadership appeal, or based on their abilities to deliver patronage or public goods. Others have argued that cleavages are important but that there is considerable variation in the social and ideological bases for partisanship across Eastern Europe. Whereas in some countries, partisan divisions are dominated by conflicts over economic liberalism, in other countries religion, ethnicity, or regional conflict is most relevant (Evans and Whitefield 2000).

Given that national parties are the key vehicles that create cohesive supranational party groups (Hix, Noury, and Roland 2006*b*), we may expect that Eastern European MEPs fit less well into the common ideological space than their Western counterparts. Moreover, given the size of expansion, this development may have consequences for the EP as a whole. If this were so, we would expect that supranational party membership is a less successful predictor of MEP behaviour in the sixth EP than it was in previous Parliaments. Moreover, low-dimensional spatial models should become less successful in accounting for observed MEP vote choices.

There is, however, also some reason to believe that the match between Eastern and Western MEPs is smoother than stated above. In a seminal article, Kitschelt (1992) argued that the transition from communism to market democracy led to a dominant 'liberal-authoritarian' division across post-Communist countries. The location of individuals along this dimension is determined by their personal resource endowments: those who expected most gains from liberalization favoured market reforms (e.g. young educated men) whereas those who benefited from state protection (e.g. the elderly) favoured a continuation of redistributive policies and price controls. Evans and Whitefield (2000) found that despite the diversity in cleavages across countries, such distributional conflict was relevant in all.

Moreover, the singular dominance of left–right socio-economic conflict in Western European countries should not be exaggerated. Center-periphery and religious conflicts have long been important in European party systems (Lipset and Rokkan 1967). Most analysts argue that a 'values' dimension has gained strength across Western Europe since the 1970s (e.g. Inglehart 1977; Kitschelt 1988). The content of this dimension differs somewhat across countries (Marks et al. 2006). In some countries, it takes a post-modernist flavour, centering on environmentalist concerns. Elsewhere, conflict over traditional values rooted in a secular-religious divide takes centre stage. In yet other countries, nationalism and immigration motivate divisions between parties. These conflicts, especially the latter two, are also highly relevant in Eastern European countries (Evans and Whitefield 1993, 2000; Zielinski 2002). An important distinction, though, is that unlike in Western Europe, the left-wing parties in the East tend more towards the authoritarian pole of this second dimension whereas the pro-market parties lean towards the more libertarian and less-traditional policies (Marks et al. 2006).[2] This may well become a point of contestation inside the supranational party groups that make up the EP, given that the positions of MEPs on the 'green /alternative/ libertarian - traditional/ authoritarian/ nationalism' (GAL-TAN) divide are important for vote choices in the EP (Thomassen, Noury, and Voeten 2004; Voeten 2005) and are highly relevant predictors for the positions of national parties on issues of European integration (Hooghe et al. 2002; Marks et al. 2006). Thus, we may expect that within party groups, an East–West divide on GAL-TAN issues becomes apparent.

5.2.2. *Expansion and national divisions*

Hix, Noury, and Roland (2006*b*) argue that the left–right divide supersedes national divisions in EP politics because in federalist systems conflicts between territorial units can be addressed through the devolution of powers, whereas conflicts between socio-economic groups are more difficult to tackle in this manner. As such, the observation that the EP is dominated by partisan left–right politics does not reflect the irrelevance of national divisions in EU politics, but rather that such conflicts are resolved in a different manner. This theory implies that decision-making procedures are centralized in a selective manner. Precisely on those issue areas in which cleavages cross-cut national divisions is decision-making delegated to supranational institutions, such as the EP. On those issues where national divisions are more prominent, one would expect to see either decentralized (national) decision-making or decisions by unanimity voting in the Council.

Yet, the new member states had little say in the allocation of competencies within the EU system. Thus, if conflicts of interests exist between the Eastern Europeans and the EU15, then those may not have been assimilated properly by EU institutions. In addition, the stalling of the EU Constitution should impress upon new members that altering the fundamental institutional characteristics of the EU through the treaty process will be exceedingly difficult. It just might be, then, that the EP will increasingly become a venue in which national divisions are on display.

All of this is premised upon the notion that new members have some national interests in common and that they can build viable coalitions with older EU members in the EP to translate those interests into policies. The most visible divide of this type has emerged in the security area, tempting US Secretary of Defence Donald Rumsfeld to divide Europe into an 'Old' and a 'New' part in which 'the center of gravity is shifting to the East'.[3] The tendentious nature of these remarks did not fail to irritate the leadership of those put in the 'Old' category. Yet, there is some truth to the notion that security issues have proven to be divisive and that the governments of the largest Eastern European countries have diverged from the 'Franco-German' axis, while building coalitions with other 'old' members (see, for instance, Jones 2004). Moreover, these issues have actually appeared in the EP as the sixth Parliament held several votes on resolutions concerning the war in Iraq and other divisive foreign policy issues.

It is plausible too, that cross-national coalitions can be built on other issues, including agriculture, regional subsidies, immigration, or religious issues. The Central and Eastern European member states tend to be poorer than their counterparts and may, at some point, form alliances with Southern countries over issues of redistribution. MEPs from heavily Catholic countries such as Poland may also form alliances with Catholics of the South about the role of values in the EU, as displayed by the debate on the EU Constitution.

If there is merit to these concerns, then we expect increased voting along national lines to the detriment of supranational parties. It may also be that within the party groups, we will witness a separation between the new Eastern European members and the EU15. The empirical analyses examine whether there is evidence for such patterns in the early goings of the sixth Parliament.

5.2.3. *Empirical strategy*

As should be clear from the discussion above, if and how expansion has affected and will affect EP politics is as yet unclear. This chapter uses a new collection of roll-call votes taken in the first year and a half of the sixth EP to confront the theoretical expectations with some preliminary data.[4] The dataset includes votes on 1,641 non-unanimous roll-calls taken before 7 April 2006. To compare the sixth EP with past Parliaments, I also rely on the exhaustive dataset collected by Hix, Noury, and Roland (2006*b*) of all roll-calls taken during the first five Parliaments.[5] Analysing roll-calls in the EP is somewhat controversial, given that only about one-third of all EP votes are recorded. The sample of recorded votes may not be representative of the overall sample of legislative votes (Carrubba et al. 2006). On the other hand, a comparison of MEP preferences derived from surveys and roll-call analysis does not find that the latter suppresses relevant dimensions of contestation among MEPs, although a distinct effect of party group pressure can be discerned from the data (Voeten 2005). Moreover, the primary task of this analysis is to compare MEP vote choices before and after expansion. Thus, the problem would be more severe for our purpose if there were evidence that practices of requesting recorded votes have changed. Nevertheless, we should apply some caution in interpreting results from roll-call analyses.

The empirical analyses focus both on the extent to which enlargement has affected the functioning of the Parliament as a whole as well as on how MEPs from the new member states have assimilated into EP politics. The analysis proceeds in two parts. The first section examines the concerns that, as a consequence of enlargement, the EP as a whole has become less dominated by partisan conflicts and more by national divisions. Moreover, this section examines whether MEPs from the new member states are more nationalistic in their vote choices than the EU15 MEPs. The second section uses empirical spatial models to examine the ideological underpinnings of vote choices in the EP.

5.3. Partisan and national divisions in the European Parliament

5.3.1. *Formal affiliations with party groups*

A first issue is to establish whether MEPs from the new member states formally affiliate themselves with the different EPGs to the same degree as their counterparts from the EU15. In Chapter 2 we observed that while MEPs from Central and Eastern Europe are slightly more likely to be unaffiliated with any party group than MEPs from the original fifteen, the overwhelming majority of Eastern MEPs (94 per cent) formally belong to a supranational group. Sixty per cent of Eastern MEPs are members of the 'big two' party groups that have dominated EP politics: the PES (Socialists) and the EPP/ED (Conservatives and Christian Democrats). This is slightly less than for the EP15 (66 per cent) but not by much. In general, there is little evidence that formal affiliations are markedly different for the new members.

5.3.2. *Partisan and national divisions*

More important than evaluating formal affiliations is to ask what proportion of the variation in actual roll-call vote choices is accounted for by partisan affiliation and nationality, respectively? An obvious starting point for answering this question would be to calculate the percentage of roll-call vote choices that are predicted correctly if we assume that each MEP votes with his or her party group/national delegation. The higher this percentage, the more informative the classification of MEPs into party/national groups is about actual parliamentary behaviour. A problem with this approach, however, is that the resulting classification percentages are not easily comparable across time: classification percentages may increase because voting becomes more partisan/nationalist or simply because the size of majorities in the EP increases.[6] I therefore use a fit statistic common in non-parametric statistics: the Average Proportional Reduction in Error (APRE), which is defined as follows:

$$\text{APRE} = \frac{\text{Total variation} - \text{Variation explained by partisanship (or nationality)}}{\text{Total variation}}$$

In the context of roll-call voting, total variation can be defined as the number of MEPs in the minority categories (e.g. 'no' and 'abstain' if the plurality vote is 'yes'). The variation explained by classifying MEPs into party groups (or national delegations) is the number of MEPs that votes against the plurality within the MEP's party/country. So, APRE becomes:

$$\text{APRE} = \frac{\sum_{j=1}^{K}(\text{Overall minority vote} - \text{Within party(or country) minority vote})_j}{\sum_{j=1}^{K}(\text{Overall minority vote})_j}$$

Figure 5.1 graphs the APRE for party and national groups. I have divided each of the Parliaments into twelve-month periods (these do not coincide perfectly with calendar years). The last two data-points are from the sixth Parliament. It is immediately obvious that membership in EPGs is much more informative about MEP vote choices than nationality.

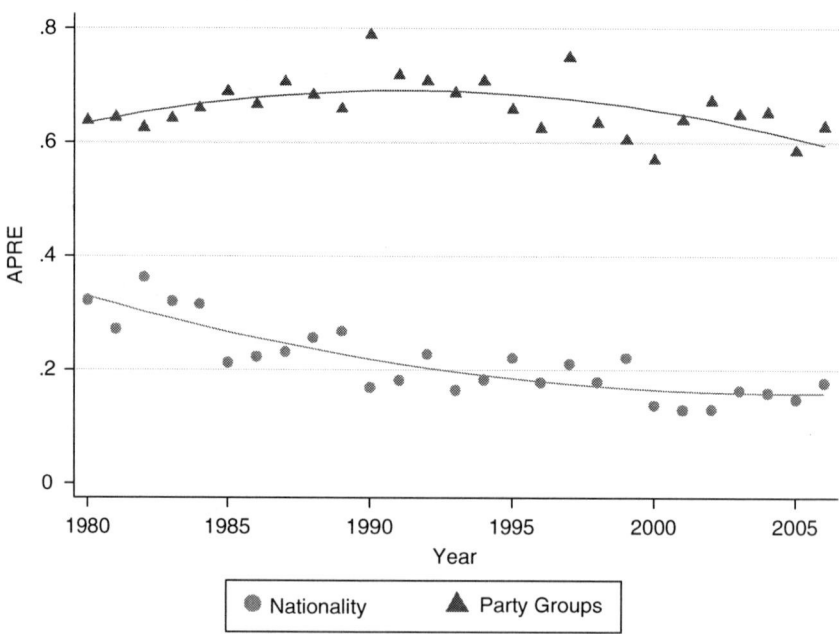

Figure 5.1. Proportion of variation in roll-call voting explained by nationality and party group

There is no evidence that the early sessions of the sixth Parliament initiated a departure in the extent to which nationality or partisanship account for variation in MEP vote choices. Nationality accounted for about one-third of the variation in the first Parliament. Its impact then declined sharply throughout the first four Parliaments, after which it stabilized. In the early goings of the sixth Parliament, the variation explained by membership in national groups was about half of what it was in the first EP. The sharpest shift away from voting along national lines came with the election of the third EP.

The importance of partisanship increased gradually in the early years, peaked in the third Parliament and then appeared to decrease somewhat. This is consistent with the substantive observation that the third Parliament represented the heyday of 'Grand Coalition' politics, characterized by frequent deals between the EP's two main party groups (EPP and PSE), whereas EP politics became increasingly characterized by left–right competition afterwards (Kreppel and Hix 2003).

The story told by Figure 5.1 is rather different, however, from a similar graph created by Hix, Noury, and Roland (2006*b*, Figure 5.2). According to that analysis, the relative cohesion of parties gradually *decreased* until 1994 and sharply *increased* after that (exactly the opposite of Figure 5.1). The difference is in the methodology. Hix et al. compute cohesion scores for party groups and divide these scores by the overall cohesion of the Parliament.[7] They then take the average of the party group cohesion scores as a measure for the importance of party groups in the EP. The appendix to this chapter explains why this approach renders results that are theoretically untenable and, more generally, that cohesion scores should not be used to conduct analyses of variance. Empirically, the problem with these relative cohesion scores is that they overcorrect for sizeable observed fluctuations in the overall cohesion of the Parliament (see Appendix).

5.3.3. *National considerations*

Are national interests a more prominent concern for MEP delegations from the new Eastern European countries than for their counterparts from the EU15? Such comparisons are usually made by comparing the cohesion scores of MEPs across countries. A major problem in such exercises is that we ought to control for the previous observation that the EPGs tend to be very cohesive: one national delegation may look more cohesive than another simply because it is dominated by members of a single party group or by a stable coalition of party groups. I propose an imperfect but

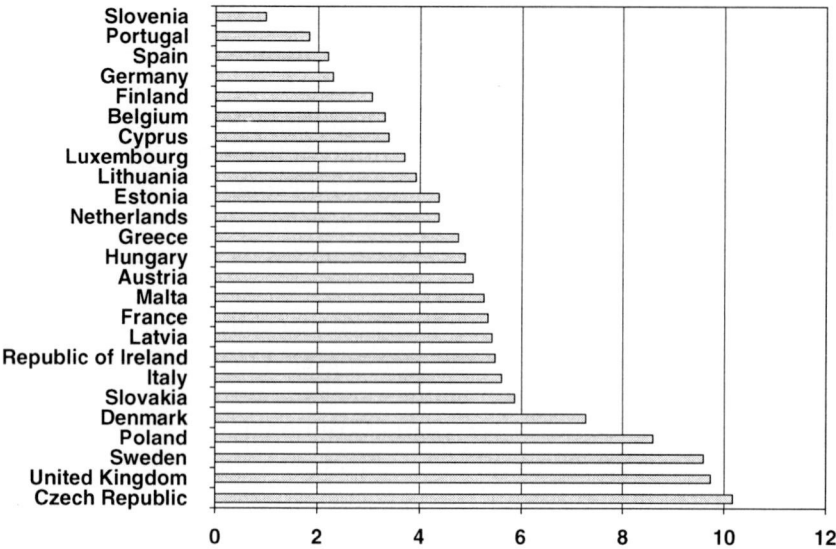

Figure 5.2. Percentage of RCVs on which MEPs vote against party group but with national delegation plurality

intuitive and powerful alternative indicator: the percentage of all vote choices that go against the observed plurality EPG position but with the observed plurality of the national delegation.[8] This should serve as a useful indication of the extent to which national considerations override partisan considerations in the vote choices of MEPs.

As Figure 5.2 shows, among the EU15, MEPs from the UK, Sweden, and Denmark depart most frequently from their EPG's position in order to vote with the main tendency within their national delegations. On the other hand, MEPs from Spain, Portugal, Germany, and the BeNeLux countries relatively rarely diverge from their party groups in order to vote with their national delegations. Again, these results diverge from analyses using cohesion scores. For example, Hix and Noury (2006a, Table 5) find that the UK is the least cohesive delegation, suggesting that it exhibits little national-based voting. This result probably occurs because the British Conservatives frequently defect from the EPP-ED positions on issues of European integration, thus lowering the number of Grand Coalition votes on which a national delegation is perceived as 'cohesive', albeit for reasons that have little to do with voting along national lines.

Figure 5.2 provides a mixed answer to the question that motivates this section. On the one hand, there is no evidence that the Central and Eastern

European delegates are generally more concerned with national considerations than their EU15 counterparts. On the other hand, MEPs from the two largest newcomers, Poland and the Czech Republic, exhibit high rates of defections from party groups in favour of national delegations. While these defection rates are not higher, or at least not noticeably so, than for some of the more eurosceptic EU15 delegations, this is an indication that national-based voting is important to the largest new members.

5.4. Ideological structures

5.4.1. *Low-dimensional spatial models*

A second aspect of the structure of party competition is its ideological underpinnings. It has long been argued that legislative decision-making is more predictable and stable when it occurs in a low-dimensional ideological space. As such, scholars of the US Congress have developed methods for fitting low-dimensional spatial models to observed roll-call voting matrices (Poole and Rosenthal 1985, 1997; Poole 2005). These methods have also been applied to the EP (Hix 2001; Noury 2002; Hix, Noury, and Roland 2006*a*). These studies have revealed the existence of a fairly stable two-dimensional ideological structure. The first, and dominant, dimension divides MEPs along the familiar left–right socio-economic continuum. The second dimension separates those MEPs with relatively favourable and unfavourable opinions towards furthering European integration.

Figure 5.3 plots the estimated ideal points of MEPs in a two-dimensional spatial model.[9] The model is estimated using the non-parametric optimal classification algorithm (Poole 2000) because in parliaments with strong party discipline there are serious violations of the parametric assumptions underlying W-NOMINATE (Rosenthal and Voeten 2004).

The results support the continuation of the aforementioned ideological structure (see also Hix and Noury 2006*a*). From left-to-right, the Greens, Socialists, Liberals, and Conservatives are located along the first dimension. On the left bottom are the left-wing anti-Europe parties, whereas the Independence and Democracy members are appropriately located towards the bottom right of the picture (albeit in a more dispersed way). The wayward group of EPP-ED MEPs on the anti-Europe side of the rest of the party consists mostly of Conservatives from the UK, whose scepticism of intensifying the European project is well-documented. Similarly, within

The Legitimacy of the European Union after Enlargement

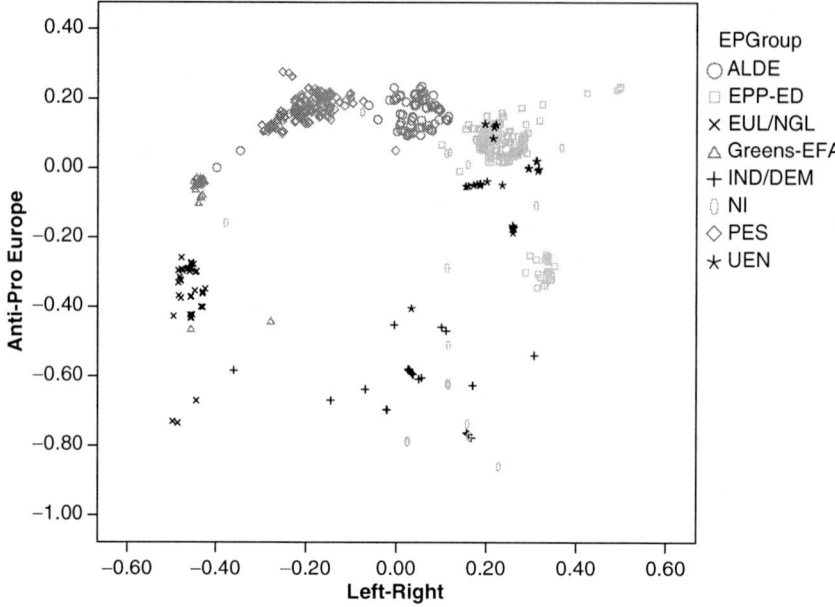

Figure 5.3. Distribution of MEP ideal points in the sixth parliament (based on optimal classification)

the UEN the Polish and Italian members are further to the bottom of the second dimension (more anti-European) than the other members of their party group.

Figure 5.4 shows that the fit of the low-dimensional spatial models to the observed data has also not decreased in the sixth Parliament. The figure plots the APREs for one-, two-, and three-dimensional models. The basic intuition behind the APRE is similar to that discussed before: the APRE for a one-dimensional model indicates the proportion of the variance in RCV behaviour that can be explained by ordering MEPs along a single dimension, where variance is defined by the number of choices that are unexplained by the baseline model that 'everyone votes with the plurality'.

Most importantly, there is no evidence that expansion has made the Parliament less structured from an ideological perspective. Quite to the contrary, a one-dimensional model fits the data better for the sixth Parliament than for any other Parliament. Instead, from an ideological perspective, the fifth Parliament is the least cohesive (perhaps due to the issue of

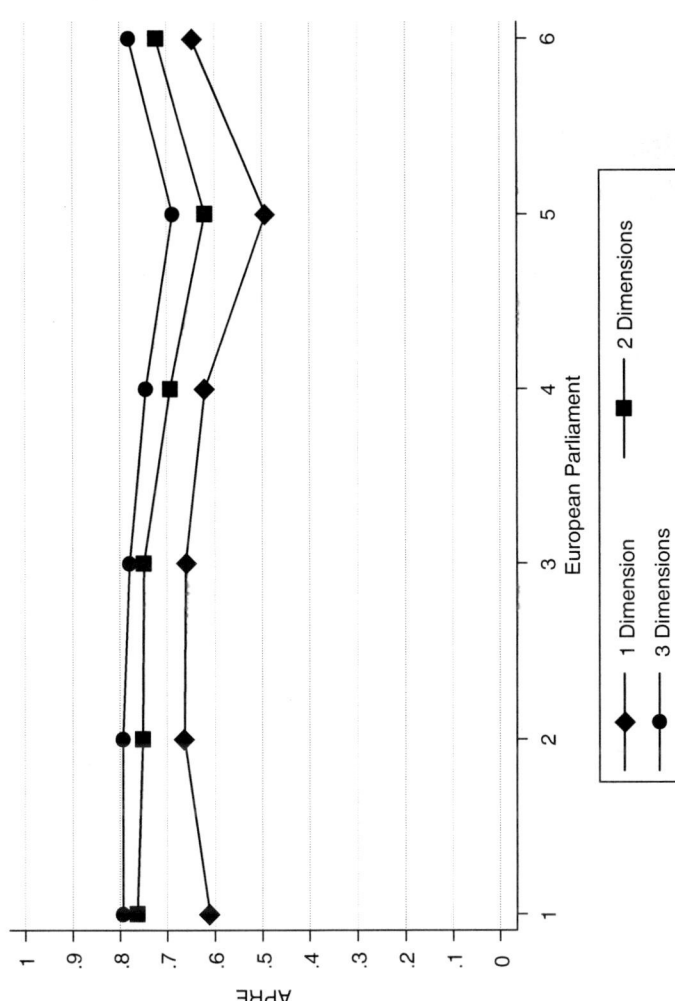

Figure 5.4. APRE of one-, two-, and three-dimensional spatial models to roll-call voting in the five EPs (based on non-parametric model)

enlargement). Thus, at least from an evaluation of the early voting, fears that enlargement undermines the low-dimensional ideological nature of the EP appear unwarranted. This could of course be because controversial issues are kept off the agenda until more is known about the behaviour of the new MEPs.

5.4.2. Fit of Eastern MEPs into the ideological structure

To say that enlargement has not altered the overall ideological structure of EP politics is not the same as to claim that Eastern and Central European MEPs fit in the same way into the ideological space as MEPs from the EU15. A first indication is that the vote choices of Eastern MEPs are not explained as well by the two-dimensional spatial model as the vote choices of other MEPs. On average, the two-dimensional model from Figure 5.3 explains 91.6 per cent of the vote choices of Eastern MEPs, against 93.4 per cent of vote choices made by the MEPs from the EU15, and 94.5 per cent of choices by the non-Eastern European new members. An ANOVA analysis determines that this difference is statistically significant.[10] Moreover, this effect remains significant and substantively important after controlling for the most obvious alternative explanation. In general, legislators with extremist preferences fit the spatial model less well (see Poole and Rosenthal 1997). In a multiple regression analysis with MEP classification as the dependent variable and the squared MEP ideal points as independent variables, Eastern MEPs are estimated to have 1.8 per cent lower classification percentage than their counterparts ($p = .000$).

Thus, MEPs from Central and Eastern Europe fit less comfortably in the EP's ideological structure. Closer analysis reveals that this result is primarily due to the poor fit of Polish MEPs: On average, the two-dimensional model explains 89.4 per cent of their vote choices correctly, whereas 95.6 per cent of the vote choices of German MEPs are accounted for by the two-dimensional model. These differences are quite large in the context of empirical spatial models. We should note, however, that Polish MEPs are not noticeably less predictable (from an ideological perspective) in their vote choices than Danish and Swedish MEPs, who also exhibit a poor fit to the model.

A second concern may be that the ideal points of Eastern MEPs are not motivated by ideology to the same extent as those of EU15 MEPs. Table 5.1 reports the results from a regression analysis that explains MEP ideal points on the two dimensions from Figure 5.3 using data on the ideological positions of their national parties (see also Hix, Noury and Roland

Table 5.1. Regression of expert judgments of national party positions on MEP ideal points (robust standard errors clustered on national party membership)

Panel A: First-dimension coordinates (left–right positions)

	EU15		Central/Eastern Europe	
	B	S.E.	B	S.E.
(Constant)	−.914***	.027	−.664	.179
Pro–anti Europe (1–7)	.035***	.015	−.020	.016
Economic left–right (0–10)	.069***	.010	.104***	.018
Gal/Tan or new politics (0–10)	.063***	.014	.056***	.012
N	483		129	
R_{adj}^2	.845		.656	
S.E. estimate	.100		.129	

Panel B: Second-dimension coordinates (pro–anti integration)

	EU15		Central/Eastern Europe	
	B	S.E.	B	S.E.
(Constant)	−.565***	.089	−.600***	.174
Pro–anti Europe (1–7)	.106***	.013	.141***	.020
Economic left–right (0–10)	.026**	.012	−.033***	.010
Gal/Tan or new politics (0–10)	−.023	.014	.008	.011
N	483		129	
R_{adj}^2	.713		.711	
S.E. estimate	.112		.134	

2006a). These data are based on expert surveys conducted in 2002 among all EU members (see Marks et al. 2006). The survey includes expert judgments about the extent to which a party supports European integration, a party's position on the economic left–right dimension, and a party's position on the GAL/TAN new politics dimension discussed earlier.[11]

Panel A shows that, for the EU15, an MEP's position on the first dimension is primarily a function of its national party's economic left–right and GAL/TAN positions and to a lesser, but significant, degree of its stands towards European integration. For Eastern European MEPs, economic left–right is by far the most important,[12] and positions on EU integration are insignificant.

Panel B shows that, in accordance with the casual interpretation discussed earlier, pro-anti Europe positions of national parties are by far the most important variables explaining variation along the second dimension of contestation.[13] There is one striking difference between the regression coefficients for Eastern and EU15 MEPs: among the EU15, parties on the economic right appear more favourably disposed towards European integration, whereas among Eastern Europeans, this relation appears to be the opposite. As a whole, however, it appears that the perceived policy stances of Eastern European national parties explain the roll-call voting behaviour of Eastern European MEPs rather well. Moreover, the structure of these policy divides is reasonably similar to that in the West, with some small but notable differences.

5.4.3. *Within party-group divisions*

A final hypothesis that warrants attention is that East–West cleavages have emerged within party groups. As speculated earlier, these may arise because Eastern national parties appear to align differently on the GAL-TAN dimension (Marks et al. 2006), because there is increased heterogeneity in income differences, because of divides over security issues, or because the new members want to alter the structure of the European project, which was largely negotiated without their input.

In order to investigate this, the empirical spatial model was applied to the two main party groups individually: the EPP-ED and the PES. Figure 5.5 shows the resulting scatter plot. Eastern European members are denoted with black two-letter country codes, EU15 MEPs are identified by grey two-letter country codes. (MEPs from the remaining two new member states are omitted.) Nearly 53 per cent of the observed variation within the EPP is explained by ordering MEPs along a single dimension (and 39 per cent of the variation among PES MEPs).[14] The second dimensions add little explanatory value.

The first dimension within the EPP-ED is very strongly correlated with variation in national party positions on European integration (Pearson $R = .83$).[15] As is evident from the graph, it is mostly the British MEPs that distinguish themselves in terms of their euro-scepticism. To a lesser extent, Swedish and Czech EPP-ED members also tend to be more on the anti-integration side. There is, however, no evidence of an East–West divide on this issue within the EPP-ED. The second dimension is correlated most strongly with national party positions on the enlargement issue ($R = .53$).[16] On this dimension, there is a significant East–West divide: the mean position of MEPs from Eastern countries is $-.06$ versus $.02$ for the EP15 ($F = 16.51$, $p = .000$). Thus, there is some evidence that issues related to enlargement divide the conservative EPG, although this dimension accounts for little variation in actual roll-call votes.

The substantive content of the dimension of contestation within the PES is different: the first dimension is most strongly correlated with GAL-TAN or libertarian-authoritarian positions of national parties (Pearson R of .400). On this issue, there is a very clear East–West divide, with Eastern

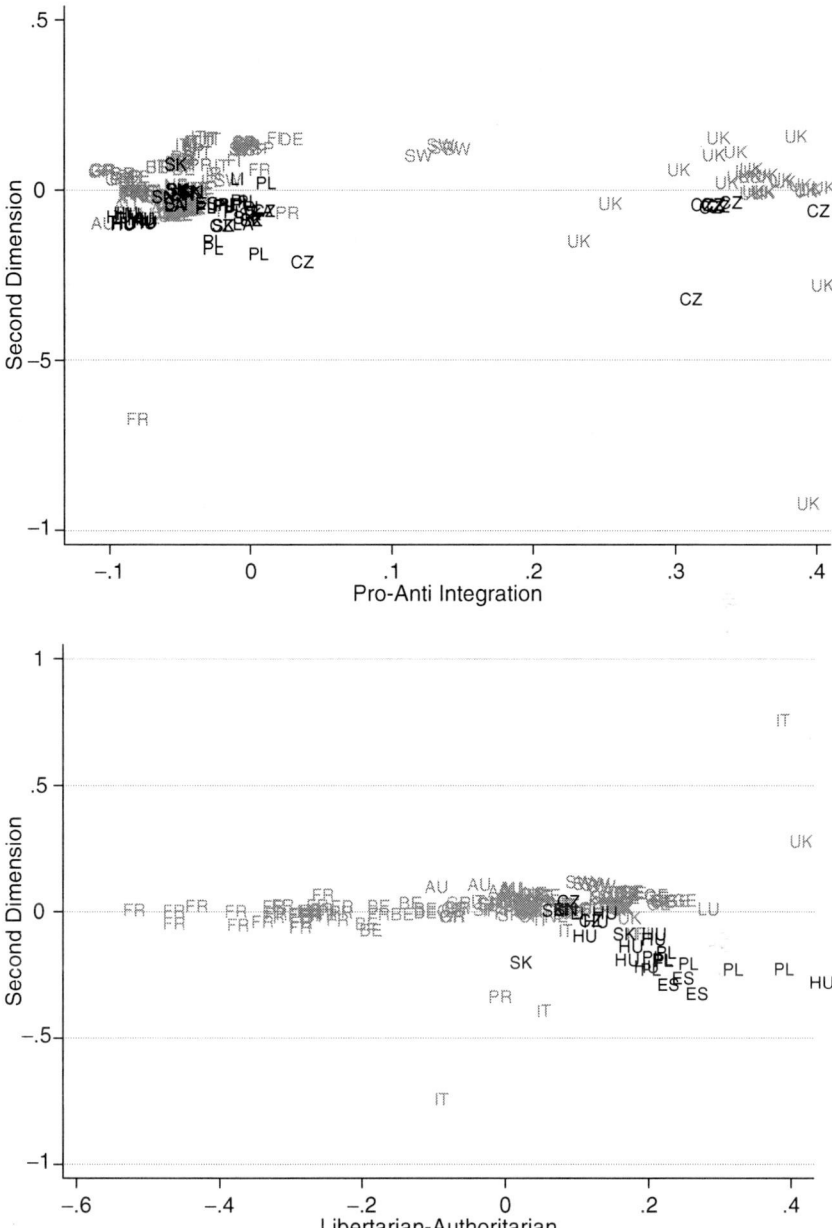

Figure 5.5. Within-party scalings of Eastern European (black) and EU15 (grey) MEPs

European members more towards the TAN (authoritarian) side of the spectrum. This confirms the finding that the national party programs of the Eastern European left are more towards the TAN side of the spectrum than those of their Western counterparts (Marks et al. 2006). This finding, however, shows that the observed ideological conflict indeed materializes in actual legislative behaviour. The second dimension again mostly captures conflict over enlargement issues ($R = .382$). In all, East–West conflict is extremely important in accounting for internal divisions within the PES.

5.5. Conclusion

This chapter has compared roll-call voting behaviour in the sixth Parliament to the preceding Parliaments in an effort to evaluate the extent to which enlargement affects politics in the EP, and thereby the prospects for supranational democratic representation in the EU. The early voting patterns reveal little cause for concern about the overall extent to which national-based or partisan and ideology-based voting characterize the EP. There are some noticeable East–West divides within parties over enlargement issues and values issues (within the PES), but as a whole East–West conflict has far from dominated EP politics, at least as revealed by roll-call voting.

One may question whether the first few years of voting records provide an accurate picture of the effects of enlargement. The answer will depend upon one's favoured theoretical perspective. Those who put great stock in socialization theories would expect that the assimilation of Eastern MEPs into EPGs will only get stronger. As such, we should expect that Eastern MEPs will fit the EP's ideological structure increasingly well and that East–West divides within party groups should gradually disappear.

Those who see politics as dominated by more fundamental clashes of interest will have a different perspective. Inequalities in income, divergent security interests, and interests over the direction of the EU are not going to disappear overnight. As the EP grows stronger and the position of the new members gets further entrenched, these new members may well seek to alter the current bases of contestation within the EP. In all, the current chapter offers no more than a preliminary look at this important issue.

More long-lasting may be the methodological contribution this chapter makes with regard to the proper evaluation of the relative influence of party and nationality on roll-call voting. I have shown that cohesion indices used in the literature improperly correct for temporal variation in the overall majority size of the Parliament. Analyses based on these indices may therefore provide a biased baseline for evaluating change in partisan voting as a consequence of expansion. I propose non-parametric analysis of variance as a better and more intuitive alternative.

Notes

1. Erik Voeten is the Peter F. Krogh Assistant Professor of Global Justice and Geopolitics at the Georgetown School of Foreign Service. An earlier version of this chapter was prepared for presentation at the University of Twente, June 16–17, 2006. I appreciate the comments by the participants at that seminar as well as by Gail McElroy.
2. This is consistent with Kitschelt's view (1992) that liberalization dominates contestation between Eastern European parties.
3. Department of Defense, Press Conference, Wednesday, 22 January, 2003 <http://www.defenselink.mil/transcripts/2003/t01232003_t0122sdfpc.html> (accessed May 27, 2006).
4. The data were collected by the author from the European Parliament's web site: <http://www.europarl.eu.int/activities/expert/pv/search/go.do>.
5. Data on the EP1-4 are available from: <http://personal.lse.ac.uk/HIX/HixNoury-RolandEPdata.HTM>. The data for the fifth parliament were kindly shared by Simon Hix.
6. Hix et al. (2006*b*, Chapter 5) make a similar point.
7. The same procedure is applied in Hix, Noury and Roland 2005 and Hix and Noury 2006.
8. A more proper way to do this would be to estimate the marginal effects of nationality in a hierarchical probit model with EPG membership as a covariate. This is complicated somewhat by the three (not necessarily ordered) vote choices.
9. One MEP, Irena Belohorská, is not plotted as her irregular vote choices (from an ideological perspective) made her an extreme outlier.
10. $F = 8.477, p = .000$.
11. For more details, see: <http://www.unc.edu/~gwmarks/data/2002%20dataset/chapel%20hill%202002%20Codebook.doc>
12. Standardized coefficient is 1.1 for economic left–right and .61 for GAL/TAN.
13. For the EU15, the standardized coefficient on the EU variable is .75, .23 for left–right. For Eastern/Central Europe, these figures are 1.1 and −.30.
14. These are APREs.
15. National party positions derived from expert survey, as in Table 5.1.
16. This is Question 11 in the aforementioned survey.

APPENDIX: CHAPTER 5

Hix et al. (2006b) calculate the following cohesion index, where Y, N, and A stand for the number of Yes, No, and Abstain choices on a given roll-call within a party:

$$\text{Absolute cohesion index (ACI)} = \frac{\max\{Y,N,A\} - \frac{1}{2}[(Y+N+A) - \max\{Y,N,A\}]}{(Y+N+A)}$$

In order to make the index comparable across time and issues, they then divide the index for each party by the cohesion index for the parliament as a whole, resulting in a Relative Cohesion Index (RCI). They then take the average RCI across parties as an indicator for overall cohesion.

	Issue 1	Issue 2	Issue 3	Issue 4	Issue 5
Party 1	100 Y	100 Y	75 Y, 25 N	90 Y, 10 N	50 Y, 50 N
Party 2	100 Y	100 Y	100 Y	90 Y, 10 N	50 Y, 50 N
Party 3	100 N	100 Y	75 N, 25 Y	90 Y, 10 N	50 Y, 50 N
Party 4	100 N	100 N	100 N	90 Y, 10 N	50 Y, 50 N
Plurality	50%	75%	50%	90%	50%
APRE	1	1	.75	0	0
ACI	1	1	.81	.85	.25
RCI	4	1.6	3.2	1.0	1.0

It is useful to walk through a stylized example to see the problems with this index. For simplicity, let us assume that we have four equally sized parties ($N = 100$). First, consider Issue 1, where two parties cohesively vote 'yes' and the other two vote 'no' (see table above). Appropriately, both APRE and RCI reach their maximum levels of cohesion. Now, suppose one party (party 3) switches uniformly to the 'yes' camp. As a result, the RCI is cut in half. So, the RCI may change dramatically due to changes in coalition formation even if party discipline stays the same. To illustrate just how sensitive the RCI is to the size of the plurality, consider Issue 3, which is identical to Issue 2 except that parties 1 and 3 have internal divisions and that the plurality size shrinks. The RCI on issue 3 is twice as high as on issue 2, even though party discipline is perfect on issue 2 and far from perfect on issue 3! Clearly, this is theoretically untenable.

Enlargement and the 'Normal' European Parliament

This oversensitivity to plurality sizes (or more precisely the ACI of the parliament) is substantively important. Figure 5.1 in Hix et al. (2006b) shows that the absolute cohesion of the EP increased from around .6 to around .7 in EPs 3 and 4, and back to below .6 in EPs 5 and 6. As such, the RCI should increase by a factor of around 1.2 as a mere consequence of these changes in majority sizes, which could be related to electoral results, coalition formation, or other factors that are unrelated to party discipline.

There is, of course, good reason to be concerned with the influence of majority sizes. The example issues 4 and 5 illustrate this point. On both issues, party membership is completely uninformative about the vote choices of MEPs. Yet, ACI is much higher on issue 4 than on issue 5 simply because the size of the majority is larger on the former issue. RCI nicely controls for this, but so does APRE: the explained variance by partisanship is correctly calculated as 0 on issues 4 and 5.

The main lesson here is that the tools of non-parametric analyses of variance are much more useful in answering the type of questions we are interested in than are relatively ad hoc cohesion indices.

Note that even though this discussion has focused on indices that characterize a parliament as a whole, it is straightforward to extend this idea to the analysis of individual parties (or national groups). Hix et al. (2005, 2006b) compute relative cohesion indices for parties to pursue an analysis across time. An index based on similar principles as APRE compares the expected minority vote based on the vote in the parliament as a whole to the observed minority vote inside a party:

$$PRE_{Party} = \frac{(\text{Expected minority vote}) - (\text{Observed minority vote})}{(\text{Expected minority vote})}$$

$$= \frac{\frac{(Y+N+A)_{All} - \max\{Y,N,A\}_{All}}{(Y+N+A)_{All}} (Y+N+A)_{Party} - [(Y+N+A) - \max\{Y,N,A\}]_{Party}}{\frac{(Y+N+A)_{All} - \max\{Y,N,A\}_{All}}{(Y+N+A)_{All}} (Y+N+A)_{Party}}$$

We should note that this index can take negative values on individual votes (unlike the APRE for the parliament as a whole) if the party is more divided than the parliament (this is a common property of adjusted measures of variance, including the much used adjusted R-squared). It is, however, a much cleaner way to correct for the problem of varying plurality sizes than RCI.

Part II

Political Support for the European Union

6

The Level of Decision Making: The Preferences of the Citizens after Enlargement

Lieven De Winter, Marc Swyngedouw,
and Bart Goeminne

6.1. Introduction

In the current system of multilevel governance in the EU, different policy issues and areas are dealt with at various levels (ranging from the local to the EU), sometimes exclusively at one level, but often by joint decision making between two or more levels. The question of whether or not the level(s) at which decisions are currently taken in different policy fields is truly the most appropriate level is one of the aspects that is supposed to affect the legitimacy and effectiveness of any democratic polity (Thomassen and Schmitt 1999*a*; Peterson 1995).

While many criteria can be taken into account to evaluate a level's appropriateness (realizing economies of scale, enhancing democratic participation and accountability, reducing the gap between policy preferences of decision makers and policy takers, etc.), in democratic polities the legitimacy of a given level of decision making is largely based on the evaluation on the part of the citizens of whether a certain division of power is right or wrong, for whatever valid or erroneous reason this judgement is based on.

In the framework of the problematic legitimacy of EU governance, the question of the appropriateness of the EU level of decision making has for a long time been dormant given the permissive pro-European consensus. Growing dissatisfaction of national governments with 'creeping EU federalism' led to the gradual introduction of subsidiarity as a principle of legitimation of EU decision making. This principle has been rapidly seized by the regions, claiming that subsidiarity also implies that some policies be decided best at the regional level. Since Maastricht and subsequent treaties, the role of the regions in EU decision making has been increasingly institutionally enshrined. All this has turned the level of decision making in the EU into one of the hot issues in the debate on the legitimacy of and the democratic deficit within the EU system of governance.

This chapter will first present a short overview of the evolution of the institutional debate regarding the appropriate levels of decision making within the EU, then offer a synthesis of the contributions of political science to this debate. Second, we will explore to what extent European citizens allocate decision-making responsibilities to the EU, the state or the regional level, and how this varies in space, over time and policy sector. Third, we will formulate a number of hypotheses – that can be tested with the data of the European Elections Studies – explaining variation of level preferences by individual attitudes and characteristics. Finally, we will test these hypotheses through multivariate analysis.

6.2. The debate on the level of decision making in the EU

The issue of the level of government refers mainly to the question – for the sectors where government regulation is considered legitimate[1] – at which level of government this regulation should occur: at the local, regional, national, European or global level, or at which mix of these levels. There is a large body of mainly theoretical and normative research that touches upon the question of the appropriate level: from ancient political philosophers (Aristotle, Thomas Aquinas, Althusius, Montesquieu, Kant, Hegel, Mill, De Tocqueville, Saint-Simon, Proudhon, etc.; see Burgess 2006), to classic and contemporary theories of federalism (Swenden 2006), theories of (minority) nationalism (McGarry and Keating 2006), Green political theory (Dobson 2000), neo-classical economic theory of federalism (Oates 1972; Peterson 1995), etc.

At the beginning of the European integration process, the level of government question was only posed in terms of EC/EU governance vis-à-vis the sovereignty of the national states and was basically treated as a typical problem of post-war expansion of forms of international governance

(UN, IMF, NATO, etc.). International organizations historically emerged and expanded in number and scope precisely because more and more issues began inherently to transcend national borders and, therefore, could only be dealt with through some form of permanent international cooperation.

In the EC/EU context, this question has focused on the policy issues and sectors in which European institutions can operate more effectively than national member states. The level of government question became politically salient in the traditional two-level debate between intergovermentalist ('sovereignist' or 'realist') and supranational ('functionalist' or 'federalist') conceptions of international organizations.

Growing critique from national governments on the practice of the EC integration process ('creeping federalism' or the emergence of a European 'Jacobine super-state'; Lodge 1996) led pro-European leaders (Tindemans report 1975; Spinelli report 1984; and finally Delors) to revive the concept of subsidiarity, in order to appease the growing tension between national governments and the European Commission. Hence, the federalist ambitions of the founding fathers of the European Community were to some extent tempered by the inscription of the principle of subsidiarity into the Maastricht Treaty, which puts a strong, albeit only symbolic, constraint on their progressive and deterministic vision on the federal outcome of the European integration process. Art. 3 of the Maastricht Treaty stated that:

> In areas which do not fall within its exclusive competence, the Community shall take action, in accordance with the principle of subsidiarity, only if and insofar as the objectives of the proposed action cannot be sufficiently achieved by the Member States and can, therefore, by reason of scale or effects of the proposed action, be better achieved by the Community... Any action by the Community shall not go beyond what is necessary to achieve the objectives of this Treaty.

Hence, only those policy sectors that cannot be dealt with effectively at the level of member states are eligible for 'Europeanization'. Still, this principle was so vague that it served predominantly political objectives, that is, putting the Eurosceptics at ease, rather than serving as a practical guideline for stipulating which policy sectors should remain national or not (Estella de Noriega 1997: 249–70). Nor was it in the beginning 'justiciable', although by now, albeit very rarely, questions of violation of the subsidiarity principle are brought before the European Court of Justice.

The subsidiarity principle was then successfully seized by the regions, promoting a 'Europe of the Regions' with a third – regional – layer within the EU system of 'multilevel governance' (Hooghe and Marks 2001).

Obviously, the theory of subsidiarity implicitly recognizes the potential role of the regional and local level of government. The institutional and symbolic recognition of the sub-state level in EU regimes was enshrined in the creation of the Committee of the Regions in 1994. The 1997 Amsterdam Treaty included a Protocol on the application of the Principle of Subsidiarity providing some safeguards against centralization by laying down certain requirements for central action.

In order to reduce the 'democratic deficit', the Commission started to actively seek more involvement of different levels of government ('as closely as possible to the citizen') and of the wider civil society at different levels, by more regularly using Green Papers and White Papers to prompt broad public debate before new proposals are submitted (cf. Prodi's White Paper on Governance). The Commission has to justify each of its new proposals in the light of the subsidiarity principle. It is to submit an annual report to the European Council, the European Parliament, and the Council of Ministers, which is also to be forwarded to the Committee of the Regions and the Economic and Social Committee, on the application of these subsidiarity clauses.

Finally, the draft EU Constitution not only included the Amsterdam Protocol on Subsidiarity of 1997, but, more importantly, elaborated a list of competences (distinguishing between 'exclusive', 'shared', and 'supporting, coordinating or complementary' powers) for different decision-making levels. The draft EU Constitution as well as the Reform Treaty of Lisbon, on the one hand, included provisions to reduce the veto power of national states but, on the other hand, also enhanced the role of national parliaments, in particular regarding their control over the respect for the subsidiarity principle. In fact, the Protocol on the Application of the Principles of Subsidiarity and Proportionality, annexed to the Lisbon Treaty, stipulates that: 'Before proposing legislative acts, the Commission shall consult widely. Such consultations shall, where appropriate, take into account the regional and local dimension of the action envisaged.' (art. 2)...'Draft legislative acts shall take account of the need for any burden, whether financial or administrative, falling upon the Union, national governments, regional or local authorities, economic operators and citizens, to be minimised and commensurate with the objective to be achieved.' (art. 5)....'National parliaments, but also the Committee of the Regions may also bring infringement of the principle of subsidiarity by a legislative act to the European Court of Justice.' (art. 8)

Hence, the question of the appropriate level of government following the subsidiarity principle has gradually been integrated into European 'basic law'. The question of the appropriate level of government spilled over from the elitist constitutional debate to the mass level in the 1990s, and therefore became a genuine legitimacy problem, due to growing disaffection of EU citizens with the EU, as well as with their national political institutions and elites (Norris 1999a). This was dramatically expressed by the rejection of the Maastricht Treaty and the EU Constitution in the French and Dutch referendums but also in other referendums on EU matters (Hooghe and Marks 2008). Yet, in spite of the growing politicization of the EU – in the sense that people, parties and social movements became aware that integration not only produces winners but also losers (Schmitter 2005: 268; Kriesi et al. 2006) – political science has up until now not contributed much to the theoretical debate regarding the level and scope of EU government (for exceptions, see Lindberg and Scheingold 1970; Scharpf 2003). Leading democratic theorists even argued that it is difficult to deduce the legitimacy of the appropriate level of government from normative political theory, and that core concepts of democratic theory like majority rule can not sufficiently provide for grounds of justification of the appropriateness of different levels of government (Dahl and Tufte 1974; Dahl 1989: 204).

At the empirical level, Sinnott (1995) underlines the fact that the legitimacy of a certain division of competencies between levels, in the end, resides mainly in citizens' preferences. He discusses three criteria for deciding on the question of which level is most appropriate. His first criterion resonates with the subsidiarity principle: the first basis for deciding the appropriate level of governance is the very nature of the issues. Some issues are intrinsically international, as they penetrate or transcend national borders, and therefore cannot effectively be dealt with at these levels. Others require a larger than national scale in order to mobilize the resources necessary to solve the problem. Likewise, some problems are so narrow that local government should best tackle them. He labels such arguments as 'endogenous' attribution of levels of governance.

The level of governance can be also attributed in an 'exogenous' way, when a given level of governance simply claims that a particular issue or policy sector explicitly lies within its legally defined sphere of competence, such as the EU Treaties (cf. the concept of EU exclusive competencies in Art. 3 of the Maastricht Treaty), or can implicitly be derived from the main institutional principles or general function as enshrined in constitutions or treaties.

Last but not least, issues can be attributed to a given level of government because the citizens, the media and political elites simply believe that this issue or sector ought to be tackled at that level ('normative' attribution of level of governance). This type of level attribution obviously has a subjective basis since it does not really matter whether the preferred level of government has the legal competence to deal with these issues, nor does it matter whether the nature of the issue in fact makes a certain level most efficient or closest to citizens' preferences to solve the issue.

Therefore the normative mode of attribution stipulates that the intervention of a political level in a certain policy sector is only legitimate if this corresponds to the 'subjective' preferences of the represented regarding the level to which they want to delegate their popular sovereignty. Even if one were to accomplish a valid 'objective' classification of policy fields by their endogenous character (for instance, by expert judgements) and attribute competencies accordingly, such a division of labour could still clash with public opinion preferences and pose a legitimacy problem.[2]

To conclude, the preferences of citizens for certain decision-making levels remains a cornerstone of the legitimacy of the EU system of democratic multilevel governance that cannot only be guaranteed by the proper application of the subsidiarity principle. We will now first explore the level preferences of European citizens and their basic variation over space, policy sector, and time. Then we will formulate hypotheses explaining variation in 2004, and subsequently test these through multivariate analysis.

6.3. Citizens' level of governance preferences over time, policy sector, and space

In comparative research, the level preferences of EU citizens have been tapped in different ways. The richest data to study the theme is offered by the European Election Studies (EES), as it allows for comparisons over time, space, and policy sectors, and also includes data regarding a large number of potential determinants of variations of level preferences.

The 1994, 1999, and 2004 EES surveys contained similar questions regarding the preferences for the European, national, or regional level of decision making. In each survey respondents were asked at which level one or more policy problems that they perceived as 'most important' were currently decided, and at which level they believed they ought to be decided. The difference between the perceived level of decision making and the preferred level of decision making taps the legitimacy deficit in terms of level of government preferences.

6.3.1. Citizens' preferences in 2004

Table 6.1 shows that for the problem citizens identified as most important in their country in 2004, 62.6 per cent believed that this problem was currently decided at the national level. About an equal proportion believed that this problem was decided at the regional (19.1 per cent) or European level (18.3 per cent). Regarding the preferred level of decision making, the latter two levels score a bit higher than the perceived level (20.1 per cent and 20.9 per cent, respectively), necessarily at the cost of the preferences for the national level (59.0 per cent). Hence, one could conclude that the legitimacy deficit in terms of level of decision making in the EU system of multilevel governance is quite small: the aggregated sum of the differences between perceived and preferred levels for all three levels amounts to only 3.1 per cent (last column Table 6.1[3]). Thus, all in all, at the aggregate level, EU citizens believe that decisions regarding important problems are taken at the level they prefer them to be taken!

However, there are huge differences between perceived and preferred levels when we break these European averages down to the country level (thus no longer weighted by country and sample size[4]). Amongst the member country populations that in 2004 prefer the European level most, we find in decreasing order Cyprus, Belgium, Austria, Latvia, Spain, and the Netherlands (in which three or more out of ten citizens prefer the European level), while those that prefer the European level least are – in ascending order – Slovenia, Italy, Sweden, Poland, Estonia, Finland, Hungary, France, and Denmark (in which less than one out of seven citizens prefer this level).

Amongst the country populations that prefer the national level most, we find in decreasing order, Slovenia, Hungary, Italy, Estonia, Poland, and the Czech Republic (in which six or more out of ten citizens prefer the national level), while less than half of the citizens of France, Belgium, Sweden Germany, and Spain – all non-enlargement states – prefer this level.

The most regional level-oriented countries are, in decreasing order, Sweden, Britain, France, Finland, Denmark, and Germany, not exactly countries – apart from the latter– with a strong regionalist tradition. Nevertheless, the current lack of competences of the regions in these countries may in fact have triggered these demands for more regional empowerment. Of the enlargement states, only Poland scores above the European average. And while we concluded at the aggregate level that EU citizens believe that decisions are taken at the level they prefer them to be taken, at the individual country level differences between perceived and

The Legitimacy of the European Union after Enlargement

Table 6.1. Perceived and preferred levels of decision making for most important problem per country and country groups in 2004 (22 countries)

	Perceived level			Preferred level			Aggregate differences Perc − Pref
	Regional	National	European	Regional	National	European	
Austria	16.1	61.7	22.1	13.3	53.1	33.6	12.9
Belgium	24.7	49.9	25.4	19.2	44.8	36.0	13.4
Britain	27.4	57.5	15.1	35.9	51.7	12.4	7.0
Denmark	21.3	66.2	12.6	27.5	59.1	13.4	3.9
Finland	19.4	62.3	18.2	28.7	59.4	11.9	11.0
France	16.0	60.2	23.8	29.0	44.7	26.2	8.9
Germany	24.2	51.3	24.5	26.2	46.7	27.1	3.6
Greece	13.3	48.7	37.9	15.8	59.9	24.3	14.9
Ireland	18.0	64.9	17.1	23.8	56.4	19.8	5.6
Italy	12.6	74.4	13.0	15.6	78.1	6.3	8.2
Netherlands	5.1	77.6	17.3	11.5	59.0	29.5	15.4
Portugal	7.2	58.5	34.2	17.4	56.0	26.6	12.7
Spain	8.1	76.5	15.4	19.0	49.7	31.3	21.4
Sweden	52.9	42.1	5.0	46.0	45.4	8.6	7.1
Old members ($n = 14$)	19.0	60.8	20.1	23.5	54.6	21.9	6.2
Cyprus	4.6	72.7	22.6	5.5	55.8	38.6	16.5
Czech Republic	19.1	56.3	24.6	16.1	62.6	21.3	4.8
Estonia	29.1	61.9	8.9	15.5	73.6	10.9	8.8
Hungary	13.4	79.0	7.6	9.7	78.2	12.1	6.4
Latvia	22.3	61.9	15.9	10.6	56.7	32.7	22.7
Poland	21.9	65.0	13.1	22.3	66.8	10.8	2.5
Slovakia	18.5	64.6	16.9	20.3	57.8	21.9	5.9
Slovenia	23.7	65.2	11.1	12.2	82.7	5.1	11.8
New members ($n = 8$)	19.1	65.8	15.1	14.0	66.8	19.2	5.1
Difference Old–New	−0.1	−5.0	5.0	9.5	−12.2	2.7	1.1
All member states ($n = 22$)	19.1	62.6	18.3	20.1	59.0	20.9	3.1

preferred levels are sometimes huge (last column of Table 6.1), with a maximum aggregate difference of 22.7 per cent in Latvia and a minimum of 2.5 per cent in Poland.

The large country differences may be due to structural features common to certain groups of countries.[5] The comparison between the old and new member states included in our analysis does reveal that respondents in the older member states not only believe that the most important problem is decided more at the European level than respondents from the new member states (by 5 per cent difference on the average), they also prefer these problems to be addressed more at the EU level (average difference of 2.7 per cent with new member states). The feeling that most important problems are decided at the national level is more predominant in the new member states (5.0 per cent difference between group averages), but old member states prefer that this level should have less power, while in the new member states there is hardly a difference between perceived and preferred importance of the national level. Regarding the regional level,[6] we find that respondents in new member states believe as much as the old ones in the current decision-making relevance of this level (in spite of the weakness of the regional level in most of these countries; Keating and Hughes 2003) but clearly prefer it to be less powerful than the current situation (9.5 per cent difference in preferences for the regional level with older member states).

6.3.2. Differences between policy sectors

As the intrinsic nature of the policy issues or sectors is the sole criteria for finding the appropriate level of decision making following the principles of subsidiarity and endogenous attribution, let us continue our preliminary exploration with an overview of variation between policy sectors, using the EES 2004 codebook's twenty-two policy sectors in which the 'most important problem' was recoded.

If we first look at the problems that citizens in 2004 perceived as the most important, we find that problems related to (un-)employment are mentioned in more than a quarter of responses given (28.2 per cent). Second comes health care (11.5 per cent). At a far lower level we find immigration, crime and violence, economy, welfare policy, wages and earnings, and pensions.

In Table 6.2, we regrouped these twenty-two policy sectors into four categories according to their degree of endogeneity[7]:

1. Genuine national matters.
2. Problems that are basically situated at the national level but whose causes or solutions are partially related to similar problems and solutions in other countries. They include mostly socio-economic policy sectors, like (un-)employment.
3. Problems with main cross-border aspects as well as problems with international but basically bilateral dimensions. Some of these issues may have larger genuine international dimensions, but these are not predominant.
4. Problems with predominantly genuine international dimensions. Sometimes this dimension is not due to the inherent cross-border nature of the problem, but to long-lasting international cooperation in the policy sector, such as the Common Agricultural Policy.

Following this aggregation per category of endogeneity, an absolute majority (58 per cent of most important problems) falls in the category 'National level related to similar problems in other countries'. The categories below and above ('Genuine national matters' and 'Cross-border problems') are situated more or less at the same level (13 per cent and 12 per cent, respectively). Note that the European/international level is quasi-absent amongst the most important problems, which reduces in practice our scale of endogeneity to the first three categories.

Regarding the gap between perceived and preferred level of decision making, we do find that most problems categorized under 'Genuine national matters' are perceived more than average (65 per cent, see Table 6.2) to be currently decided at the national level, and that respondents do not prefer (further) Europeanization (except for housing). Also most problems categorized under 'National level related to similar problems in other countries' are perceived more than average (apart from employment) to be currently decided at the national level. For pensions, taxation, economy, health care, wages and earnings, and poverty/high prices/costs of living, more Europeanization is desired, while less is wanted for inflation and infrastructure/traffic/transports. Apart from drugs, all problems categorized under 'cross border problems' are perceived more than average (i.e. 17.6 per cent) to be currently decided at the European level and respondents prefer that they all be decided (much) more than average (i.e. 20.3 per cent) at the EU level.

To conclude, endogeneity matters. In spite of large country differences, at the European average, citizens' preferences for Europeanization are rather coherent, whereby the more a policy sector is perceived to be currently most Europeanized (which is the case for most cross-border problems) further Europeanization is most called for. For most 'National level related to similar problems in other countries', we find a similar call for Europeanization, while 'genuine national matters' displays a mixed call.

6.3.3. *Differences over time*

If we compare over time the results of the eleven countries[8] that were included in 1994 as well as in the 1999 and 2004 EES survey, we notice a considerable but non-linear evolution with regard to the perception of where the decision making currently takes place for the most important problem. In 1999, respondents perceived decision making by the European level (27 per cent) to be considerably more important than in the previous and subsequent survey (18 per cent and 19 per cent, respectively). The same non-linear

Table 6.2. Most important problem and perceived and preferred levels of decision making per policy sector in 2004 (18 countries)[1]

	Most important problem (%)	Perceived level of decision making (%)			Preferred level of decision making (%)		
		Regional	National	European	Regional	National	European
Overall		17.5	65.0	17.6	20.4	59.3	20.3
Genuine national matters							
Government/politics in general	3.7	10.8	76.3	12.9	9.5	77.3	13.1
Education	1.8	17.8	60.9	21.3	18.2	64.8	17.1
Other social problems/conflicts	1.8	22.7	56.1	21.2	32.7	51.3	16.0
Other political problems/conflicts	2.2	19.1	69.7	11.2	19.0	64.8	16.2
Political fraud/corruption	1.5	3.0	70.4	26.5	14.0	65.6	20.4
Housing*	1.2	12.8	82.0	5.2	30.5	54.6	15.0
Subtotal	12.7						
National level related to similar problems in other countries							
Unemployment/employment	28.2	20.7	59.9	19.4	24.8	55.9	19.3
Pensions	2.8	10.9	79.2	9.9	9.0	76.8	14.2
Taxes/taxation*	1.0	12.6	79.3	8.1	19.8	63.4	16.7
Welfare policy	3.2	18.9	67.7	13.5	16.3	69.3	14.4
Economy	4.1	8.3	74.6	17.2	11.1	65.6	23.4
Health care system	11.5	22.2	68.9	8.9	31.3	56.6	12.2
Inflation	1.7	6.2	76.6	17.2	9.0	76.2	14.9
Infrastructure/traffic/transports**	0.6	16.5	73.8	9.7	22.5	71.5	6.0
Poverty/high prices/costs of living	1.6	19.9	71.8	8.3	18.8	54.4	26.9
Wages and earnings	3.2	13.9	69.6	16.5	8.9	70.7	20.5
Subtotal	58.0						

(Continued)

Table 6.2. (Continued)

	Most important problem (%)	Perceived level of decision making (%)			Preferred level of decision making (%)		
		Regional	National	European	Regional	National	European
Cross-border							
Immigration/integration	5.8	12.4	64.2	23.4	12.4	57.2	30.4
Crime and violence	5.4	16.6	58.8	24.6	23.9	48.4	27.7
Ecology/environment**	0.6	24.3	53.2	22.6	13.6	24.5	61.9
Drugs, drugs policy/regulation	1.7	24.4	63.5	12.1	18.5	58.0	23.6
Subtotal	13.5						
International dimension							
EU***	0.3	20.5	62.0	17.5	27.9	72.1	0.0
Other							
Other problems[2]	16.1	16.9	60.5	22.6	17.1	56.9	25.9

Legend: * Category with less than 100 units; ** Category with less than 50 units; *** Category with 19 units.

Notes:
1. For a number of countries in the 2004 European Election Studies, some of the key variables needed for the multivariate analyses are lacking, leaving us with eighteen countries (the list of 22 listed in Table 6.1 minus Cyprus, Estonia, Sweden, and the Netherlands) and 5,982 valid cases.
2. Category 'other problems' contains all problems that could not be classified in one of the aforementioned categories.

The Level of Decision Making

Table 6.3. Perceived and preferred levels of decision making for most important issue in 1994, 1999, and 2004 (11 countries)[1]

Year	1994		1999		2004	
	Perceived (%)	Preferred (%)	Perceived (%)	Preferred (%)	Perceived (%)	Preferred (%)
Regional	16	16	23	24	17	23
National	66	47	50	41	64	54
European	18	37	27	35	19	23

Notes:
1. The frequencies differ marginally from those reported by De Winter and Swyngedouw (1999). In that analysis of the 1994 data, answers to the first, second, and third most important problem and the decision-making levels were aggregated using the multiple response technique. The 1994 figures in Table 6.3 reflect now only the data for the first 'most important' problem mentioned, given the fact that in 1999 and 2004, we have level perceptions and preferences for the 'most important problem' only. Although the Netherlands are not included in our subsequent analyses (due to lack of description of the content of the most important problem), they were included to calculate the Perceived and Preferred scores for 2004, in order to be able to compare the same countries in 1994, 1999, and 2004.

pattern is found for the perceived importance of the regional level, while the perception of the relevance of the national level follows an inverse pattern (with only half of the respondents perceiving the national level as most important in 1999, against about two thirds in 1994 and 2004).[9]

More important for legitimacy, there are major shifts regarding the preferred level of decision making. The European level tumbles from 37 per cent in 1994 to only 23 per cent in 2004 (while still at 35 per cent in 1999). The regional and national levels each gain 7 per cent in importance over this period (Table 6.3).

This dramatic loss of popularity of the European level can be due to several factors. First, it is possible that the EU level effectively lost attractiveness vis-à-vis the national and regional levels. This loss of attractiveness can be due to popular dissatisfaction with the 2004 enlargement (disapproved by about half of the citizens of the EU15 in 2004; EB61 2005: 92).[10]

A closer inspection of the type of problems to which the perceived and preferred decision-making levels refer may clarify the reasons for the declining 'euro-permissiveness'. Since Table 6.2 indicated that endogeneity matters, the decline in calls for Europeanization may be due to a shift over time in the nature of the problems citizens perceive as most important, from cross-border towards more endogenously national or regional issues, such as traffic security and the fight against petty crime. Table 6.4 presents the evolution over time of the endogeneity of the policy problems examined. The problems that we classified as 'purely national' have gained in importance over the 1994–2004 period, from 3 to 14 per cent. But also 'cross-border problems' have increased, though less spectacularly. Note that in both years, the predominant category remains 'National

Table 6.4. Degree of endogeneity of most important problems in 1994 and 2004 in percentages (11 countries)

	Per cent 1994	Per cent 2004
Purely national	3.0	13.6
National with international cause/effect	77.5	62.2
National with cross border	17.4	23.6
European/international	1.5	0.6
Total	100.0	100.0

problem related to similar problems in other countries' but has lost considerable weight. Hence, the fact that the 'most important problem perceived' falls in 2004 much more under the category 'purely national' problem decided mainly at the national/regional level, can explain the drop in calls for Europeanization, but only partially, given the huge size of this drop. In addition, the national problems with cross-border features have also increased in this period, a category that tends to incite preferences for further EU empowerment, and thus one would expect calls for Europeanization to have increased in this period.

A second hypothesis is that since 1994, the policy sectors seen as the 'most important problem' in 1994 may be perceived by 2004 as having become much more Europeanized given the expansion of EU competencies, and therefore further Europeanization may be considered less warranted. However, a watertight empirical confirmation of this argument is difficult to offer since it requires a measure per policy sector of the increase of Europeanization that actually occurred in that ten-year period (Alesina et al. 2005). In addition, in 1994 respondents were offered a closed list of problems (seven common to all countries, and four country specific items), while in 1999 and 2004 the most important problem was tapped by an open question, recoded into categories not fully consistent with the ones used for recoding the 1994 survey.

To conclude, there is a wide variation in the perceived and preferred level of government, and this variation is only mildly related to the distinction between old member and enlargement states. In both groups, we find very Eurosceptic countries (Finland, Slovenia) and rather Europhile ones (Belgium, Latvia). This absence of large and robust differences between new and old states – and the wide variation within each group – calls for a wider search for potential determinants of the variations of citizen preferences for decision-making levels, such as their attitudes towards EU integration and connected issues, their general political attitudes, their socio-demographic

The Level of Decision Making

and political background characteristics. The potential impact of these determinants is formulated in the hypotheses below.

6.4. Hypotheses on citizens' preferences for level of government

We grouped our hypotheses around three sets of variables that in the literature have been identified as potential determinants of citizens' level of governance preferences, to which we have added some hypotheses of our own that follow the rationale of the hypotheses formulated by others. Most of the hypotheses found in the literature concern only the 'two-level game' between the national and EU level. Preferences for the regional level in a 'three-level game' remain a theoretically underexplored field. The design of most comparative surveys do by now include the regional level as a preferred and/or perceived level of government, but hardly any region-specific explanatory variables (apart from regional identity and attachment). Crucial variables regarding citizens' support attitudes towards their regional political system (similar to the indicators of national and EU system support listed below) are generally absent. Nor does the size of comparative surveys, usually about a thousand per member state, allow us to constitute representative regional samples within countries, and thus we also cannot test for the impact of structural regional features.

Still, we will maintain the regional level in our analyses below, even when hypotheses formulation and testing will focus on the variations of the preferences for the national vis-à-vis European level. These variations are certainly influenced by offering respondents explicitly a 'third way' to contrast national vs. EU level (the regional level being preferred by about as many respondents as the EU level, see Table 6.1).

As argued above, we expect the endogeneity of a policy problem to affect citizens' level preferences, expecting that at least a part of the citizenry would take this rational criterion into account. Unfortunately, we do not have a valid indicator of citizens' perception of endogeneity of the problem they consider most important in their country. Hence, endogeneity will be operationalized as in Table 6.2, on the basis of the authors' 'expert judgement'. Thus 'endogeneity' varies between individuals on the basis of the type of problem they picked as most important, but not on the basis of respondents' evaluation of the endogeneity of the problem (sector) they picked.

The other most central and direct determinants include, first, political attitudes towards different components of the EU and the national political system (Norris 1999b) and, second, some general political attitudes. Both types of attitudes have been shown to vary along the classical socio-demographic and socio-political variables that may also exert a direct influence by themselves, warranting their inclusion as separate independent variables in the multivariate analyses.

6.4.1. *Political attitudes towards the EU and national political systems*

As the wider definition of the subsidiarity principle introduced the notion of support of citizens for the political system, one can expect that preference for the EU or the nation state as level of decision making to be determined not only by the endogenous nature of policy problems but also by citizens' support for the various components of both the EU and the national political system (Easton 1965a; Dahl 1989: 109). System support can be disaggregated into the following components (see the introductory chapter in this book) taking into account their operationalizability with the variables included in the EES 2004 survey:

- European identity (measured by 'feeling a European citizen' and 'pride in EU citizenship'): (Bruter 2005: 119; Risse 2005; Berg 2007; Thomassen and Bäck in this book).
- Support for general EU system principles (measured by the belief that 'EU membership is a good thing', and 'support for the unification process') (Norris 1999b).
- Support for the EU's main institutions (measured by trust in the European Commission and Parliament) (Norris 1999b; Wessels in this book).
- Support for the operation of the EU system (measured by 'satisfaction with democracy in the EU' (Norris 1999b).
- Support for EU system outputs (measured by the perception that one's country and one personally have benefited from EU membership) (McLaren 2006: 38; Mikhaylov and Marsh in this book).
- Awareness of the EU as a political system (measured by 'interest in EU politics'): those that display a relatively high degree of interest in European politics will more likely prefer EU decision making, as one can assume that only a political level of which one has a minimal degree of understanding can be preferred as an appropriate level of government (cf. the notion of parochial civic culture in Almond and Verba 1963).

These components of EU system support cannot be reduced to a single scale, as preference for the EU level of government can be triggered by different components separately, or in combination. One may not feel European at all, but still believe that one's country has profited from EU membership, or vice versa. One can support the principle of EU integration but be dissatisfied with the quality of democracy in the EU. Therefore, in the analyses we will treat these components of EU system support as separate potential determinants of level preferences.

Likewise, we can expect that preferences for the national level are affected by attitudes towards the national system. We find in the EES 2004 survey the following valid indicators of various components of support for the national political system, following a similar causal rationale as for EU system support (Norris 1999*b*):

- National identity (measured by 'national pride').
- Support for the national authorities (measured by trust in national parliament and government).
- Support for the operation of the national system (measured by the degree of 'satisfaction with democracy in one's own country').
- Support for national system outputs (measured by 'approval of national government's record', and by 'retrospective' and 'prospective economic evaluations'): since national governments usually claim credit when the economy fares well (but blame 'Brussels' if things go wrong), we can presume that positive economic evaluations (retrospective as well as prospective) would lead to a higher support for the national level.
- Awareness of the national system (measured by the degree of 'interest in national politics').

As argued above for the EU system, these components of national system support also cannot be reduced into a single scale.

6.4.2. *General political attitudes*

Amongst general political attitudes that can be expected to exert an impact on preference for different levels of government we include:

- left–right attitudes: one can expect that left-oriented people, in light of the (historical) association between internationalism and socialism, will give more preference to the European level, while right-wing respondents will favour the national level more, given the general association between national conscience and a conservative outlook (Huber and Inglehart 1995: 84; Goetz and Hix 2001: 59; Eurobarometer 67 2007: 142). On the other hand, several authors find that the relation between Euroscepticism and the left–right scale is U-shaped, with the extreme left and extreme right being most Eurosceptic (for entirely different reasons), while the mainstream parties are more Europhile (Hooghe, Marks and Wilson 2004; Schmitt and Thomassen in this book).

- Ethnocentrism (measured by the 'fear of foreigners to take the jobs of "nationals"' and by 'the need to reserve social welfare benefits to nationals but not immigrants from other EU countries'): since for many Europeans, the EU is associated with economic globalization and immigration (presumably menacing autochthonous employment and undermining their welfare state benefits), we can expect that people with a more ethnocentric attitude to opt more often for the national level (Banting and Kymlickz 2003).
- Political information-seeking behaviour (measured in terms of 'watching news on TV' and 'reading newspapers'): the Eurobarometers indicate that 'opinion leadership' (a composite measure that includes these two variables) is associated with pro-European attitudes.

6.4.3. *Socio-demographic and socio-political variables*

Eurobarometer surveys (for instance EB67: 142–5), indicate that citizens' level preferences are associated with certain individual socio-demographic and socio-political characteristics for a variety of reasons. The individual socio-demographic and socio-political characteristics (included in the EES 2004 survey) that can be expected to exert an impact on preference for different government levels include:

- *Education*: respondents with higher levels of education may tend to grasp more easily the cross-border dimension and interdependency of complex problems and therefore opt more for the decision-making level apt to deal with such problems, that is, the EU.
- *Age*: young people generally display more pro-EU attitudes on a variety of indicators (EB67: 145) probably because of their more open attitude to the 'wider world' than older generations more attached to their 'church tower' (Inglehart 1970), and they can therefore be expected also to prefer more readily the EU as decision-making level.
- *Gender*: men generally display more pro-EU attitudes on a variety of indicators (EB67: 145), supposedly for the same reasons differentiating younger and older generations.

- *Subjective social class*: Fligstein (2008) argues that objectively mainly managers, professionals, and other highly educated people have benefited from cross-border transactions. The Eurobarometers also indicate that generally workers, the unemployed, homemakers, and pensioners are less supportive of the EU than employers, cadres, and the higher educated. Hence we can expect that the higher the level of subjective class identification, the stronger the preferences for the European level.
- *Union membership*: since the working class is organized more than other classes in nationally embedded trade unions, membership in a trade union may enhance a preference for the national level (see reasoning as above). In addition, trade unions in the EU have generally been critical of the too strongly market-oriented integration process, while they promote a 'social Europe' (Schmidt 2008).
- *Religion*: Catholicism is traditionally associated with internationalism (given its tradition of centralized church governance from the Vatican) as well as with European integration (at least in its founding phase), while Protestantism and Greek Orthodoxy were more associated with the nation state (Lipset and Rokkan 1967c; Inglehart and Norris 2004). Thus, we may expect Catholics more than Protestant and Orthodox believers to more easily accept decision making by supra-national institutions, not only by 'Rome', but also by 'Brussels'.

6.5. The level of decision making: Explaining the preferences of citizens

In order to estimate the effect of attitudes towards the EU and national political systems,[11] general political attitudes, and the classical socio-demographic and socio-political variables[12] on the preferred level of decision making, a multinomial logistical model was run. Table 6.5 offers an overview of the strength of the effect of each of the potential determinants on the choice of government level. The strength can be deduced from the ratio X^2/df, that is, the larger the ratio, the stronger the effect.

Controlling in this model for the effect of all the other variables formulated in the hypotheses, endogeneity of the most important problem has the strongest effect, whereby preference for national-level decision making is comparatively strongest for problems related to 'genuine national matters', while the European level is most preferred for 'cross-border problems'.[13]

Table 6.5. Preferred level of government (European, national, regional) for solving most important problem (multinomial logistic model; all 18 countries combined)

Variables	DF	X^2	Sign.	X^2/df
Endogeneity of most important problem	6	95.6	0.000	15.9
Trust in European political institutions	2	18.7	0.000	9.4
Unification	2	10.9	0.004	5.5
Feeling European citizen	4	16.1	0.003	4.0
Trust in national political institutions	2	9.4	0.009	4.7
Retrospective economic evaluation	2	26.0	0.000	13.0
Ethnocentrism in terms of scarcity of jobs	2	11.1	0.004	5.6
Education	2	10.5	0.005	5.3
Religion	8	46.6	0.000	5.8
Likelihood ratio	11,882	10,220.9		
N		5,982		

As far as the indicators of support for the EU and national system are concerned, we find the expected positive effect for trust in European political institutions, and also (albeit weaker) for 'feeling European citizen' and 'support of EU unification'. Inversely, we find the expected (but rather weak) effect of trust in national political institutions on preference for national-level decision making. Retrospective economic evaluation exerts a strong effect (nearly as strong as endogeneity) in favour of preference for regional-level decision making.[14] Only one general political attitude is (moderately) important: ethnocentrism in terms of scarcity of jobs. Finally, of the classical socio-demographic and socio-political variables, only education and religion exert a significant (but rather weak) impact. As expected, we find that the higher the level of education, the stronger the preference for the European over the national level. Contrary to our hypothesis, Catholicism has hardly any impact on level preferences. Protestantism does exert the predicted anti-European effect.[15]

Hence, we have not found results that contradict the predictions formulated in our hypotheses, but, of course, many hypotheses did not produce statistically significant results as we controlled for all other variables formulated in the hypotheses.

More puzzling are the results when we divide our eighteen countries in old and new member states (not reported in Table 6.5). On the one hand, we do find basically the same results[16] for the twelve old member states, which is not surprising given their numerical strength in the survey. On the other hand, not a single predictor is significant for the six postcommunist states analysed as a separate group. And this lack of significant relations cannot be attributed simply to the difference in sample size

(n = 4,639 vs. 1,343), as close inspection shows that the effects that are strong and significant in old member states are usually very weak and completely insignificant in new member states. Nor are any of all the other variables included in our hypotheses relevant for explaining variation in level preferences in new member states.

6.6. Conclusion

The question as to which decision-making level is most appropriate to deal with different policy problems is a central aspect of the legitimacy of any multilevel political system. With regard to the level of government in the EU, the discussion is structured around the meaning and application of the principle of subsidiarity, permitting EU action when member states or regions cannot sufficiently act to solve a problem, or when for reasons of scale or effects, actions could be better achieved by the EU.

This question of which issues or policy sectors are by their endogenous nature subject to Europeanization (or regionalization) is difficult to answer in the real world, as many problems have local, regional, national, European, and even global implications. In addition, European as well as national or regional governments can only gain legitimacy when the public agrees with the basic rules of a political system, including the division of labour between different levels of government. Therefore the opinion of European citizens regarding the appropriate level of government in the EU (European, national, regional) is crucial for a given or future division of power between these levels to gain or retain legitimacy.

For the whole of the twenty-two countries included in the 2004 EES survey, the national level is preferred by about six out of ten respondents, the rest spread about equally between the European and regional level. There is large variation over space, not only between old and new member states (the latter preferring even more the national level), but in each group country variations are often large.

As far as variation over time is concerned, the three EES surveys show that the European publics of the eleven countries included in the 1994 survey have by 2004 gradually lost their enthusiasm for the EU as the most appropriate level for solving the most important problem they perceived, in favour of the national level. The inclusion of eleven new member states in the 2004 survey (among which eight of the 2004 enlargement) further enhances the aggregate preferences for the national level.

From a wide variety of theories we have deduced a large number of hypotheses regarding the individual level factors that may influence citizens' preferred level of government and tested them through multinomial logistic analysis. Of all the potential determinants (including numerous EU and national system support indicators, some general political attitudes, and the classic socio-demographic background variables), those that produce significant effects include (in decreasing order of importance) endogeneity of the most important problem, several indicators of system support for the EU and the national state, ethnocentrism, education and religion.

All multivariate analyses were also run separately for the group of old member and 2004 enlargement states. We find that in the old member states the comprehensive model was largely confirmed, while in the new member states all the comprehensive model determinants exercise no or only a weak and usually highly insignificant effect. This surprising and puzzling outcome suggests that preferences for decision-making levels in the new member states are either genuinely unstructured, or determined by factors alien to the theoretical literature developed until now to explain level preferences in Western European member states. This calls for the formulation of alternative hypotheses and the construction of valid survey indicators that may capture better the 'hidden' structure of preferences in the new member states.

Notes

1. Regarding the question of the 'scope' or 'breadth' of government, there is a large body of theoretical and empirical research. For the most comprehensive empirical research to date, see the 'Scope of Government' volume of the *Beliefs In Government* project (Borre and Goldsmith 1995).
2. Survey research indicates in fact considerable differences between level and scope preferences of European publics and EU elites (MEPs, members of national representations and governments, Commission officials and experts), the latter tending to be more Europhile (Beyers and Dierickx 1997; Egeberg 1999; Schmitt and Thomassen 2000; Hug and König 2002; Aspinwall 2002; Hooghe 2003).
3. Sum of differences between perceived and preferred levels for all three levels are divided by two, in order to avoid double counting differences.
4. Data were weighted by party vote (including non-voting) as this is the variable for which weights for the largest number of cases are available.
5. Given the large level preference differences between countries, we examined the impact of structural features of each country that according to the literature can be expected to affect preferences for government levels. They included the

duration of EU membership, membership of the Schengen and Eurozone, the size of a country, the openness of a country's economy, human development/quality of life index, inflation rate, general government deficit and general government expenditures, and the degree of decentralization. A multinomial multilevel model was run, controlling for the micro-predictors found to be significant in the multinomial model reported in Table 6.5, but did not produce any significant result (at the .01 level) for the contrast between preference for the national vs. the European level.

6. Note that the Swedish survey included as first option 'regional/local' and also a category 'a combination' (of levels). The first category was recoded in 'regional', while combinations were assigned to missing values, as there was no indication about which levels one wanted to combine. The Italian survey included apart from the three common categories also categories of 'municipality' and 'province' which were recoded into 'regional'. We can assume that these additional categories have affected the scores on our three common categories, but we can not ascertain to what degree (De Winter 2008).

7. We are quite aware that the question of which issues or policy sectors are eligible for endogenous internationalization is not easy to answer. There is no consensus on the range of problems that due to the 'endogenous' nature of the issue belong to the remit of local, regional, national, European, and international governance. The degree of endogenous internationalization of an identical policy issue can also vary between countries. First, certain countries can be considered being the cause of the problem suffered by others, as would be the case for a strongly air-polluting country surrounded by cleaner neighbours. For the latter, the problem of air pollution is endogenously international, for the former it is in the first place a problem that can and should be solved by the national government. Second, in some countries, a particular level of governance (national, regional and local) can be better equipped to deal effectively with an issue than the same level in another country. This can be due to economy of scale effects, depending on the size of the territory covered and material resources and expertise different levels of governance have at their disposition. For instance, the German Land governments are much better equipped to deal with environmental problems than the sub-state level in non-federal states. Third, the degree of interdependency of economic and social systems may vary considerably: in an autarchic economy, the need for international collaboration and governance may be less strong than in open economies where prices, wages, interest rates, etc., are highly dependent on the policies and economic fortunes of their main trading partners. Therefore our coding could certainly be fine-tuned, for instance by asking in each country the view of experts in specific policy areas on the degree of endogeneity of the policy sector and on its variation over time. Evidently, this is a huge research project by itself. For some attempts see Giscard d'Estaing (1990), Conclusions of the Presidency of the European Council of Edinburgh of 1992 (Bull. EC 12-1992);

Wessels and Kielhorn (1999). For estimations of the actual 'task expansion' of the EU level per policy sector, see Alesina et al. (2005) and Börzel (2005).
8. Belgium, Denmark, Germany, Greece, Spain, France, Ireland, Italy, the Netherlands, Portugal, and the UK.
9. Maybe this was caused by a conjunctional effect, that is, the end phase of a decade of national implementation of the Maastricht criteria and the rapidly approaching introduction of the Euro, combined with a decade of 'Europe of the Regions' hype (Keating 2008).
10. Unfortunately, the 2004 EES study does not include a precise question about the desirability of the 2004 enlargement, only a general question regarding the support for further unification, which may mean widening yet also deepening of the integration process.
11. For 'Trust in European political institutions' we combined trust in European Commission and European Parliament. Interest in European politics is a six-item scale ranging from 0 (= 'no interest') to 10 (= 'a lot of interest') including the following variables: watch a programme about the election on television, read about the election in a newspaper; talk to friends or family about the election; attend a public meeting or rally about the election; look into a website concerned with the election; interest in the campaign for the European Parliament elections. Trust in national political institutions: combination of trust in country government and country parliament.
12. Age was recoded into five categories (18–24; 25–34; 35–49; 50–64; 65+); education was measured by the age when respondents stopped full-time education; religion was recoded into five categories (Roman Catholic, Protestant, Orthodox, Other, None).
13. While we only report on determinants that reach a significance level of .01, the model did contain all the other variables mentioned in the hypotheses, as controlling for these variables improves the quality of the estimators. This analysis was complemented with a separate analysis of the net effects of each category of the categorical variables on the basis of the parameter estimates of the multinomial logistic model. For the metric variables net effects were estimated using the 'additive logistic regression parameters' on the binary variables 'regional vs. European' and 'national vs. European', with 'European' as reference category. These analyses (not reported) corroborate the specific direction of the expected effects formulated in the hypotheses.
14. This may suggest that one's individual economic evaluation may be influenced by the perception of the prosperity of one's region, rather than of one's country as a whole.

15. Orthodox religion has a strong pro-European and anti-regional effect, but this is due to the specific Greek configuration (combining strong pro-European attitudes with politically irrelevant regions, as reflected in Table 6.1).
16. With the exception that on the one hand ethnocentrism and education are no longer significant while on the other hand gender, which had already a moderate effect in the overall analysis, now becomes also statistically significant.

7

Policy Performance and Support for European Integration

Slava Mikhaylov and Michael Marsh

7.1. Introduction

Following Easton's conceptual framework discussed in the introductory chapter, a hierarchical relationship exists between three objects of support: output support, support for institutions, and support for the community. The latter two objects of support are examined in turn in two subsequent chapters on trust in European political institutions and the relationship between citizenship and identity in the European Community. This chapter focuses on the first object of support – support derived from the accrued material benefits of EU membership.

Public perceptions of benefits accruing from EU membership have been explained previously in terms of national economic circumstances (economic growth rates, inflation, unemployment, share of intra-EU trade, and EU contributions to the national budgets), subjective evaluation of economic well-being (the 'feel-good' factor), and socialization (duration of membership in the EU) (Marsh 1999). The wider literature on support for the EU is generally consistent with this set of results, suggesting a strong utilitarian basis for such judgements. However, in recent years, identity (or the Haasian 'shifting loyalties' in general) became the focus of much theoretical and empirical research aiming to explain public perceptions of European integration. It has also been proclaimed that in the context of general public support for the EU, 'identity rules': while utilitarian factors are taken into account by citizens, 'the conceptions of group membership are more powerful' (Hooghe and Marks 2004).

Policy Performance and Support for European Integration

This chapter assesses the extent of utilitarian roots for the perception of benefits from membership in EU member states comprising different accession waves over the period from 1984 to 2005. We examine economically driven explanations provided in the literature and evaluate whether they remain consistent over a much longer time period than utilized in any of the previous studies. The time period covered includes a major qualitative change in the nature and functioning of the EU, and consequently possible changes in the degree to which people approve EU outputs as well as the basis on which they do so.

7.2. Previous research

Support for European integration is affected, and at least partially driven, by the anticipated benefits of European integration to individuals in member states (Gabel 1998*b*). The influence of policy output on the level of both general and specific support for a political system has been highlighted in Easton (1965*a*). As argued in Marsh (1999), the functionalist, and later neo-functionalist, central premise is that well-performing institutions are invested with more authority; that is, states and pseudo-states, like the EU, are judged on their relative effectiveness in performing a service. Within the neo-functionalist approach, the assumption is that performance is being evaluated via its impact on functional social groups. More specifically, citizens in social groups that expect to receive benefits from EU policy output will welcome the integration process and the economic liberalization associated with it. Anderson and Reichert (1996), Gabel and Palmer (1995), and Gabel (1998*a*, 1998*b*) showed that citizens with relatively low levels of competitive advantage in an integrated economic environment (like the working class and generally citizens with lower levels of human capital) are likely to be negatively predisposed towards the EU. At the same time, people with high levels of human capital (education and specific occupational skills) are likely to be positively disposed towards closer integration. However, if functional social groups are re-defined within a European rather than a national context, national governments can be viewed as playing a role of mediating institutions with people pressing national governments for more benefits for their countries from the EU (Marsh 1999).

The most direct form of benefit consists of transfer payments made from the EU budget, where citizens of countries that are net beneficiaries of EU transfers would be more supportive of the EU than citizens of donor countries (Anderson and Reichert 1996; Whitten, Gabel, and Palmer 1996; Medrano

2003; Brinegar, Jolly, and Kitschelt 2004; Hooghe and Marks 2004). A related utilitarian perspective focuses on another aspect of direct cost/benefit calculations, the existing extent of economic integration. This has been operationalized in several aggregate level studies as the proportion of trade with EU countries in total trade of a country (Eichenberg and Dalton 1993; Gabel and Palmer 1995; Anderson and Reichert 1996; Bednar, Ferejohn, and Garrett 1996; Gabel and Whitten 1997; Eichenberg 1999; Marsh 1999; Palmer and Gabel 1999). This sort of utilitarian consideration could be seen as a very direct feature of EU integration.

In addition to such direct benefits, there is a second economic explanation of public support for European integration that bases its account on more indirect influences on perceptions. This extends the logic of comparative studies that link macroeconomic conditions to citizen approval of government performance (Eichenberg 1999) to explain how national economic circumstances can influence perceptions of the EU. It is assumed that people perceive national economies to be affected by the EU policy output, and base their evaluations of EU effectiveness on the performance of their national economies. Evidence for this indirect political economic model of EU support has been presented in a number of studies (Dalton 1993; Anderson and Kaltenthaler 1996; Bednar, Ferejohn, and Garrett 1996; Eichenberg 1999; Eichenberg and Marsh 1999). Duch and Taylor (1997) show that the link between economy and public support for the EU is the result of citizens' evaluation of the national economy. Although evidence is not consistent due to different model specifications, several studies found a negative relationship between public support for integration and inflation (Eichenberg and Dalton 1993; Anderson and Kaltenthaler 1996; Bednar, Ferejohn, and Garrett 1996; Eichenberg 1999), although Palmer and Gabel (1999) found no significant relationship. Unemployment has been shown to have a weak relationship (Anderson and Reichert 1996; Bednar, Ferejohn, and Garrett 1996), while the economic growth rate is weakly positively related (Eichenberg and Dalton 1993; Anderson and Reichert 1996). At the same time, Gabel and Whitten (1997) found no significant relationship between inflation, unemployment, and economic growth and citizens' support for EU integration.

In the same vein, a related explanation positing a different mechanism, but a similar pattern of association, focuses on the fact that citizens rely on domestic cues (proxies) when formulating their attitude towards the EU (Hooghe and Marks 2005) as, typically, they are neither interested in, nor informed about, the EU. Evaluations of the EU can be contextualized in domestic politics, which provides shortcuts for the respondents when answering survey questions on Europe (Franklin, Marsh, and McLaren 1994; Franklin, Van der Eijk, and Marsh 1995; Anderson 1998; Sánchez-Cuenca 2000; Rohrschneider 2002; Ray 2003).

All economic explanations of support for the EU can be generalized as representing the relationship between a poor economic situation in a country and a negative perception of its citizens and between a good economic situation and positive perceptions of the EU. Arguably, this is weakened by the mediation of national political competition, since government might well seek to take credit for good times and blame the EU for bad ones (Marsh 1999). However, the opposition may argue that the government ought to take the blame for bad times and should not always take credit for good times, so it is reasonable, even allowing for such mediation, to hypothesize a relationship between local economic performance and EU support. However, alternative hypotheses, which suggest a negative rather than a positive relationship with some economic variables, are also plausible. When the national economy is actually doing well, people might be more inclined to see the EU as an unnecessary interference. When it is doing badly, they look to the EU for salvation.

A third explanation is couched in terms of socialization. Arguably, it will take time for people to see benefits. Many economic explanations are supplemented by the suggestion that membership will bring about more positive feelings with time. This 'socialization' argument may be seen to depend on the accumulation of outputs, but could also stem from the greater awareness of the EU that comes from longer membership (Inglehart and Rabier 1978; Eichenberg and Dalton 1993; Anderson 1995a; Anderson and Reichert 1996).

For some analysts, all utilitarian accounts are strictly limited. The research agenda in the early 2000s has been dominated by non-utilitarian explanations for why citizens would perceive the EU in a positive light, regardless of whether or not their economy performs well, and focuses on the concept of identity. It is argued that the EU could be seen as a threat to non-material well-being. In particular, 'national identity' has been identified as a constraint on citizens' support for European integration (Van Kersbergen 2000; Medrano and Gutiérrez 2001; Carey 2002; Christin and Trechsel 2002; McLaren 2002). Although several authors identified strong national attachment as being positively related to the desire for further European integration (Marks 1998; Haesly 2001; Risse 2002; Citrin and Sides 2004; Marks and Llamazares 2007), citizens with an 'exclusively' national identity have been shown to perceive European integration as a threat (Hooghe and Marks 2004, 2005). Risse (2005) points out that an identity shift from the national to the European level has traditionally been linked to the material benefits received through European integration, and later augmented by the concept of socialization, i.e. the slow embedding of European-ness in national identities. This particular non-utilitarian explanation is picked up in two subsequent chapters, and, in particular, in Chapter 9, while here we focus largely on utilitarian explanations.

More general are suggestions that the potency of some explanations may vary across countries. It has been suggested that public support for European integration in the new member states may be defined by people's desire to cement democratic transition in their countries (Rohrschneider 2002). In fact, Rohrschneider and Whitefield (2006) show that in new member states, economic explanations, while still playing a role, are less important than concerns about democratic performance, values, and identity in shaping public perception of the EU. More generally, countries have probably joined the EU for different reasons, and publics in those countries have been encouraged to see the benefits of the EU in different lights. In Ireland, for instance, material benefits were always prominent in campaigns about EU membership and in subsequent referendums on further integration. Yet for countries joining later, even in second wave countries – Spain, Portugal, and Greece – the link with liberal democratic Europe was an important way to strengthen democracy, an argument also made in the new member states joining in 2004. This obviously poses the question of how far any utilitarian account will be equally persuasive for all member states, which we will address in this chapter.

A second source of variation is time. The EU now is a rather different institution to what it was twenty-five years ago, when the second wave of accession took place, let alone fifty years ago when it was founded. It has many more powers over many more policy areas: in effect, there are more outputs, and many of these are not economic ones. It has been suggested, most recently by Eichenberg and Dalton (2007), that this has consequences for our understanding of the dynamics of EU support, with utilitarian calculations having much less significance in more recent years. Therefore, we will also examine the stability over time of economic and some non-economic explanations.

7.3. Public perceptions of benefits

There are a number of measures of public perceptions of the EU and its institutions available from the Eurobarometer, but relatively few that have been asked repeatedly over a long period. The most appropriate for the purpose here, where the objective is to consider how citizens view the

Policy Performance and Support for European Integration

outputs of the Union, is the so-called 'benefits' question: 'taking everything into consideration, would you say that [country] has on balance benefited or not from being a member of the EU?' This is one of a number of items that seem to tap aspects of overall support for integration, the others being questions tapping support for 'unification', asking would respondents be sorry if the EU were to be scrapped, and whether their country's membership of the EU was a good thing. The benefits question seems best suited to analyse policy outcomes – the basis of what Easton called 'specific' support – while it has been argued that the unification question best measures what Easton called 'diffuse' support. That said, it is also easy to exaggerate the real difference between these four questions, as each may be shown to tap a common attitude towards the regime of the EU (for a good review and analysis see Scheuer 2005: 3–7 and 49–50). Certainly there have been no successful attempts to validate these questions as operationalizations of the different Eastonian concepts. However, in terms simply of face validity, the benefits question seems best suited to our task here, and while a more broadly based measure might well be preferable as an overall indicator of EU support, we do not see that it would be a better measure of outputs.

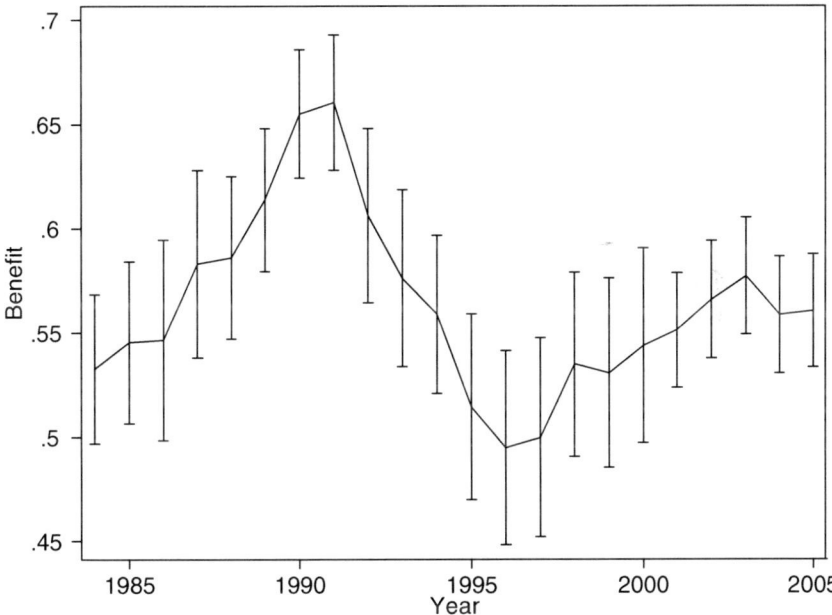

Figure 7.1. Time-series cross-section plot for average benefit perception in EU member states (in a year with standard errors shown by vertical bars)

Figure 7.1 shows the overall level of perceived (national) benefits across the member states since 1984, the first year for which the data are available. This is a cross-national average. It is evident that the perceptions of the EU as beneficial have followed a cyclical pattern. They grew steadily more positive until 1991, only to fall equally steadily for the next five years, after which they have again risen fairly steadily, without regaining

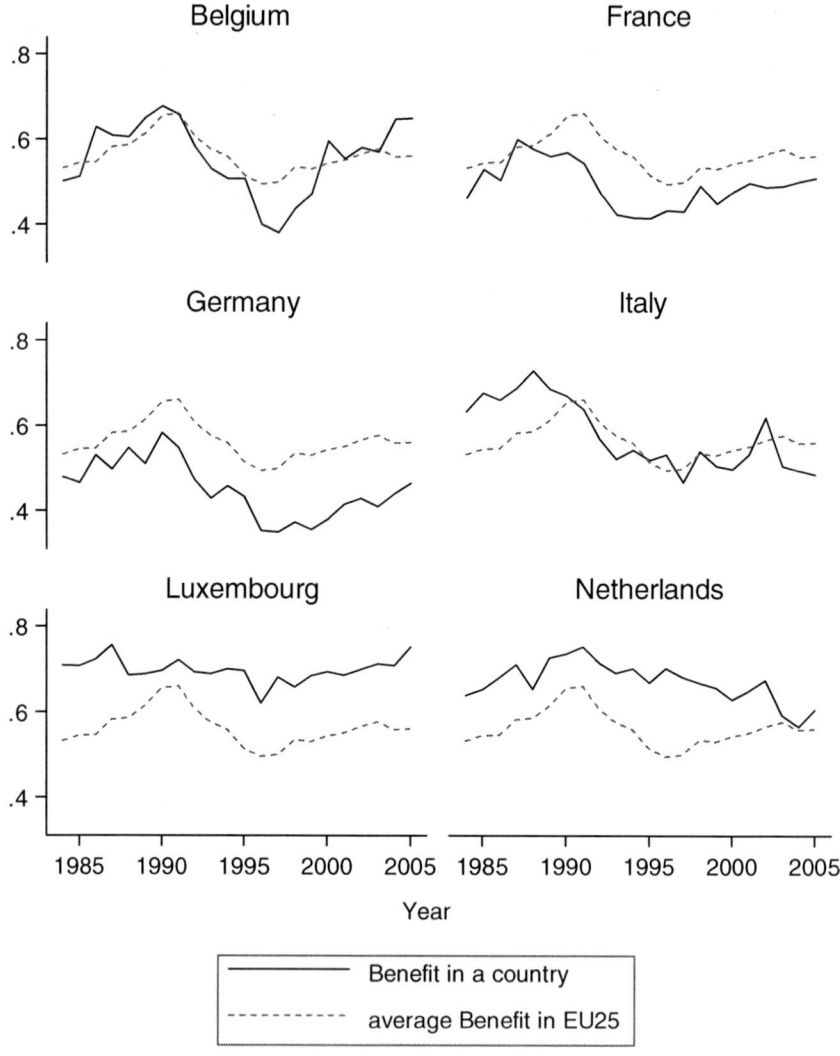

Figure 7.2. Perceptions of benefit from EU membership in the founding six members and average perception in the EU25

Policy Performance and Support for European Integration

the heights of 1991, when an average of 66 per cent in each country saw the EU as beneficial for their country. However, the bars around this line indicate that this average has quite a high standard error, indicating a lot of disparity across countries. In fact it seems that disparity increased after 1991 and became smaller only a decade later.

Of course, the membership of the EU has not been consistent across this period, as new members joined in the 1980s, the 1990s, and most recently in 2004. In Figures 7.2 through 7.4 we show the trends in each of the various waves of accession. We are looking here to see how well member states in each wave fit with the overall trend. The original six (Figure 7.2) show significant variations in the levels of positive perception, but most countries follow broadly the same trend. The only clear exception is the Netherlands, where support has declined steadily from the early 1990s and shows no sign of recovering.

Figure 7.3 focuses on states in the enlargement waves prior to 2004.[1] The states in the first wave show rather different patterns: in Ireland and Denmark perceptions are increasingly positive while in the UK the pattern echoes the EU average, although perceptions are much more negative. In contrast, the states joining in the 1980s all show significant increases

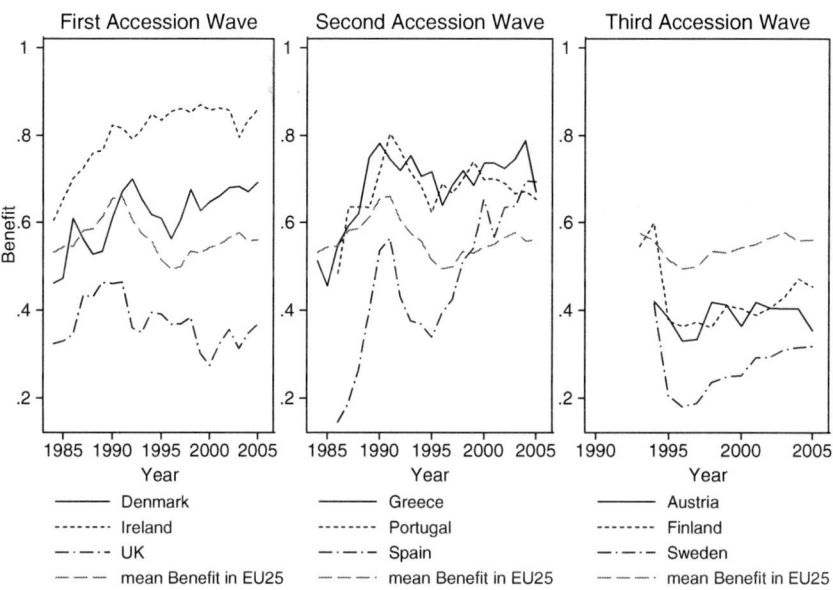

Figure 7.3. Perceptions of benefit from EU membership in the countries of the first-, second-, and third-accession waves and average perception in the EU25

in positive perceptions in the first few years. This increase has levelled off in Greece and Portugal, but has continued upwards in Spain. In the 1990s accession states, perceptions are much more negative, and a trend upwards from the late 1990s can be observed only in Sweden.

Finally, the ten new accession states (Figure 7.4) follow diverse patterns with some striking variations in responses over the short time over which data have been gathered.[2] In general, most started below the EU average,

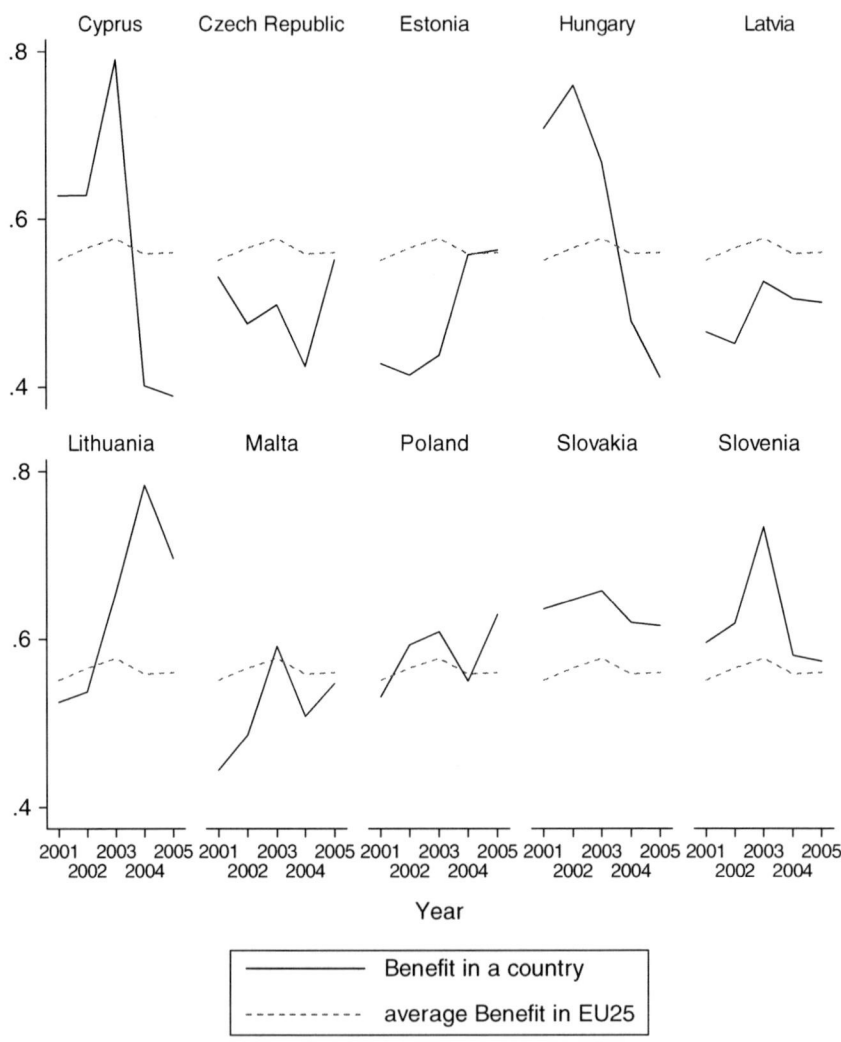

Figure 7.4. Perceptions of benefit from EU membership in the countries of the fourth accession wave and average perception in the EU25

Policy Performance and Support for European Integration

and show upward or stable trends with support trending downwards in Cyprus, Hungary and, perhaps, Slovenia.

Figure 7.5 shows a single trend line for each of these five sets of states. It demonstrates that in broad terms there is a similar pattern over time for each set: a rise until the early 1990s, followed by a clear decline (wave 1 may be an exception here), and then a recovery from the late 1990s. In other words, the sort of pattern observed for the EU25 as a whole in Figure 7.1 is not much affected by the varying composition of the EU. In particular, the decline in the early 1990s was amplified by the accession of Sweden, Finland, and Austria, but exists independently of that compositional change. Moreover, the inclusion of ten new states in the 2000s is not responsible for the recovery of support. It has been suggested that there is growing convergence in support for the EU across the member states (Eichenberg and Dalton 2007). This is not really very apparent in Figure 7.5. Support levels were in fact more similar around the time of the

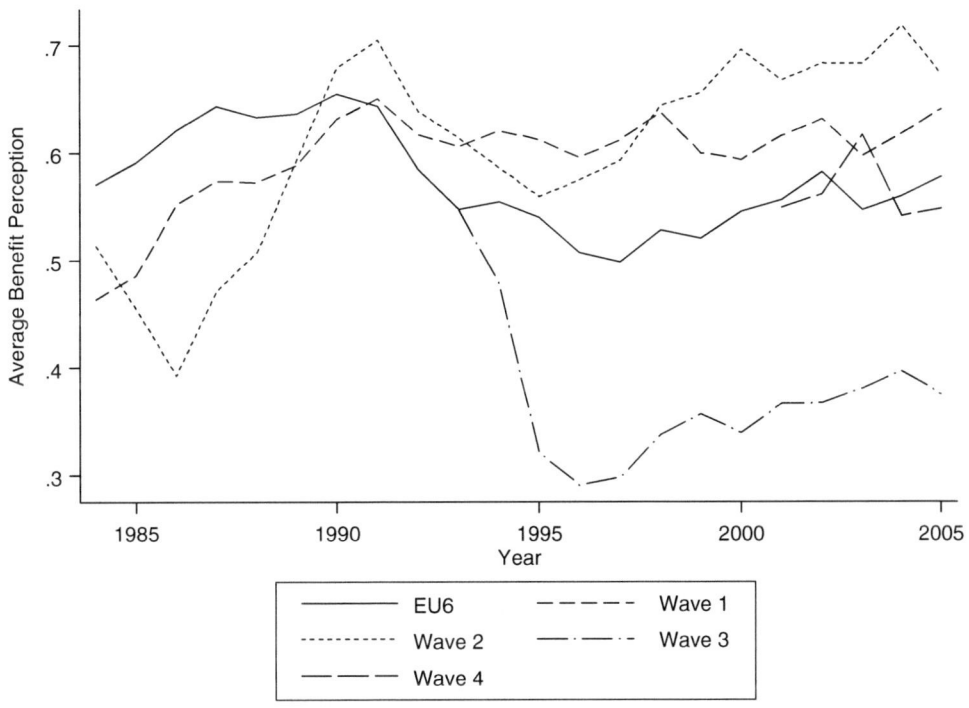

Figure 7.5. Average perceptions of benefit from EU membership in the founding six members and in countries of subsequent accession waves

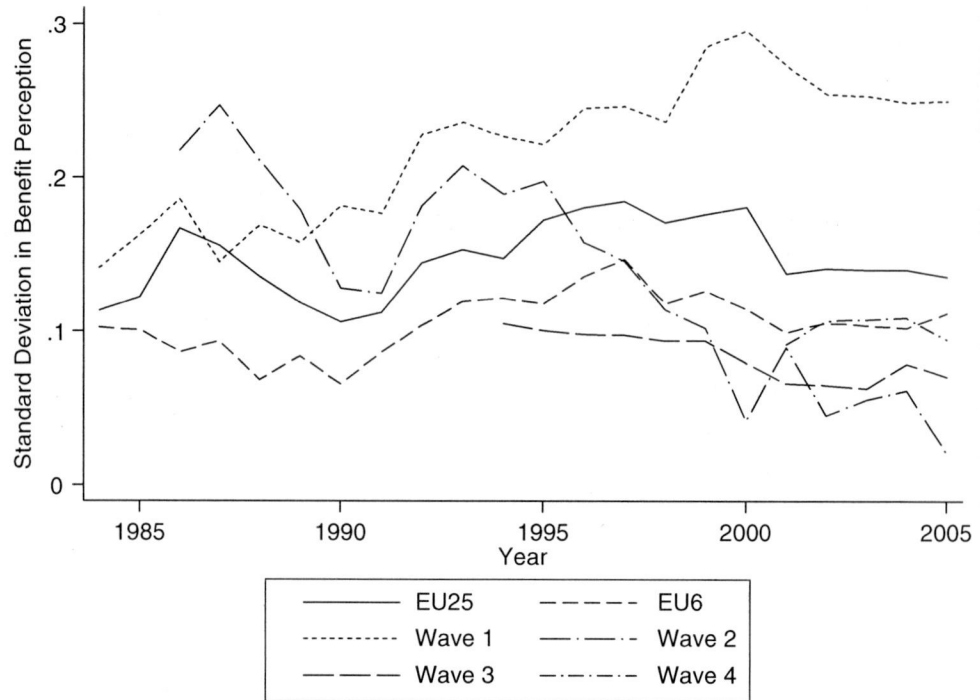

Figure 7.6. Standard deviation in perceptions of benefit from EU membership within founding six members, within subsequent accession waves, and overall in the EU25

Maastricht Treaty in 1992 than they have been over the last few years, even leaving aside the states in the third wave of accession, who certainly increase the degree of diversity.

In fact, as Figure 7.6 shows most clearly, diversity in perceptions of benefit from the EU also seems cyclical. After a short rise and fall initially, the lowest level of diversity was in 1990–1991. After that, diversity increased until 2000, when it returned almost to the level of 1992 (Figure 7.6).

It is clear that there is considerable diversity in terms of countries' perceptions of the EU, both in terms of different levels at any one time, and in terms of the changes in levels over time, with Spain and Ireland showing a considerable increase and the Netherlands a marked decrease in positive perceptions of the impact of EU membership. What we seek to do in the next section is to explain some of that diversity.

7.4. Explaining diversity and change

As we have seen in our summary of previous explanations of EU support, there are several different explanations that have been examined, each of which has been consistent with some of the evidence put forward. Here we focus on the three explanations with the separate question of identity picked up in later chapters. The first explanation considered in this chapter is the direct economic benefits of membership, such as the impact of transfer payments; the second explanation concerns the more indirect benefits evident in national economic indicators, such as growth and employment; and the third is the impact of time, or socialization. The basic model to be estimated is:

Benefit = intra-EU trade as % of all trade +
         net budget transfers +
         unemployment +
         inflation +
         log (GDP per capita in PPP) +
         log (number of years in the EU) +
         country (full set of country dummies) +
         u

The dependent variable is constructed as the proportion of respondents who considered that their country benefits from the EU membership. While there are alternative ways of deriving a measure from the benefit question, such as subtracting negative from positive responses, we chose this as it is the most straightforward and is less inclined to vary wildly, which is the case for the most obvious alternative. In addition, this approach allows us to reduce the random variation in our dependent variable measure that may have resulted from aggregation (subtracting negative from positive evaluations) and alternative handling of the 'don't know' category in the data.[3] For the EU15 member states the data are taken from the Eurobarometer trend file (1984–2002), and individual Eurobarometers from 2002 to 2005. For the new member states the data are from the Candidate Countries Eurobarometers (2001–2003) and from the general Eurobarometers for 2004 and 2005. Pre-accession, the 'benefit' question was asked as 'advantage', but it is treated as the same question here.

The data on budgetary transfers are taken from the Statistical Annex to the European Commission report 'Allocation of 2005 EU expenditure by Member State' (Tables 7.3f and 4f therein), which covers expenditure allocation from 1992–2005. Time-series were extended from 1984–1992 based on the annual reports by the European Court of Auditors in the Official Journal. Other economic data are largely from Eurostat, supplemented where necessary (in the case of the new member states) from the World Bank World Development Indicators (WDI). Unemployment (as percentage of total labour force) data for all countries are from WDI. Data for pre-unification Germany are for West Germany and taken from the OECD Main Economic Indicators (historical series). The consumer price index is used here as a measure of inflation. Personal income is operationalized as GDP per capita in purchasing power parity (in current international dollars) and following general practice in the field is rescaled here as a natural logarithm. Intra-EU trade is the data from Eurostat on the share of exports to and imports from the EU member states in the total trade of a country. Socialization is operationalized as the number of years since the Treaty of Rome for the original six EU members, and the number of years since accession for all other countries. This analysis follows that of Marsh (1999) by operationalizing socialization as a natural logarithm of the membership time. This allows the effect to diminish over time, a logical necessity as support as measured here cannot exceed 100 per cent. This is different from other operationalizations used in the literature that allow socialization to grow in an unbounded way by taking simply the number of years that a country has been a member of the EU (e.g. Anderson and Reichert 1996; Gabel 1998b).

7.5. Analysis

There are a number of considerations to be taken into account before estimating this model. They are detailed in a technical appendix and briefly overviewed here. A first consideration is the obviously different levels of positive feeling in each country. While we do want to explain such differences, the existence of what might be essentially national-level peculiarities could bias our search for more general patterns. The normal solution to this is to include a set of country dummies.[4]

A second consideration is the result of our estimation on groups of EU member states after each accession wave. Here, analogous to our first consideration, peculiarities shared by groups of accession states could bias our search for more general patterns within all EU member states. For example, countries in the third accession wave (Austria, Finland, and Sweden) may share some characteristics that would set them aside from the EU12 group of member states. At the same time, countries of the third accession wave may be similar in certain characteristics to Denmark and the UK from the first accession wave. This similarity (or dependence) within our estimation panels, especially in combination with autocorrelation in our data, would bias standard errors in our estimation results if ignored.

A third consideration is whether the series themselves are stationary, that is, do the mean and variance of each series remain stable over time, even if the sample size increases? It is well-known that standard regression analysis on data series that follow a non-stationary process produces spurious results. Our tests of the data suggest that the series are stationary, thus allowing us to proceed with standard estimation techniques.

In estimating the model we opt for a conservative approach that takes into account all three considerations. In particular, we estimate the model by ordinary least squares with Driscoll and Kraay (1998) standard errors.[5] We have estimated the model for the full EU25 as well as for sets of countries comprising the EU after each enlargement wave (i.e. EU6, EU9, EU12, and EU15). This allows us to see how robust the findings are across different sets of states without having to estimate models on what would be very small samples. Estimates are shown in Table 7.1. A graphical representation of the results reported is presented in Figure 7.7, which indicates the confidence interval for the coefficient for each variable and for each of the sets of EU member states. The results in the graphical presentation are of the estimates on standardized variables, which makes

Table 7.1. Utilitarian model of EU support

	EU6	EU9	EU12	EU15	EU25
Inflation	0.008	0.005	−0.000	−0.004	−0.004
	(0.004)	(0.004)	(0.003)	(0.003)	(0.003)
Unemployment	−0.013	−0.012*	−0.014***	−0.015***	−0.015***
	(0.003)	(0.004)	(0.002)	(0.002)	(0.002)
Transfers	0.248	−0.133	0.257	0.453*	0.422*
	(0.292)	(0.321)	(0.200)	(0.172)	(0.188)
Trade	0.876**	0.530*	0.384**	0.426**	0.449**
	(0.162)	(0.177)	(0.121)	(0.122)	(0.121)
Log (income)	0.040	−0.070	−0.127***	−0.099***	−0.094***
	(0.044)	(0.035)	(0.020)	(0.021)	(0.023)
Socialization	−0.258*	0.044	0.119***	0.065	0.059*
	(0.097)	(0.061)	(0.008)	(0.024)	(0.022)
Constant	0.612	0.862*	1.339***	1.208***	1.172***
	(0.287)	(0.288)	(0.216)	(0.195)	(0.215)
R-sq (within)	0.461	0.166	0.390	0.352	0.342
RMSE	0.048	0.060	0.062	0.061	0.061
N	132	198	260	293	313

* $p < .05$, ** $p < .01$, *** $p < .001$.
Note: Driscoll–Kraay SCC standard errors in parentheses.

The Legitimacy of the European Union after Enlargement

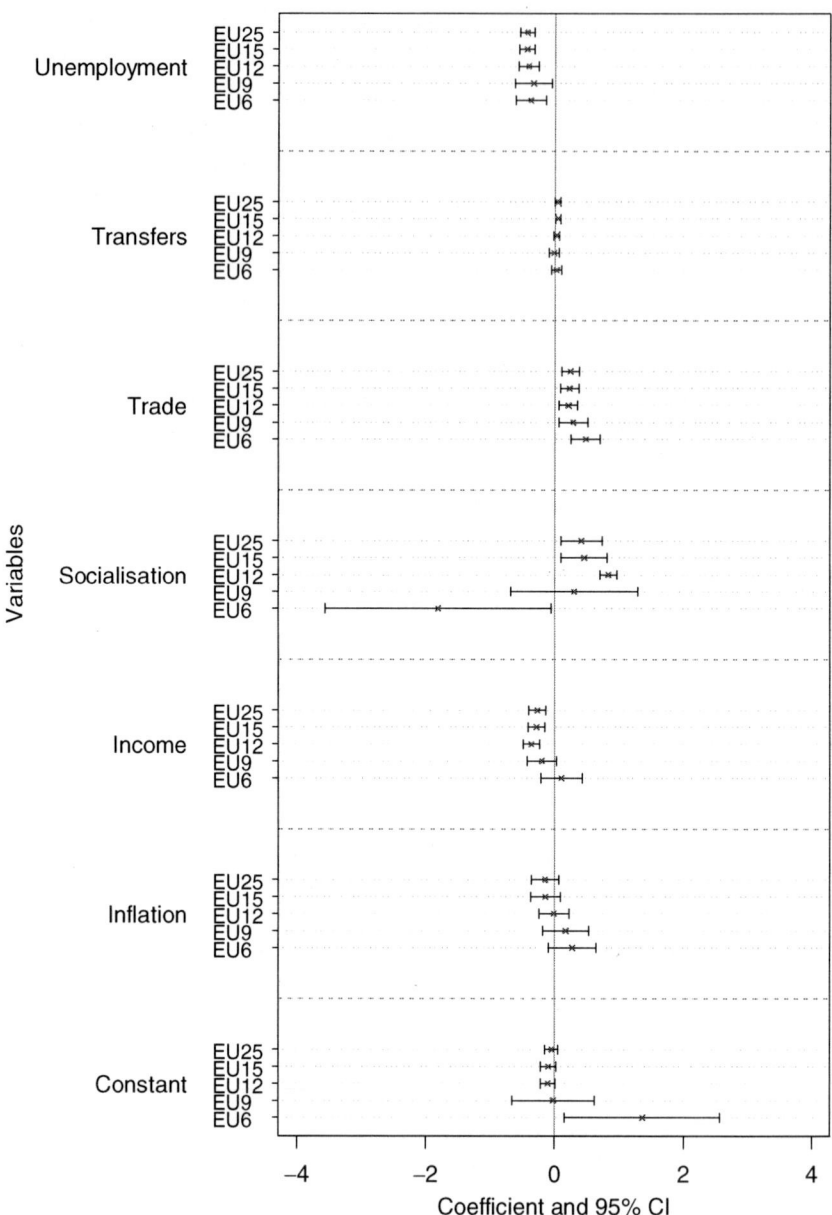

Figure 7.7. Estimation results of the utilitarian model after each accession wave
Note: 95 per cent confidence interval around coefficients for each standardized variable.

Policy Performance and Support for European Integration

it easy to see how the magnitude as well as the significance of the coefficients change with the enlargement of the EU.

For the EU25 the results suggest that a combination of direct and indirect economic effects, as well as socialization, all go some way to explain popular responses to the EU's outputs. There are significant direct effects. Transfer payments via the EU budget and the extent to which trade is intra-EU are both significant. It also seems to be the case that people respond to domestic economic considerations and are inclined to give the EU credit for 'good times'. The unemployment variable is significant, as is income, but inflation, which has been found to be significant in several other studies, is not significant here. Socialization is also important, with the accumulation of years of membership associated with more positive feelings.

These findings hold in large part for each set of EU member states, although there are exceptions. The most important is that transfer payments matter only for the larger number of countries and not for the EU6, EU9, and EU12. This is not simply that similar results become insignificant when the N is smaller. The coefficients themselves are much smaller, and negative in the case of the EU9. A second exception is the income variable, but only the EU6 really looks different here, and even then the difference between the coefficient for the EU25 and that for the EU6 is only just significant. The third concerns socialization. The effect is strongest for the EU6, although it is not positive as we expected, but negative. Positive effects are most marked for the EU12, but generally positive for all but the EU6.

The model seeks to explain the movement around the average public perception of the EU benefit *within* each member state. The R^2 is .34 indicating that 34 per cent of the variation within countries over time is explained by the model. This pattern holds across all sets of EU member states, but it is evident that it is much better for EU6 countries, where R^2 is .46, than for the EU9, where it drops to .17. In essence this would suggest that the utilitarian model is best suited to explain popular perceptions of EU outputs within the six founding countries, but it does hold up reasonably evenly for all the remaining sets of EU member states, with the possible exception of the first wave: Denmark, Ireland, and the UK.[6]

Eichenberg and Dalton (2007) argue that utilitarian concerns have become less important, and place the Maastricht Treaty at the heart of that change. Thus we should in essence face two distinct periods in the history of the EU. This suggests that the model estimates should be significantly different before and after Maastricht. We test this proposition by estimating the structural stability of our model over two periods: the first being the time up to and including 1993 and the second being after 1993.[7] We find that for the EU6 group of countries the model has been structurally stable across these two time periods. That is, estimates of parameters do not seem to differ (in statistical terms) between their values before and after the Maastricht Treaty. However, there is structural change in the way the utilitarian model explains people's benefit perception in other groups of EU member states (EU9, EU12, EU15, and EU25). However, when we look at the stability of the individual parameter, rather than in the set of parameters as a whole, only socialization (not for EU12) and transfers differ significantly in their values before and after Maastricht. In general then, while we agree with Eichenberg and Dalton (2007) that Maastricht has significantly altered public perception of the EU, we find little evidence that most of the utilitarian factors in the model have a different impact after 1993.

7.6. Conclusions

This chapter explored the perceptions of EU outputs within the mass public, asking how much these have varied across time and space and how far we can explain that variation by reference to objective considerations of material gain as opposed to non-utilitarian considerations such as local national identities. We certainly do see changes in perceptions across time. In broad terms, perceptions of benefits have first risen, then fallen, and now seem to be rising again. This is not simply a consequence of the changing composition of EU. In fact, this sort of pattern is characteristic of most waves of accession, if with different degrees of clarity and of course at different levels of overall support. It has been suggested that there is growing diversity in national reactions to the EU, but we find little sign of this.

In looking to explain these variations we find that utilitarian considerations matter. Direct utilitarian benefits in terms of trade and transfer payments are associated with variation, as are changes in national economic performance, with the EU seemingly rewarded for good times. We have looked closely at various groups of EU members after each accession wave, and this finding is quite consistent across these groups, although there are differences: transfer payments, in particular, are more important in the larger groups and the effect of socialization is much clearer for the EU6 group of countries than any other.

If we look at this cyclical pattern in the light of our model, we see clearly that the model predicts just this cycle of surge and decline, which peaked in 1991 around the time of Maastricht and reached a trough in 1996, only to rise again to reach another peak on the eve of the 2004 accessions. Our model predicts just such a pattern, although the first peak is 1990 and the trough is in 1995. As is typical of such models, the hills and valleys of our predicted cycle are also less distinct than are those in the real world. Perhaps other sources of explanation, and other variables, can better match the real terrain, but the performance of this very simple, purely utilitarian, model is quite impressive at an aggregate level.

We have seen that the parameters of the model are fairly stable across the different waves of accession. At this lower level of aggregation, within each accession wave, the performance of the model is also fairly consistent, at least to the extent of reflecting the general trend of support – up, down, or pretty flat – in each of those groups. What is not explained are the sudden increases in negative perceptions following entry in the wave 3 countries – Sweden, Finland, and Austria. The predicted trend was an upward one, a trend visible in the data in Figure 7.3 only if the first entries are discounted. The equally sharp increases in support in the first couple of years of membership of the wave 2 countries are also remarkable and not captured in our model, although the broad upward trend in our predicted model is consistent with the trends in Figure 7.3.

There are perhaps only two countries where the pattern is clear and is not consistent with our utilitarian model. One is the Netherlands, where the gradual disenchantment with the benefits of membership since the early 1990s is not reflected in the underlying material changes. A more striking expectation, and the most striking negative result in our analysis, is the case of the UK. There, support has fallen since the early 1980s, and fallen sharply from the relative heights achieved in the early 1990s. Predictions from our model suggest support should have risen steadily, rather than fallen steadily from around 1993.

Leaving the special case of the UK aside, the model is quite consistent across member subgroups, but given the huge changes that have taken place with the EU since 1983, when this series of measures started, it would hardly be surprising if the models were unstable across the time period as a whole. In particular, the growing interventions in macroeconomic freedoms that date from the early 1990s might well increase differences between countries, while the growing scope of EU policy making could lead to more negative reactions based on non-utilitarian considerations. However, while we find limited evidence of the existence of two distinct periods in EU (before and after 1993), the utilitarian explanation of support seems to remain stable in time, a result that runs counter to the recent findings of Eichenberg and Dalton (2007).

We find more stability over time and, when it comes to national economic indicators, a different set of significant effects than some previous studies have found. It is obvious that more work needs to be done to resolve some of the inconsistencies in results from different analyses. Moreover, as discussed in the introductory chapter, while outputs should contribute initially to what Easton called 'specific' support, they could also – in time – encourage diffuse support, a supposition behind the neo-functionalist interpretation of EU development. The next two chapters investigate this argument further, analysing the spill-over effect from output support to support for institutions and to support for the community.

Notes

1. Here we designate four accession waves as follows: 1st wave (Ireland, Denmark, the UK), 2nd wave (Greece, Portugal, Spain), 3rd wave (Austria, Finland, Sweden), and 4th wave (Cyprus, Czech Republic, Estonia, Hungary, Latvia, Lithuania, Malta, Poland, Slovakia, and Slovenia).
2. The question asked by Eurobarometer in these countries before accession concerns 'advantage' rather than 'benefit' perception. See discussion in the next section for more details.
3. We thank Cees van der Eijk for pointing this out to us.
4. Such models are usually referred to as fixed effects models.
5. See Technical Appendix for details.
6. It seems that the weaker fit for the EU9 group of countries is due to weakness of socialization in that group, and to a particularly poor fit for one country: Ireland.
7. See Technical Appendix for details.

APPENDIX: 1 CHAPTER 7

EU25 IN-SAMPLE DATA SUMMARY

Variable		Mean	Std. Dev.	Min.	Max.	Observations
Benefit	Overall	0.5608	0.1537	0.1442	0.8701	$N = 313$
	Between		0.1307	0.2575	0.8022	$n = 25$
	Within		0.0713	0.2370	0.7881	Mean $t = 12.52$
Inflation	Overall	3.6114	3.3809	−0.7078	23.0211	$N = 313$
	Between		2.0664	1.0962	10.7123	$n = 25$
	Within		2.4617	−4.4641	15.9202	Mean $t = 12.52$
Unemployment	Overall	8.5804	4.1016	1.5000	23.9000	$N = 313$
	Between		3.8460	2.6682	18.3500	$n = 25$
	Within		2.3592	0.7954	16.0304	Mean $t = 12.52$
Transfers	Overall	0.0077	0.0159	−0.0100	0.0624	$N = 313$
	Between		0.0114	−0.0055	0.0331	$n = 25$
	Within		0.0087	−0.0262	0.0463	Mean $t = 12.52$
Trade	Overall	0.6642	0.0787	0.4962	0.8568	$N = 313$
	Between		0.0783	0.5443	0.8280	$n = 25$
	Within		0.0330	0.5641	0.7440	Mean $t = 12.52$
Log(income)	Overall	9.9204	0.3764	8.9807	11.2195	$N = 313$
	Between		0.2478	9.4597	10.4606	$N = 25$
	Within		0.2950	9.0855	10.7461	Mean $t = 12.52$
Socialization	Overall	2.8212	1.0523	0.0000	3.8918	$N = 313$
	Between		1.4004	0.3466	3.6367	$n = 25$
	Within		0.4377	0.7044	3.7001	Mean $t = 12.52$
EU feeling	Overall	0.5490	0.1120	0.2754	0.9257	$N = 313$
	Between		0.0935	0.3838	0.6923	$n = 25$
	Within		0.0603	0.3894	0.8359	Mean $t = 12.52$

APPENDIX 2: CHAPTER 7

It has now become customary in political science to use the Beck and Katz (1995) panel corrected standard errors (PCSE) method estimating models with time-series cross-section (TSCS) structure. Quite often researchers use PCSE without giving a second thought to underlying assumptions or justifying their estimation method theoretically. Simple citation of the Beck and Katz 1995 article seems to suffice. Neil Beck half-jokingly suggests that P in PCSE has become understood to stand for Panacea and not Panel (Beck 2007). Practical researchers have been repeatedly warned against using the PCSE method as a quick fix in TSCS models (Beck and Katz 1995, 1996, 2004). Recent analysis of published work in leading political science journals presented in Wilson and Butler (2007) shows that only a relative minority heeded to Beck and Katz's cautionary note. Hence, not to appear on Wilson and Butler's 'naughty' list for Christmas, in this Technical Appendix we go through several methodological and theoretical considerations justifying our choice of estimation method.

A first consideration that was contemplated for estimation of the model is our specification of the model as a fixed effects model. In such models the set of independent variables is essentially the variation around national means. Because it is a fixed effects model, the assumption is that the relationships between dependent and independent variables are the same for each country. We tested the fixed effects assumption of the model against random effects model (a possible alternative) using the Hausman test, and the general validity of fixed effects using the standard F-test. Both tests support estimation of the model through a fixed effects specification.

A second consideration is whether the series themselves are stationary or not, as performing standard regression analysis on non-stationary series produces spurious results (Greene 2003). When a dependent variable and a covariate follow a random walk (that is, the series are not stationary), Granger and Newbold (1974) showed that the usual t-statistics from standard regression technique (OLS regression) provide spurious results. We tested the data for the presence of unit roots, but found no significant sign of unit root processes in our data. We used a Fisher's test, proposed in Maddala and Wu (1999), which combines p-values from independent unit-root tests for each panel. It is based on p-values of individual Augmented Dickey—Fuller unit root tests (Dickey and Fuller 1979) and assumes that all series are non-stationary under the null hypothesis with the alternative hypothesis being

Appendix

that at least one series in the panel is stationary. The test has also been suggested as a preferred choice in case of cross-sectional correlation, when standard alternatives (the Levin-Lin and Im-Pesaran-Shin tests) are invalid (Maddala and Wu 1999). We tested different alternative specifications of the test (with and without the trend) but the results are unchanged.

A third consideration is how far there is spatial correlation within our panels, something that would bias our standard errors if we ignored it. Our discussion in the second section gives reason to expect some spatial correlation. Under the assumption that cross-sectional dependence is caused by unobserved common factors, uncorrelated with included covariates, the effect would be translated through the disturbance term. In that case, cross-sectional correlation is the average absolute value of the off-diagonal elements of the cross-sectional correlation matrix of residuals (De Hoyos and Sarafidis 2006). Estimates of cross-sectional correlation in our data range between 0.24 in the original six countries (the same for accession waves 1 and 2), 0.26 in wave 3, 0.42 in wave 4, 0.34 in EU9, 0.374 in EU12, 0.409 in EU15, and 0.421 in EU25. This is a descriptive and intuitive result rather than a useable test statistic. We cannot resort to any spatial dependence statistical tests due to the particular structure of our data (N/T ratio) and generally small sample size.[1] However, cross-sectional correlation results appear to be high enough to suggest that cross-sectional dependence may be present in our data to a degree of affecting the estimation results.

The effect of cross-sectional dependence depends heavily on the magnitude of cross-panel correlation and the nature of dependence. However, typically standard fixed- and random-effects estimators remain consistent, but inefficient, and estimated standard errors are biased (Baltagi 2005). In particular, Beck and Katz (1995) showed that, in the presence of group-wise heteroskedasticity and cross-sectional and temporal correlation, which is a standard situation in time-series cross-section models, regular assumptions about the error-term are violated, and models estimated by feasible generalized least squares (standard approach in such circumstances) in finite panels produce overly optimistic results (anti-conservative), with standard errors usually biased downwards. Beck and Katz (1995) propose a correction for two of these problems – groupwise heteroskedasticity and contemporaneous correlation of the disturbances – in their PCSE methodology.

We tested for the presence of temporal correlation in our data using the Arellano–Bond test (Arellano and Bond 1991) and the Wooldridge test for serial correlation in the errors of a linear panel-data model (Wooldridge 2002). These tests suggest that autocorrelation features in our data. The PCSE approach does not correct for autocorrelation, requiring it to be corrected before applying PCSE, but neither does it account for temporal heteroskedasticity (another persistent feature in time-series data and present in our data here) (Beck and Katz 2004; Kittel and Winner 2005).

One popular way to account for autocorrelation is by including lagged dependent variables (LDV) among the covariates in the PCSE estimation model (Wilson and Butler 2007). However, if autocorrelation is persistent after the inclusion of LDV the coefficient estimates are biased (Beck and Katz 1996; Wilson and Butler 2007). From the theoretical point of view, we believe that including lagged popular perception of the EU benefits (LDV) is not justified in our model. Moreover, tests for autocorrelation in the PCSE estimation of our model with LDV included among covariates point to remaining autocorrelation, potentially biasing coefficient estimates.

Taking into account considerations discussed above, and the fact that we are interested above all in the temporal component of the model, we opt for a fixed effects model estimated by ordinary least squares with Driscoll and Kraay (1998) standard errors. Driscoll and Kraay (1998) proposed a nonparametric covariance matrix estimator, which produces heteroskedasticity and autocorrelation consistent (HAC) standard errors that are robust to general forms of temporal and spatial dependence. Furthermore, Driscoll and Kraay (1998) show with evidence from Monte Carlo experiments that their estimator is independent of the cross-sectional dimension of the data, which is particularly important to political scientists usually operating with finite samples. Hoechle (2006), who adopted the estimator for use with unbalanced panels, shows that in the presence of spatial correlation, which we suspect exists in our data, the Driscoll–Kraay estimator performs much better than standard existing estimators. Generally, Driscoll and Kraay (1998) apply Newey and West (1987) HAC correction to a sequence of cross-averages of the moment conditions (Hoechle 2006). Here we use the default lag length of two, which is the first step in Newey and West (1994).

Regarding our tests of structural stability of the model, we create dummy variables for two periods (1984–93 and 1994–2005) and interactions of these period dummies with all our covariates. We estimate a general model, which includes all our covariates for full-time sample and interactions for a second sub-sample (this is more numerically stable than estimating a model with interactions for both sub-samples). This fully interacted model is fitted for our consistent spatial sub-samples (i.e. groups of EU member states after each accession wave: EU6, EU9, EU12, EU15, EU25). We then conduct a Wald test for a linear hypothesis that parameters in the second temporal sub-sample equal the first sub-sample. This test is equivalent to a Chow test for structural break.

Note

1. For an overview see Anselin (2001).

8
Trust in Political Institutions

Bernhard Wessels

8.1. Introduction

The last chapter dealt with output support from a utilitarian perspective. In terms of the Eastonion framework (see introductory chapter), this chapter goes a step further up in the hierarchy of objects of support and explores the levels of trust in institutions at the national and the European level. Since the major concern of this book is representation and accountability, analysis will be restricted to institutions that are functionally concerned with both aspects, that is, parliaments and governments. More precisely, we will analyse the development of trust in the respective national parliament and the European Parliament (EP) and trust in the respective national government and the governing bodies of the EU, namely the European Commission and the Council of Ministers, and try to explain their dynamics since the early 1990s. In a second step, we will look into the cross-national situation after the Eastern enlargement in 2004.

In analytical and political terms, trust in political institutions is an essential element of the democratic legitimacy of decision making and the regime as such. Furthermore, trust can be regarded as a resource or an asset of a political system allowing for relative autonomy of governance. The very nature of trust is that, with regard to political actors or institutions, it is an advance 'payment' resulting from the expectation that they will do a proper job or function properly in the future (Luhmann 1968; Preisendörfer 1995). In this sense, trust is a buffer against temporary output fluctuations (Kaase 1979). It is based on retrospective evaluations that are translated into expectations for the future. Theoretically and within the Eastonian framework of political support, one can argue that repeated positive experience translates into generalized attitudes, that is, trust.

Since the early 1990s, the EU was institutionally on course for further integration, deepening and widening at the same time. Its speed even accelerated over recent years: first, with the enlargement of the EU by ten new member states that implied crossing the so-called iron curtain and taking on board eight new democracies in Central and Eastern Europe and, second, with the preparations for a EU constitution. These developments toward a politically integrated Europe did not find unanimous support. It rather seems that public support for European integration has decreased since 1992. This decline in the mid-1990s has been called the 'post-Maastricht blues' (Eichenberg and Dalton 2003), and a reason for these blues is seen in the increasing awareness of European citizens that integration might not only bring benefits, but also entail some costs, produce new risks, harm national democracy, etc. (Eichenberg and Dalton 2003; Netjes and Edwards 2005).

In particular, the biggest enlargement of the Union since its formation has obviously produced stress and raised the question whether the EU is still on due course. Indications were the referenda in France and the Netherlands in which the European constitution failed to gain support from the majority of the population. These developments apparently alarmed the European Commission, which launched its 'Plan-D for Democracy, Dialogue and Debate' in October 2005. The Commission's analysis reads as follows:

> Faced with declining confidence in political systems, the Commission believes that it is important to ensure that representative democracy continues to maintain the trust and involvement of Europe's citizens. The latest Eurobarometer survey shows that public approval of the European Union has steadily decreased over recent months. Whether in terms of trust, image or assessment of EU membership, all the indicators have fallen. A similar decline is seen in the public approval of and trust in the national political process. While membership of the European Union is still supported by 54% of EU citizens, the image of the European Union has steadily decreased in citizens' eyes with only 47% of respondents giving a positive response. Trust in the European Union has dropped from 50% of citizens trusting the EU in autumn 2004 to 44% in spring 2005. (European Commission, COM (2005) 494 final: 3)

The crucial question is, however, how this trend has come about. The short-term development has to be seen in relation to long-term developments. If the diagnosis of the Commission is correct and 'people need to feel that Europe provides an added value' (European Commission, COM (2005) 494 final: 3), the question arises at what point did the people in Europe lose this feeling. The history of European integration has been characterized by a permissive consensus due to the achievements it provided, in particular with regard to economic benefits and peace. Is there an indication that this consensus no longer exists, and, if so, what are the implications for trust in representative institutions?

8.2. Trust in institutions: Concept, hypotheses, and prior research findings

The 'post-Maastricht blues' clearly highlights increasing discomfort with the EU development over more than a decade (Eichenberg and Dalton 2003; Netjes and Edwards 2005). Based on the observation that support for European integration seems not to be as self-evident in the 1990s and the new century as in the 1980s (Norris 1999*b*), one might speculate how this would affect trust in political institutions.

The classical starting point for an analysis of political support and attitudes toward political objects is the concept developed by Easton (Easton 1965*b*). According to his concept, orientations toward political objects must be conceptualized hierarchically. Easton differentiates between three object levels and two modes of orientations. The object levels are the authorities, the regime, and the community; the modes of orientations are either specific or diffuse.

The theory of political support suggests that positive experience with concrete political objects may spill over to positive orientations toward political objects at a more abstract level. Thus, positive experience with political authorities results in specific support for them. If this positive experience is not challenged, specific support of authorities transforms into diffuse support first of the authorities, then of the regime. 'Such attachment may be a product of spill-over effects from evaluations of a series of outputs and performances over a long period of time' (Easton 1975: 446). This is a typical process of generalization indicating that the term diffuse may be misleading since it denotes generalized evaluations. Therefore, Fuchs (1993) has proposed differentiating between specific and generalized orientations. Easton himself speaks of a 'generalized attachment to political objects' (Easton 1975: 444).

Political trust has a very particular character since the distinction between specific support (related to what an object does) and diffuse or generalized support (related to what an object represents) is somewhat blurred. Political objects can be evaluated with regard to either their performance (what they do) or their quality (how they do it). Both criteria are evaluative, one more instrumentally, the other more morally (Fuchs 1989). As the definition of trust as an 'output effect' (Gamson 1968; Easton 1979) suggests, trust is somewhat in between or a mixture of both instrumental and moral standards of evaluation.

However, research on support for national governments and European integration suggests that instrumental, utilitarian considerations may be more relevant for trust than moral standards. Thus, this perspective will be the focus here.

In his early study of European integration and support for institutions, Handley (1981) found a situation apparently very similar to the present situation. The crisis of support for European integration and European institutions in the 1970s marked a pivotal change in post-World War II history. Handley discovered that the interdependencies between public opinion, national policies, and European integration had never been as high as in the 1970s. In the 20-year period before 1970, there was no strong co-variation between (national) economic development and the evaluation of the EC. This changed in the 1970s. Furthermore, the crisis of support was associated with the enlargement of the Community. These findings suggest that there may be strong interdependency between the national and the European level of support.

Subsequent research has validated the strong link between support of European integration and (national) economic performance (Eichenberg and Dalton 1993; Gabel and Palmer 1995; Gabel 1998*b*;). This is not only true with regard to generalized support for European integration or the EU polity, but also with regard to specific support in referenda (Christin and Hug 2002).

Two general hypotheses can be drawn from these considerations:

H1: Trust in political institutions is instrumentally driven. The better the socio-economic performance is, the higher the trust.

H2: There are spill-over effects from national economic performance to the evaluation of the European level. This implies that trust in European institutions co-varies with national economic performance.

Furthermore, one can assume that instrumental evaluations are stronger when they apply to actors or institutions that are assumed to be responsible for or to have an impact on performance. Thus, a third hypothesis reads as follows:

H3: Since governments are comparatively more strongly evaluated in terms of what they do, trust in government is more performance-driven than trust in parliaments.

A fourth hypothesis concerns spill-over effects on trust from evaluations of a series of performances over a long time period. Marsh (1999: 100) argues that people learned to approve of the EU in the same way that they acquired party identification and, due to positive experiences, support showed an upward trend. This concerns specifically the EU and does not necessarily relate to national institutions. Thus, one would expect:

H4: The length of EU membership breeds consent, that is, the longer the membership, the higher the trust in European institutions.

In the following, these hypotheses will be investigated. In a first step, the longitudinal perspective before enlargement is explored; in a second step, a cross-country analysis after enlargement is performed.

8.3. The development of trust in national and European political institutions

There is a great variety of political institutions, both at the national and the European level. As already mentioned, here the focus will be on institutions primarily related to representation and accountability, and analysis will be restricted to the major and functionally equivalent institutions at both levels. These are parliaments and governments. With regard to parliaments, both political levels have the same institutions at least as far as the label is concerned. This is not the case with regard to government. At the European level, the Commission and the Council share this role to some degree, the Commission being the administrative executive (and the legislative initiator) and the Council being the political executive. Thus, analysis will concentrate on trust in parliaments on the one hand and on trust in national governments, the Commission, and the Council on the other hand. Unfortunately, the time series is not very dense, covering only nine cross-sections between 1993 and 2006, and the wording of Eurobarometer questions changed between 1993 and 1999 (Table 8.1).

From the perspective of the 'post-Maastricht blues', one should expect trust in European political institutions to decline. This follows from the concept of political support that assumes spill-over effects from support

The Legitimacy of the European Union after Enlargement

Table 8.1. Questions on trust in institutions in the Eurobarometer (EB) surveys

EB No.	Year	Month	Wording
39	1993	4	Which of the following do you trust or not, to check how European Community decisions are carried through... (READ OUT)?
51	1999	4	
55	2001	5	
56	2001	11	
61	2004	5	
62	2004	10	And, for each of them, please tell me if you tend to trust it or tend not to trust it?
63	2005	5	
64	2005	10	
65	2006	5	

for authorities to support for regimes (Easton 1965*b*). Thus, the result of the empirical observation comes as somewhat of a surprise. Trust in the European governmental institutions and, in particular, the EP is higher in the most recent decade than in the 1990s (Figure 8.1).

Whereas the European Commission and the Council of Ministers faced declining trust between 1993 and 1999, but then recovered fast, the EP continuously gained support. Between November 2001 and May 2004, trust in these EU institutions seems to have reached a plateau. The development of trust in national parliaments and national governments is very similar to that of trust in the governmental institutions until 2002, but it then experiences a notable decline. One observation should be highlighted first of all: There is a considerable upward movement in trust, in particular in national institutions between May and November 2001. In its report on the survey, the European Commission attributes this to the terrorist bombings that took place on 11 September 2001 in the United States. This shows the high sensitivity of trust to *major* events. In May 2004, all European institutions gained more trust than their national counterparts on the EU's cross-country average (the mean of country means). This finding is certainly not in line with the 'post-Maastricht blues' and seems to indicate that citizens chose to detract trust from the nation-state rather than from the EU.

The second observation is that there is a noticeable, dramatic drop in trust between May and November 2004. This is the development that alarmed the European Commission and coincided with the Eastern enlargement and the signing of the Constitutional Treaty in Rome on 29 October 2004.

Huge differences between member states are hidden behind this general development. There are some particular patterns that have to be mentioned.

Trust in Political Institutions

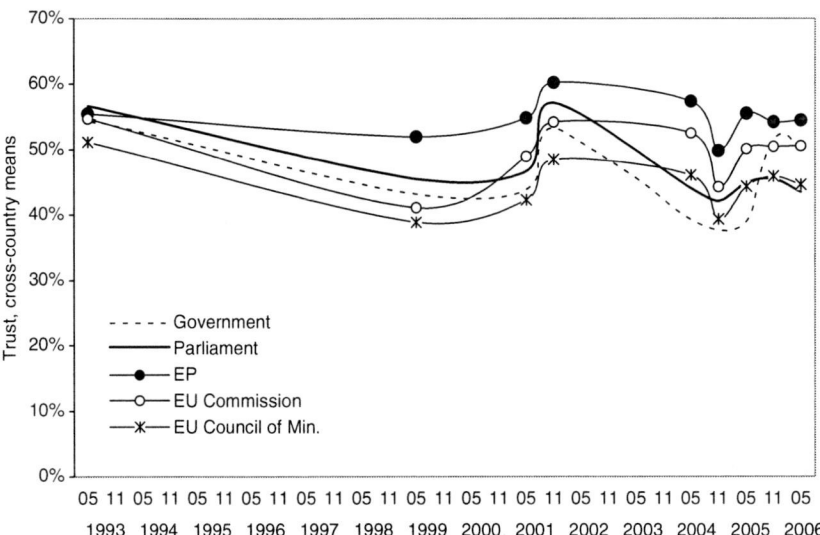

Figure 8.1. Trust in national and European political institutions

Note: 1993 EU12, afterwards EU15. Calculating 1999 for EU12 (i.e. excluding Austria, Finland, and Sweden), the difference to the EU15 mean is 1.9 per cent at maximum, which implies that the time comparison is not distorted by using only twelve countries in 1993.

Until the Eastern enlargement, the citizens of Luxembourg show the highest or close to highest trust in all five institutions. In contrast, British citizens seem to be the most sceptical of all people. Of all member states they show the lowest trust in any of the five institutions. Besides this finding, which may be attributed to different (political) cultures, trust in the national parliament is highest in the Netherlands and Finland, lowest in Italy and France. Trust in national governments on average is again highest in the Netherlands and Finland, lowest in Italy and Belgium. The EP is trusted most by the citizens of Italy and Ireland and least in Sweden and Austria. Trust in the European Commission is also highest in Italy and Ireland and lowest in Germany and Sweden. Finally, the Council of Ministers is trusted most in Ireland and Greece, and least in Austria and Germany.

Furthermore, comparing trust across levels, that is, comparing national parliaments to the EP and national governments to the Commission and the Council, huge variations across countries can be observed. In Denmark, the Netherlands, Sweden, and the UK, trust in national institutions is higher than in EU institutions for all three pairs of comparison. In contrast, in seven countries (Belgium, France, Greece, Ireland, Portugal, and Spain) trust in EU-level institutions is higher than in national institutions. The remaining countries show mixed patterns. On average from 1993 until May 2004, the EP draws higher support than national parliaments in eleven countries, the European Commission and the Council of Ministers in seven countries out of fifteen.

The question is whether the general trend can be ascribed to common causes despite the great differences between countries. As mentioned above, prior research suggests such commonalities, putting emphasis on performance and benefits (see also the previous chapter). In order to pursue the hypotheses formulated above, more specifications are necessary to formulate a model explaining the dynamics of trust in institutions.

Hypothesis 1 states that trust is performance-driven. It assumes that economic conditions that are beneficial to the people increase their willingness to put trust in acting institutions. If the conditions are not beneficial, trust is withdrawn. The economic performance measures that are most easily accessible for citizens are economic growth, unemployment, and inflation. Information on these three characteristics of an economy is widely published in the mass media and figures prominently in the political debate. An evaluation on this basis is principally related to the notion of socio-tropic reasoning. But it refers to an egocentric perspective concerning personal fears or expectations as well. Within the framework of the nation state, positive economic growth, low inflation, and low unemployment should benefit parliament and government with regard to trust. However, if hypothesis 2, which assumes spill-over effects, is correct, these factors should also produce higher trust in European institutions. Since spill-over is an indirect effect, one might expect the impact of economic performance on trust to be higher for the national than for the European institutions. A similar logic applies to hypothesis 3, which assumes that economic performance matters more for trust in government than for trust in parliament. The fourth hypothesis relates to experience with EU membership and says that, as experiences with the EU are mainly positive, the length of membership in the EU should increase trust in EU institutions.

The implications for national institutions can be manifold. If there is a real trade-off in trust, which can only be assumed if there is a zero-sum game, the correlation should be negative. However, the Luxembourg example shows that such a direct trade-off is unlikely. Obviously, a nation can trust *all* institutions more than all other nations do. If one assumes that there is a spill-over effect from the national to the European level but length of membership only affects the European level, all other things being equal, there should be no relationship at all, though the gap

Trust in Political Institutions

Table 8.2. Expectation regarding the correlates of the development of trust in longitudinal perspective

	National Parliament	National Government	European Parliament	European Commission	Council of Ministers
Inflation (price index), $t-1$	−	−	−	−	−
Growth rate, $t-1$	+	+	+	+	+
Unemployment rate, $t-1$	−	−	−	−	−
Membership length at time of Survey	no	no	+	+	+

between the national and the European level should widen with length of membership. Theoretically, there is no reason to expect any impact of the length of membership on trust in national institutions. Table 8.2 summarizes the expected effects.

The model to be tested uses annual objective economic data instead of perceptions. Since these annual figures are only available at the end of a year or early in the following year, the economic variables from one year before the survey are used.

To test the model, an aggregate data set has been constructed for which cases are defined by country and time point. The model includes the levels of trust (in per cent) in the five institutions as dependent variables. Independent variables include economic growth of the country in the year before the survey (Eurostat data), inflation in the year before (price index from International Financial Statistics (IFS), International Monetary Fund), unemployment rate of the year before (IFS, International Monetary Fund), and length of membership in the EU at the time of the survey. Ordinary least square regressions with random effects have been performed using robust standard errors to test the hypotheses.[1]

The results clearly support hypothesis 1 with regard to the impact of inflation and economic growth. High inflation leads to a decrease of trust, high growth rates lead to an increase of trust. For unemployment, the hypothesis is corroborated for national parliaments and governments, but not for European institutions except for the EP, on which it shows a positive, but statistically insignificant influence. Thus, the hypothesis of instrumentally-driven trust is supported in general. The spill-over hypothesis (hypothesis 2), however, is only partly backed. Hypothesis 3, which claims a stronger impact of performance on trust in government than on trust in parliament, is corroborated in terms of inflation and growth (Table 8.3).

Finally, the fourth hypothesis, on length of membership and trust, is quite strongly supported and shows the highest significance of effects for

Table 8.3. Regression of trust in representative institutions on economic performance and length of EU membership, 1993–2006

	National Parliament Coef.	National Government Coef.	European Parliament Coef.	European Commission Coef.	Council of Ministers Coef.
Inflation (price index), $t-1$	−0.273*	−0.385***	−0.094	−0.090	−0.122
Growth rate, $t-1$	0.623	1.418**	1.160**	0.681	0.601
Unemployment rate, $t-1$	−0.798*	−0.738*	0.637*	0.579	0.527
Membership length at time of survey	−0.200***	−0.154*	0.219***	0.202***	0.157*
Constant	86.705***	89.877***	50.243***	46.807***	46.963***
R-squared	0.152***	0.205***	0.149***	0.096***	0.072*

Aggregate data, stacked, $n = 132$; EU 15.
Estimates with robust standard errors.
Significance level: ***< .005; ** < .01; * < .05.

European institutions. Furthermore, there is also a clear, but negative impact of the length of membership on trust in national parliament and government. This distinct and strong effect comes as a theoretical surprise, since it seems to indicate a trade-off between trust in national and European institutions.

A test of three models, in which the trade-off in form of the balance of trust in (*a*) the national parliaments versus the EP, (*b*) the national government versus the European Commission, and, (*c*) the national government versus the Council of Ministers is the dependent variable, shows that length of EU membership is highly significant in all three. Furthermore, explained variance in these models (at 29 per cent) is much higher than in the models using simple proportions of trust. Empirically, this provides support for a trade-off in trust between political levels. These results are in stark contrast to the theoretical expectation that there should be no relationship between trust in national institutions and length of EU membership.

Theoretically, only one, although not irrelevant, perspective can be consistently applied to this finding. A zero-sum game is only sensible if one assumes that, because of European integration, trust in national institutions declines in the long run. This would support Scharpf's argument that there is a double democratic deficit in the EU, both at the national and the European level, with the national level losing effective control over policies (output legitimacy) and the European level lacking input legitimacy (Scharpf 1996). If this were the correct interpretation of the empirical results presented here, it would indicate that this double deficit was no longer a problem of political scientists alone but also of the people. And this would signify a problem for nation state democracy in the long run. However, empirical evidence for such a strong interpretation is rather weak. Furthermore, Figure 8.1 above indicates that national institutions can regain trust. On average, there is a steep increase of trust in national government following the rather dramatic decline in November 2004 and a slight increase of trust in the national parliaments. European institutions are also recovering somewhat from the November 2004 dip. Thus, national institutions can regain trust without a decrease of trust in European institutions. Therefore, the interpretation of our findings in line with Scharpf is questionable.

8.4. Trust in national and European political institutions after Eastern enlargement

Turning to the situation after enlargement, more emphasis will now be placed on single country profiles as well as differences between old and new member states, and a more thorough explanatory model will be introduced. For the cross-sectional perspective, data from the European Election Study 2004, conducted mainly in June, in some countries fieldwork lasted until autumn, will be used. For the developments since 2004, Eurobarometer surveys will be employed.

Turning first to differences between the fifteen old and the ten new member states, it becomes clear that at European election time in 2004, citizens in old member states trusted their national institutions more than the European ones, parliaments coming first at both levels, followed by governmental actors. For the new member states the pattern is almost the reverse. Citizens in these countries trust their national institutions least and European institutions most, and governmental actors more than parliaments. However, the Council of Ministers attracts the least trust of the European institutions (Figure 8.2).

The situation after the EP elections held in June 2004 looks quite different than in the earlier period. Before the 2004 European Elections, trust in national institutions was higher than trust in EU institutions in only four of the old member states (Denmark, the Netherlands, Sweden, and the UK). A few months later, European institutions prevailed over national ones in only three of the old member states (Portugal, Italy, and Ireland). These changes are obviously event-driven. Enlargement and the discussion about a European constitution are the likely candidates for this

The Legitimacy of the European Union after Enlargement

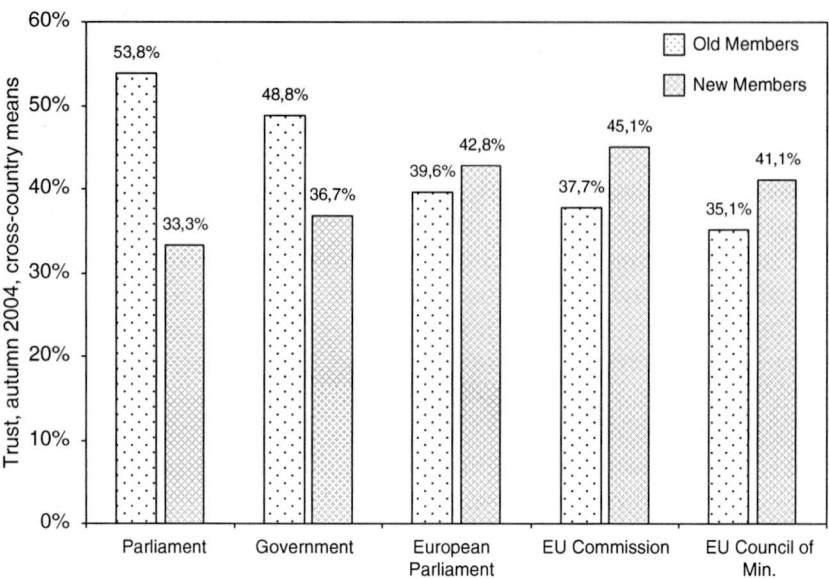

Figure 8.2. Trust in institutions in the old and new member states, 2004

Source: European Election Study 2004 (mainly June, some countries had fieldwork until autumn) trust scale (1 no trust; 10 full trust) recoded to 1 through 5 = 0; 6 through 10 = 1; percentage with the value of 1. Cross-country average based on equal sample weights.

'revival' of the nation state. Whether this trend will hold for the future is an open question.

As shown in Figure 8.3, in 2004, trust in the national parliament was highest in Denmark, Luxembourg, Cyprus, and Finland and lowest in Poland, the Czech Republic, Slovakia, and Latvia. Trust in national governments shows the same pattern. The comparison of trust in national and in European institutions yields a rather clear pattern. Where trust in national institutions is rather low, trust in EU institutions is higher. The most obvious differences are between the old and new members, with the exception again of Portugal, Italy, and Ireland.

In light of recent developments, it is an open question whether the instrumental perspective still contributes to trust in the institutions. Therefore, an explanatory model will be tested at the individual level. At the aggregate level, prior research and also the analysis in this chapter have found ample evidence for the utilitarian, instrumental explanation. Positive performance of the economy helps governments (Eulau and Lewis-Beck 1985; Anderson 1995b), the EU (Eichenberg and Dalton 1993), and political authorities in general. This has not only been demonstrated with macro-data on economic performance, but also with individual-level data

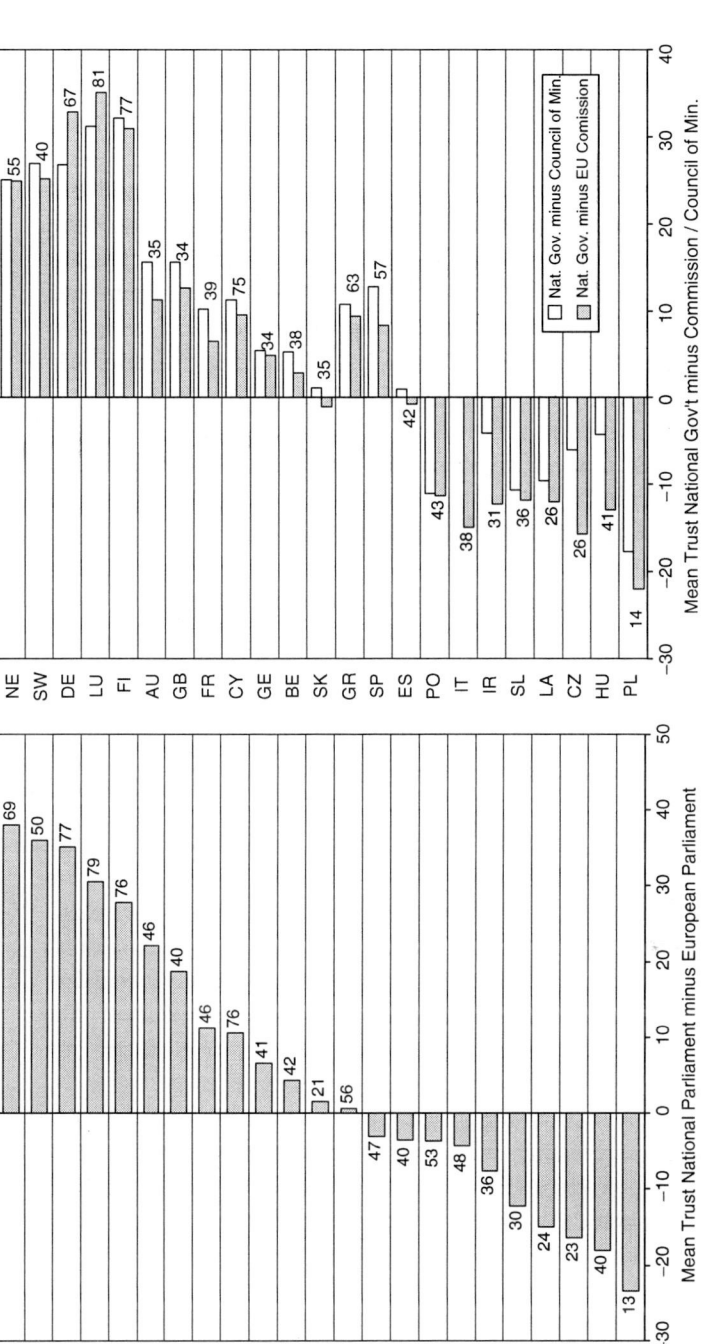

Figure 8.3. Difference in support for national and EU institutions – parliament and 'government.' (*a*) Trust in the national parliament and the EP and (*b*) trust in the national government and European 'government'

(Bars indicate the mean difference in trust of national parliament minus trust in the EP, and trust in national government minus trust in European 'government', respectively; figures indicate percentage of trust in national parliament, and percentage of trust in national government, respectively.)

on perceptions of the economy and the individual socio-economic situation (Eulau and Lewis-Beck 1985; Gabel and Whitten 1997). Thus, it is worthwhile to develop a model of trust in institutions taking the insights of this research into account.

The model used here has commonalities with other models of political support, but it is also different. Like the other models, the one used here combines micro- and macro-economic conditions. As in the aggregate model, macro-indicators were not included if it was doubtful whether citizens are informed and sophisticated enough to understand their implications. Thus, whereas foreign trade figures, EU net benefits, etc., are excluded, unemployment, an obvious candidate for observation in day-to-day life, is included. The expectation is that unemployment is attributed to the policy failure of national institutions. Thus, higher unemployment should decrease the trust in national institutions but not affect European institutions significantly.

In addition, a number of individual-level variables concerning the economic situation are included. The questions on the retrospective and prospective state of the economy (socio-tropic) are directly related to macro-economic performance. Here again, the expectation is that the institutions of the nation state are more affected.

Furthermore, as Gabel (1998*b*) has demonstrated, the competitive situation in labour markets plays an important role for support for European integration. The more the fear or the risk of being affected by the internationalization of labour markets, the less supportive of the EU citizens are. Since the aim is to include indicators that are not only relevant for European but also for national institutions, only rather basic indicators are used here: unemployment and employment status, 'worker' versus others. In other respects, the argument is very much the same again: for fear about the internationalization of the economy, either national institutions are blamed because they do nothing about it, or European institutions are not trusted because they promote economic liberalization.

The evaluation of the incumbent government and voting behaviour are also included. It is expected that the evaluation of a national government or voting for a party in government has a clear impact on trust in national institutions. More specifically, if the national government is approved through positive evaluation or by voting for one of the parties in government, trust in national institutions will be high and trust in European institutions comparatively lower.

Another variable used in the model is trade union membership (in the household). At the national level, this is an indication for social capital and social inclusion, thus positively related to trust. At the European level, trade union membership marks an ideological position opposed to liberalization and globalization for which European institutions stand and, thus, it is expected that union membership will be negatively related to trust.

Interest in politics as an indicator of access to and awareness about political information is also included. Prior research indicates that political interest goes along with positive attitudes toward political institutions. Whether the reason for this is that the more informed have a more differentiated worldview or whether this is an indication of political inclusion and integration is a question still to be answered by research.

Finally, a dummy variable for old versus new member states is included to capture the obvious differences. The model will not include dummies for countries (fixed effects), since the economic variables replace country dummies with content that matters according to the model's assumptions.

As shown in Table 8.4, the model shows significant deviations from the aggregate model. All the macro-variables, the economic ones and length of EU membership, produce unexpected results. Obviously, the effects of these variables are totally blurred due to the event effects, mainly the 'institutional stress' produced by enlargement. This does not mean, however, that utilitarian considerations do not matter. The respective individual-level variables, that is, positive retrospective and prospective evaluations of the economy, show strong effects in the expected direction. Furthermore, effects are stronger for national-level institutions (strongest for government, as expected) than for trust in European institutions. Government approval as indicated by a positive evaluation or a vote for a party in government also reveals very strong effects in the expected direction, again stronger for the national level than for the European level.

The socio-demographic variables, that is, trade union membership, being unemployed, and being a worker, that also are related to particular socio-economic interests basically show the expected results. Being unemployed or being a worker goes together with less trust in institutions and, in particular, in European institutions. Union membership as an indication of social and political integration at the national level shows positive effects there and no effects for European institutions. The expectation that union members do not trust European institutions due to the perception that European integration goes together with globalization of the economy is not supported. The models for trust in parliament and government have quite strong explanatory powers. This does not apply to European institutions, but the models are still satisfactory with an explained variance of around 10 per cent.

Table 8.4. A utilitarian model of trust in institutions

	Trust (1: not at all; 10: fully trust)			
	National Parliament	National Government	EP	EU Commission	EU Council of Min.
	B	B	B	B	B
Constant	6.851***	4.526***	2.395***	-0.898	-0.898
Inflation (price index), t−1	-0.026***	-0.015***	0.014**	0.042***	0.042***
GDP growth, t−1	-0.099***	-0.038***	-0.027*	-0.037**	-0.037***
Unemployment rate, t−1	-0.083***	-0.043***	-0.038***	-0.001	-0.001
EU membership in years	-0.005***	-0.003*	-0.002	-0.004**	-0.004*
Voted for a party in government	0.509***	0.987***	0.333***	0.338***	0.338***
Old members (1; else 0)	0.461***	0.154*	-0.271***	-0.210**	-0.210***
Interest in politics	0.136***	0.099***	0.186***	0.196***	0.196***
Prospective (socio-tropic)	0.288***	0.309***	0.279***	0.266***	0.266***
Retrospective (socio-tropic)	0.153***	0.192***	0.113***	0.085***	0.085***
Government approval	1.189***	2.156***	0.647***	0.623***	0.623***
Trade union member	0.256***	0.121***	-0.013	0.005	0.005
Unemployed	-0.217**	-0.107	-0.555***	-0.455***	-0.455***
Worker	-0.297***	-0.241***	-0.281***	-0.380***	-0.380***
Adj. R-square	0.243	0.354	0.094	0.097	0.116

Missing: listwise.
Weight: equal sample size.
Significance level: *** < .001; ** < .01; * < .05.
Source: European Election Study 2004.

Trust in Political Institutions

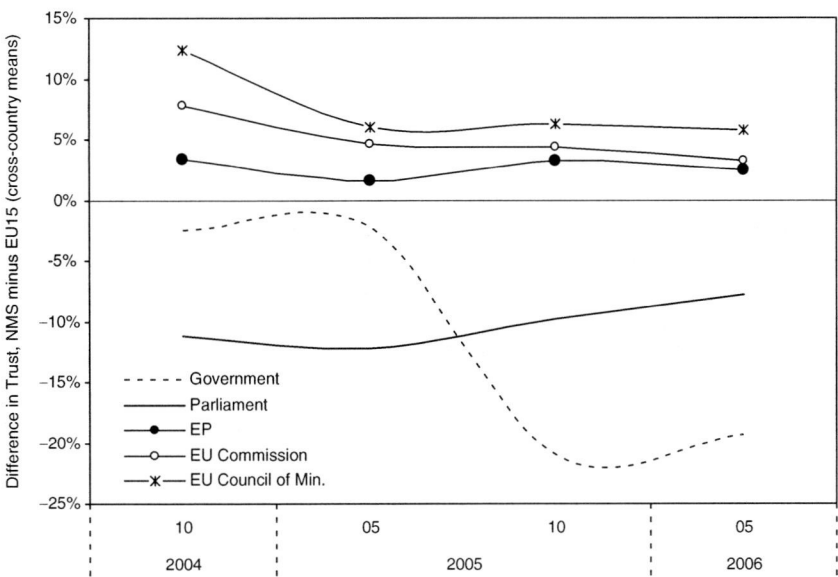

Figure 8.4. Differences in trust in national and European institutions between old (EU15) and new member states (NMS)

The instrumental, utilitarian explanation of trust in institutions holds up in general, but the particular situation with the enlargement has probably weakened its powers. It may well be that more political considerations have gained importance and will continue to do so in the future. This may also be a result of the disparity and differences between members after enlargement.

Heterogeneity has increased with enlargement and has been on the rise since then, at least with regard to trust. The balance in the mean trust in institutions between new and old member states has changed in the time period between October 2004 and May 2006, in particular with regard to national governments. On the one hand, it seems to be a stable pattern that citizens in the new member states trust European institutions more than citizens in the old member states. In contrast, trust in national institutions is considerably lower in new than in old member states, and trust in national governments has experienced tremendous change. The gap between new and old members has widened enormously (Figure 8.4).

8.5. Discussion

In this chapter, trust in political institutions as one element of political support has been investigated from the perspective of the legitimacy of the EU after Eastern enlargement. The basic concern was trust in political institutions that are functionally responsible for the provision of representation and accountability. These institutions are parliaments and governmental institutions, both at the national and the European level.

As a first step the development of trust in national parliaments and governments, the EP, the European Commission, and the Council of Ministers from 1993 until 2006 has been analysed. Between 1999 and May 2004, trust in European institutions increased. This is in contrast with prior research findings on the so-called post-Maastricht blues. Trust in national institutions sharply declined after 2001. On average, in the period from 1993 to May 2004, trust in national institutions was higher than in European ones in only four out of fifteen countries. Previous research suggests that the explanation for the development of trust can be found in instrumental, utilitarian considerations and evaluations of the citizens. Our test of a regression model of levels of trust on economic performance is largely in line with prior findings on support for European integration.

The model also shows that membership experience contributes positively to trust in European institutions. Results even suggest that there is a trade-off in trust between the national and European level. This interpretation, however, can be made only with strong assumptions. Theoretically, it is not reasonable to think of trust in different political objects as a zero-sum game. The basic and strong assumption to be made relates to Scharpf's consideration of a double democratic deficit. This is only plausible if citizens believe that the nation state's capacity for problem solving suffers from European integration and an increasing authority at the European level.

The development after enlargement shows that this does not necessarily happen. After 2004, trust in national parliaments increased somewhat, whereas trust in national governments increased tremendously. Still, in the same period trust in European institutions increased as well. This (partial) revival of trust in national institutions is probably a result of the 'institutional stress' caused by two events: enlargement and the discussion about the European Constitution. However, the test of a micro-level model proves that utilitarian considerations still contribute to trust after enlargement.

Nevertheless, heterogeneity within the EU has increased tremendously due to enlargement, and the development of trust between the European elections of 2004 and May 2006 indicates that differences between new and old member states are even on the rise. With this growing heterogeneity, it seems quite likely that the mechanisms for generating trust will also become more heterogeneous. New factors may gain in importance, or known factors may change relevance. The performance-driven basis for trust may be complemented or contradicted by cultural and identity questions, with nationalism overriding rationalism. This increased heterogeneity is challenging the progress of European integration. The conflict between the new member Poland and the old members at the EU summit meeting in June 2007 demonstrated this. Fears and hopes about European integration and its consequences have to find a new balance—in the old as well as in the new member states. The 'revival' of trust in the nation state is not so much related to the performance of nation-state actors, but is rather a reflection of the developments at the European level. Perceived risks and fears may change the mechanisms of generating trust and support in the future, and this may increase the relevance of political – in contrast to instrumental – considerations.

Note

1. In order to check for country-level effects, fixed effect models have also been estimated, showing basically the same results with regard to the direction of effects, but making most estimates statistically insignificant. This is due to the relation of the relatively high number of variables (19) and low number of cases (132) in such a fixed effect model. In order to check the reliability of the results, homogeneity of variance tests and tests of the significance of paired country comparisons have been performed with the estimated values of the random effect model. Tests show that the assumption of homogeneity of variance across countries is not violated and that only about 10 per cent of the paired comparisons show a significant difference between countries at a 5 per cent level. These significant country differences are not systematic or patterned. Thus, the results of the random effect model can be regarded as reliable.

9

European Citizenship and Identity after Enlargement

Jacques Thomassen and Hanna Bäck

9.1. Introduction

In this chapter we focus on the first dimension of legitimacy distinguished in Chapter 1, the dimension of identity and citizenship, from the perspective of the citizens themselves. Thus, the aim of this chapter is to try to assess the effect of the 2004 enlargement on the legitimacy of the European Union (EU) with regard to the dimension of identity.

For this purpose we should first clarify what we mean by a European demos and a European identity. It is beyond dispute that the very idea of democracy, and of people's sovereignty, presupposes the existence of a people, a *demos*. What is disputed is what 'the people' really means. A basic issue is whether 'the people' is a more or less legal construct, in the sense of all people who are subject to the jurisdiction of a particular polity, or whether the notion of 'the people' is based on a more sociological, or even ethnic concept, which stresses the subjective affiliation of the people with a community as a prerequisite for the constitution of a *demos* as a collective actor. These different interpretations lead to different conclusions with regard to the feasibility of European democracy and possibly to different conclusions with regard to the effects of the 2004 enlargement.

In the next section, we present a short summary of this debate. We make a distinction between people's identification with a political community or *sense of citizenship* and their *sense of communal identity*. The latter might enhance the former but the two concepts are not identical. In section three we develop an operationalization of these two concepts and discuss some potential problems with answering our research question. In section four we present an analysis of the degree to which people across the EU have developed an identification both with the EU as a political community and with the Union as a social community, focusing on the effect of the 2004 enlargement on this development.

9.2. European identity and European citizenship

Different views on the feasibility of a legitimate democratic system at the level of the EU are partly due to different historical views on the relationship between citizenship and nationhood. According to nineteenth century German philosophers like Fichte and Herder (Bruter 2003), nations are based on a common culture, in particular a common language. Part of the literature on the feasibility of a legitimate European democratic political system reflects the view that the establishment of a legitimate democracy requires the pre-existence of a collective identity. According to Graf Kielmansegg (1993), for example, the concepts of *demos* (*'Volk'*), community (*'Gemeinschaft'*), and nation are almost identical. Once one accepts this view, the verdict on the feasibility of a European democracy is obvious. A democratic constitution in itself cannot establish a legitimate European democracy. As long as there is no European community, every attempt to establish a democratic Europe is bound to fail. The EU is far from being a community with a common identity. The European people do not share a common language; they lack memories of a common history that might help to develop a collective identity; and they do not take part in a common 'European' public sphere (*'Oeffentlichkeit'*, Kielmansegg 1993). In a similar vein, Scharpf (1999) argues that the democratic principle of majority rule will only be accepted in polities with a 'thick' collective identity, that is, in polities based on pre-existing commonalities of history, language, culture, and ethnicity. Because such a collective identity does not exist at the level of the Union, input-oriented legitimacy is out of reach for the EU for the foreseeable future:

Given the historical, linguistic, cultural, ethnic and institutional diversity of its member states, there is no question that the Union is very far from having achieved the 'thick' collective identity that we have come to take for granted in national democracies – and in its absence, institutional reforms will not greatly increase the input-oriented legitimacy of decisions taken by majority rule (Scharpf 1999).

According to this view, input-oriented legitimacy requires a pre-existing collective identity. This same philosophy is reflected in the famous decision of the German Federal Constitutional Court on the compatibility of the Maastricht Treaty with the German Basic Law (BVerfGE 89, 155 – Maastricht). According to this decision, as no European *demos* has developed yet, democracy cannot be exclusively grounded at the European level (Shaw 1997: 35).

However, the argument that a *demos* and citizenship require the pre-existence of a community with a collective or national identity is anything but generally accepted. An alternative view allows for the possibility that European citizenship need not be the political projection of a collective European identity, but can essentially be regarded as a purely legal construct: 'Citizenship should be the ultimate basis of legitimation for institution-building, not ambiguous cultural identities' (Delanty 1995: 163). This seems to be consistent with the history of many nation states. The argument that a shared common identity, a *demos* in the ethno-cultural sense, should precede the constitution of a *demos*, in the sense of a community of citizens sharing the rights and duties of citizenship, has little ground in history. In many European countries the formation of the state preceded the development of the nation (Fuchs 2000: 230).

This view is shared by David Easton. First, he makes a clear distinction between a *sense of social community* and a *sense of political community*. The sense of *social* community is an indication of the cohesiveness of *society*. The sense of *political* community 'indicates political cohesion of a group of persons [...] the feeling of belonging together as a group which, because it shares a political structure, also shares a political fate' (Easton 1965a: 185). But in Easton's view even a sense of political community is not a prerequisite for a feasible political system:

> [...] [T]his approach does not compel us to postulate that before a political system can exist or even if is to persist, a sense of political community must first rise to some specified level. Although we may adopt the degree of mutual identification as one kind of measure of the input of support for the political community, it is conceivable that for considerable periods of time, the sense of political community may be low or non-existent. [...] It is possible for a political structure to bind a group together before feelings of mutual identification have emerged. We may go further. Frequently the imposition of a common division of political labor has itself made possible the slow growth of sentiments of political solidarity; this reverses normal expectations of the significance of sentiments of solidarity as a pre-condition for the emergence of a political community. A political community may precede and become a condition for the growth of a sense of community (Easton 1965a: 185–6).

While this view explicitly accepts the reciprocal reinforcement of ideas of community and the practice of citizenship, it reverses the causal sequence. In line with this view one may well argue that the constitution of a

European democratic polity and the establishment of a European citizenship by the Maastricht Treaty ['Every person holding the nationality of a Member State shall be a citizen of the Union' (Article 8.1)], is a prerequisite for the development of a European identity. To borrow a phrase from O'Leary: European citizenship may be regarded as an 'evolving concept': starting from the free movement of persons, through its legal formalization, to a full-fledged identity (O'Leary 1996).

However, the argument that the *demos* need not be defined in terms of an exclusive identification of the people with a cultural or social community does not imply that there is no empirical relationship between the two, or that this relationship would be unidirectional. It is generally recognized that the feasibility and stability of a democratic political system are related to its political culture. Notwithstanding a formal definition of a *demos*, a democratic community undoubtedly benefits from citizens identifying themselves with the *demos* as a collective entity and with other members of this *demos* (Fuchs 2000: 219). But the essential thing is that the identification with a European *political* community is not the same thing and might take priority over a cultural identification with a European collective community (Habermas 1994).

Different positions taken in this essentially normative debate can have far reaching implications for the further process of European integration, as the verdict of the German Constitutional Court on the Treaty of Maastricht proves. However, the two different views on the meaning of a European *demos* and their mutual relationship have empirical implications as well. The main empirical component of this debate refers to the relationship between the sense of community and the sense of citizenship, and in particular to the causal sequence of this relationship. Does the development of a sense of citizenship depend on the pre-existence of a sense of community, or can it develop despite a lack of a sense of community and can it in turn be instrumental in the development of feelings of community? In this chapter we try to answer these questions empirically, and we now turn to discussing our data and methods.

9.3. Conceptualizations, operationalizations, and methods

9.3.1. *Conceptualizations*

The argument in the previous section implies that social, cultural or national identity should conceptually be clearly distinguished from the concept of citizenship. McCrone and Kiely (2000: 25) define the difference as follows: 'nationality and citizenship actually belong to different spheres of meaning and activity. The former is in essence a cultural concept which binds people on the basis of shared identity – in Benedict Anderson's apt phrase as an "imagined community" – while citizenship is a political concept deriving from people's relationship to the state. In other words, nation-ness and state-ness need not be, and increasingly are not, aligned.' Citizenship is usually conceptualised as a package of rights and duties bestowed on individuals by the state. Marshall (1950) described citizenship as 'a status bestowed on those who are full members of a community. All who possess the status are equal with respect to rights and duties with which the status is endowed'.

In a more or less similar way,[1] Bruter (2003) makes a distinction between the *civic* and *cultural* component of a European political identity. The European *civic identity* of people can be understood as the degree to which they see themselves as citizens of a European political system, whose rules, laws, and rights have an influence on their daily life, whereas *cultural identity* refers to citizens' identification with their political system as an institutional frame, that is, their state. Civic identifiers will identify with European integration as a political project whether or not they feel a sense of commonality *a priori* with the citizens of the Union. In Bruter's conceptual framework the 'European cultural identity of citizens is best described as individuals' perceptions that fellow Europeans are closer to them than non-Europeans. That means that cultural identity refers to their identification with their political community as a human group, regardless of the nature of the political system' (Bruter 2003: 155–6).

In our conceptualization of the *sense of citizenship*, we try to stay as close as possible to Marshall's definition. In our view, the concept of European citizenship implies that European citizens are prepared to accept that all citizens of the (enlarged) Union are entitled to all rights that come with the citizenship of the Union. Examples of these rights are the rights of free movement and residence, voting rights in municipal elections, diplomatic protection, and the right of appeal to EU institutions. The willingness of citizens across the Union to accept these rights as applying equally to the citizens of each and every member state is a first indicator of a sense of European citizenship. A second indicator of European citizenship is the extent to which people *consider* themselves as citizens of the EU, in addition to, not necessarily instead of, considering themselves as citizens of their country. Our indicator of the cultural or social component of identity is based on the *sense of community* as originally developed by Deutsch et al.

(1957). It is defined as 'a matter of mutual sympathy and loyalties; of "we-feeling", trust and mutual consideration; of partial identification in terms of self-images and interests; of mutually successful predictions of behaviour, and of cooperative action in accordance with it' (Deutsch et al. 1957; also see Niedermayer 1995; Scheuer 1995; Sinnott 1995).

9.3.2. Operationalizations

In the European Election Study 2004, which was conducted in twenty-four of the twenty-five member states immediately after the elections for the European Parliament in June 2004, a number of questions were included asking to what extent people across Europe are willing to accept citizens from other EU countries as fellow European citizens, entitled to all the rights coming with European citizenship. In this paper we analyse three statements about citizenship rights, all asking on a four-point scale (strongly agree to strongly disagree), whether the respondent agrees with the statement: 'Please indicate how strongly you agree or disagree with the following three statements. When jobs are scarce, employers should give priority to [COUNTRY] people over citizens from other EU member-countries who want to work here.'; 'Citizens from other EU member-countries who live in [COUNTRY] should be entitled to vote in local elections.'; 'Citizens from other EU member-countries who live in [COUNTRY] should not be entitled to social security or unemployment benefits.'

To measure the respondents' sense of European citizenship we make use of two questions in the EES survey. First, we use the question, 'Do you ever think of yourself not only as an [COUNTRY] citizen, but also as a citizen of the European Union?'. Here the response categories are, 'often', 'sometimes', and 'never'. Second, we use the question, 'Are you personally proud or not to be a citizen of the European Union?', where the response categories are, 'very proud', 'fairly proud', 'not very proud', and 'not at all proud'.

The *sense of community* as introduced by Deutsch has several components. Because of the limited space in the EES questionnaire the operationalization had to be limited to only one of these components, *mutual trust*. This is an important component as it can be considered as a measurement of European social capital. This aspect of the sense of community is measured by the following question: 'Now I would like to ask you a question about how much trust you have in people from various countries. Let's start with the Austrians: do you trust them a lot or not very much? And the Belgians?' This question was then repeated for the people of twenty-eight countries in total, including the Bulgarians, the

Romanians and the Turks, in addition to the people of the then twenty-five member states.

9.3.3. *Methodological considerations*

As mentioned above, the main empirical component of the debate on European identity and citizenship summarized in section 2 refers to the causal sequence of the relationship between the sense of community and the sense of citizenship. Establishing the causal sequence between these two phenomena is not easy. At a single point in time we can establish the correlation between them, but we can never give a definite answer to the question of the direction of causality. Even the access to panel data would not solve the problem. Feelings of citizenship can be assumed to belong to the category of basic attitudes that will not easily change during people's lifetime. Basic attitudes and values are mainly developed during people's adolescence and tend to be persistent during their lifetime (see a.o. Inglehart 1977). As far as changes at the level of society as a whole occur, they are most likely due to generation replacement. The assessment of such a process requires the availability of comparable data over a long period of time. As we will see, that requirement is met – at least to some extent – for one of the variables in the equation, the sense of European citizenship, but not for the sense of community.

What we can do is test the validity of the argument on one side of the debate: the question of to what extent formal European citizenship breeds both feelings of citizenship and a sense of community? There are two ways of doing this. Where a longer time series on feelings of citizenship is available, we can test the hypothesis that feelings of citizenship will gradually increase with the length of membership. Of course, such a longer time series is only available for older member states. In case only cross-sectional data are available, a positive relationship between the length of membership of a country and the feelings of citizenship and community of its citizens can be interpreted as evidence in support of the hypothesis. The more specific question we address is to what extent the 2004 enlargement had an effect on the development of feelings of European citizenship and community? Such an effect might occur either because the enlargement had an effect on these feelings among the citizens of the older member states and/or because the citizens of the new member states had different feelings than their counterparts in the older member states. In the next section we empirically assess to what extent membership does indeed breed feelings of citizenship and a sense of community, as indicated by feelings of mutual trust.

9.4. An empirical analysis of citizenship and trust

9.4.1. *Sense of citizenship*

Above, two sets of survey questions on citizenship were introduced, three on people's recognition of the citizen rights of their fellow European citizens, and two on people's self orientation as a European citizen. In order to see to what extent the conceptual difference between these two sets of attitudes corresponds with the way people's attitudes are constrained in reality, we first computed the correlations between these items and then explored their scalability. The correlation coefficients are presented in Table 9.1. The mutual correlations between the three items on citizen rights are quite low, ranging between .16 and .20. Not surprisingly, the scalability of the items is also low.[2] The correlation between the two self-orientations is much higher (.56). Because of the low mutual correlations between the first set of items we do not attempt to scale them. Instead we present our findings for each item separately.

In Table 9.2 a simple descriptive analysis of the variables on citizenship is presented for each country. For this purpose the five variables were dichotomised; and here only the pro-European answers are presented. The countries are grouped in order of their admission. A summary measure for each group of countries is also presented.

The percentages in the first column of Table 9.2 leave little doubt about people's attitudes towards a free labour market. In all member states except Germany and Denmark, a majority is against it – in some countries this majority is even close to 100 per cent. There is a clear difference though between the older member states in North-Western Europe and the new member states in Central and Eastern Europe. All six founding member states are among the ten most liberal countries of the enlarged Union. Therefore, it is tempting to attribute this difference to the longer process of socialization into the idea of a European political community that the people of these countries have been subjected to. However, since Austria,

Table 9.1. Correlations between items on citizenship

Q17: Employment – priority to citizens of [country]				
Q18: Citizens of EU countries entitled to vote in local elections	−.17			
Q19: Citizens of EU countries entitled to social benefits	.19	−.20		
Q23: Not only [country] citizen, but also European citizen	−.21	.19	−.14	
Q24: Proud of EU citizenship	−.16	.20	−.13	.56
	Q17	Q18	Q19	Q23

Note: All coefficients are significant at the .01 level (two-tailed).

The Legitimacy of the European Union after Enlargement

Table 9.2. Attitudes on European citizenship (per cent pro-European)

Country	European citizenship				
	Labour market	Elections	Social benefits	European citizen	Proud to be European citizen
Belgium	34		57	67	62
France	48	60	66	73	75
Germany	54	60	75	61	54
Italy	31	60	81	78	76
Luxembourg	31	63	82	70	79
Netherlands	28	59	72	49	29
Original six	38	60	72	66	63
Britain	43	61	55	40	47
Northern Ireland	25	33	43	36	32
Ireland	26	71	61	69	76
Denmark	51	63	62	57	54
1973 enlargement	40	65	59	55	59
Greece	18	60	68	75	63
Portugal	27	70	69	79	77
Spain	19	74	76	59	77
1980s enlargement	21	68	71	71	72
Austria	37	62	65	56	41
Finland	20	64	70	66	38
Sweden	30		49		38
1990s enlargement	29	61	61	61	39
Cyprus	9	46	81	84	77
Czech Republic	9	48	48	46	36
Estonia	16	47	58	46	28
Hungary	5	40	41	24	59
Latvia	11	37	53	42	26
Poland	10	79	71	53	54
Slovakia	8	63	59	51	46
Slovenia	15	55	63	60	46
2004 enlargement	11	53	56	46	42

Note: The percentages for the summary measures for each group are the unweighted averages of the country percentages.

For the 1973 enlargement, Northern Ireland was excluded because otherwise its weight compared to Britain would have been too high. For the 2004 enlargement, Cyprus was excluded to avoid giving it too much weight in the summary measure.

Britain, Denmark, and Sweden are also part of this group of ten, this interpretation is disputable. The more positive attitudes in these countries might just as well be due to a longer tradition in liberal democracy with its self-evident value of equality for all citizens. But an equally plausible explanation is that the differences are due to differences in economic development.

It is remarkable that despite the fact that 'Polish plumbers' have become proverbial for the fear that after enlargement Western Europe will be flooded by cheap labourers from Central and Eastern Europe, this fear is not reflected in these figures. It is not the people in Western Europe, but those in Central and Eastern Europe that are most inclined to reject a free labour market. On average not more than 11 per cent of the people from these countries are willing to accept this. It is not unlikely that a general feeling of being economically behind Western Europe is responsible for this more negative attitude. Compared to the attitudes on an open labour market, a surprisingly large number of Europeans accept the entitlement of people from other EU countries to national social security and unemployment benefits. The length of membership does not really make a difference. Also, the right to vote in local elections is accepted by a clear majority of the people across Europe.

The percentage of people who see themselves, at least sometimes, as European citizens, in addition to being citizens of their own country is on average above 50 per cent. Also, in just above half of the countries a majority of the people are proud to be a citizen of the EU. However, for both questions there is a huge variation across countries. There does not seem to be much of a pattern in the extent to which people across Europe differ in their reaction to either question, at least not if we try to interpret the existing differences in terms of the length of membership of people's home country. In general, the people from the new member states in Central and Eastern Europe are less inclined to see themselves as European citizens, or to be proud of being citizens of the Union, than people in the older member states, but this is not a uniform pattern. The differences between some of the founding member states (the Netherlands and Luxembourg, for instance) are as large as between any other pair of countries. In particular the percentage in the Netherlands on the second question is strikingly low.

Summarizing, these cross-sectional data do not clearly support the hypothesis that formal citizenship breeds feelings of citizenship. The Eastern enlargement does not seem to have contributed to the development of a European political community. On all variables but one (proud to be a European citizen), this group has the lowest score of all successive enlargement groups. The question is whether this result holds when we study citizenship across time.

Only on the question of whether people consider themselves as European citizens (in addition to being a citizen of their country) is a longer time series available. In the Eurobarometer, a question asking whether the respondent feels like a citizen of the EU (besides feeling like a citizen of their own country) has frequently been asked since 1984.[3] In Figure 9.1 the trend of the answers to this question is shown separately for each of the successive enlargements. The graphs present the percentage of people in a country in a given year saying that they often or sometimes feel like they are citizens of the EU.

The Legitimacy of the European Union after Enlargement

What is most striking in this figure is the clear difference between the groups of countries that joined the Union in the successive enlargements. The percentage of people willing to think of themselves as European citizens is highest in the original six member states. This is what we should expect if the sense of citizenship, or the sense of political community, is a function of the length of membership, that is, if formal membership breeds a sense of citizenship. However, we should then also expect that the sense of citizenship in new member states would gradually increase and move towards the level of the older member states. This, however, is not the case. There are no linear trends towards an ever higher level of citizenship, but only fluctuations that affect the several groups of countries to more or less the same extent. As a consequence, the differences between these groups of countries are not becoming smaller over time. On the contrary, they seem to become even larger. The first enlargement in 1973 brought in three new member states, two of which (Britain and Denmark) were exceptionally eurosceptic and have remained so ever since. Only since the turn of the century have they seemed to move somewhat in a more positive direction, but because this is a general turn, the differences remain at least as large as

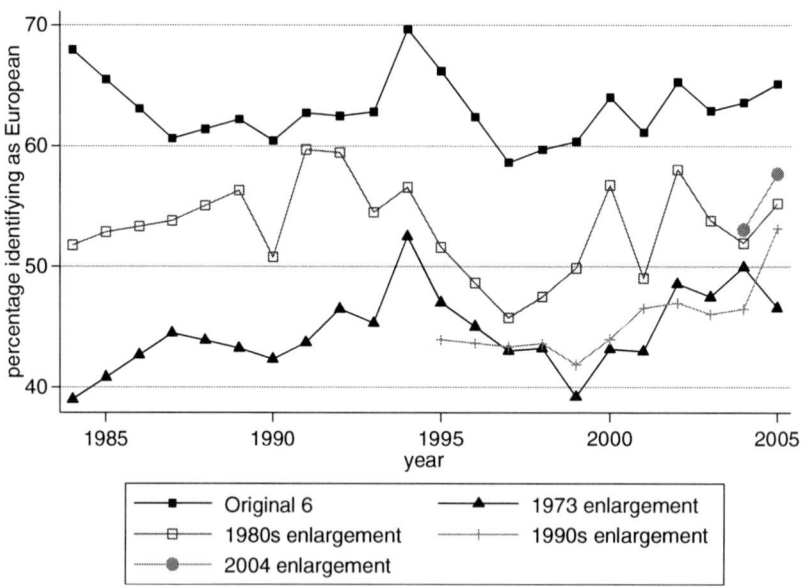

Figure 9.1. Successive enlargements and feelings of European citizenship

they were. The southern enlargement countries entered the Union with on average a much higher level, at about the same level as the original six, and remained close to them ever since.

The general conclusion suggested by these findings is that feelings of being part of a European political community have historical roots and are hardly affected by the duration of membership. Therefore, admitting new member states with a eurosceptic citizenry might have a persisting effect on the development of a European political community.

In order to fully investigate whether EU membership affects the sense of European citizenship, we have also performed a multivariate analysis, where we control for a number of factors that vary across time and across countries. The dependent variable used in this analysis measures the percentage of people in a country in a given year saying that they often or sometimes feel like they are citizens of the EU (until 1992) or see themselves as at least partly European (after 1992). Covering all of the EU25 countries over the period 1984–2005 (but only during the time that the countries have been members) gives us a dataset of over 300 country-year cases. The main independent variable in our analysis is a variable measuring the number of membership years that a country has experienced at a specific point in time.[4] The other independent variables are taken from different data sources and describe the economic situation in a country at the same point in time.[5] The results from this analysis are presented in Table 9.3.

Model 1 presented in Table 9.3 shows that when we only include the variable measuring EU membership years, this variable exerts a significant and positive effect. This gives some support to the hypothesis that the duration of membership increases the sense of European citizenship. In Model 2 the control variables measuring the economic situation in the country are included, in order to gauge whether the effect of membership years is a spurious correlation, created by the fact that economically advanced countries are more likely to be in the EU and citizens of these countries are also more likely to identify themselves as European citizens. Even when these variables are included, we see a positive and significant effect of the length of membership. Thus, we so far find support for the membership hypothesis.

However, in these models we cannot separate the effect of entering the EU at a specific point in time and the continuous effect of being an EU member. Therefore, we include a set of country dummies in Model 3, that is, we perform a country fixed effects regression, focusing only on the variation across time.[6] In this model, length of membership no longer exerts a significant effect on sense of European citizenship. Thus, the effect of length of

Table 9.3. Regression analysis with European identity as dependent variable

	Percentage sometimes/often identifying as European		
	(1) Bivariate	(2) Multivariate	(3) Country-fixed effects
Membership years	0.003** (0.001)	0.004*** (0.001)	0.001 (0.002)
Net EU transfers	—	−0.665 (0.269)	0.728 (0.457)
GDP per capita (logged)	—	0.002 (0.020)	−0.041 (0.042)
Growth	—	0.000 (0.002)	−0.003 (0.002)
Inflation	—	0.006*** (0.002)	0.001 (0.002)
Unemployment	—	0.004** (0.002)	−0.007*** (0.002)
EU trade	—	0.356*** (0.069)	0.052 (0.112)
Number of observations	313	313	313
Number of countries	25	25	25
Adjusted (overall R^2)	0.206	0.262	0.699 (0.052)

Note: Significant at ** the .05 level, *** the .01 level. Entries are unstandardized regression coefficients with standard errors in parentheses (panel corrected standard errors obtained using STATA:s xtpcse command). Fixed effects regression results obtained using STATA:s xtreg, fe option.

membership (in Models 1 and 2) is probably explained by the fact that early entry into the Union gave a country's citizens a high identification with the EU, whereas the level of identity does not seem to increase continuously with the number of years that a country has been a member.[7] Therefore, we find no convincing evidence in support of the hypothesis that formal citizenship breeds feelings of citizenship. Since the 2004 enlargement brought in a number of countries with a low sense of citizenship, this might have a lasting effect on the development of citizenship in the Union.

9.4.2. Sense of community – mutual trust

As we observed above, mutual trust is one of the main components of Deutsch's concept of a sense of community. A sense of European community can only exist if the people of the EU evaluate each other positively, that is, if they trust each other. The level of trust flowing within the European community is a good indicator of how integrated this community of a still increasing number of national citizenries potentially is (Delhey 2005). Again, we are particularly interested in the question of to what extent the 2004 enlargement affects the mutual trust among the peoples of the Union.

Previous research shows that it is highly unlikely that people from older member states will immediately embrace the people from the 2004 accession countries. In the 1994 European Election Study people from the then-fifteen member states were asked whether they would welcome each of a number of countries as new member states of the EU. Whereas countries like Switzerland and Norway would have been most welcome, most can-

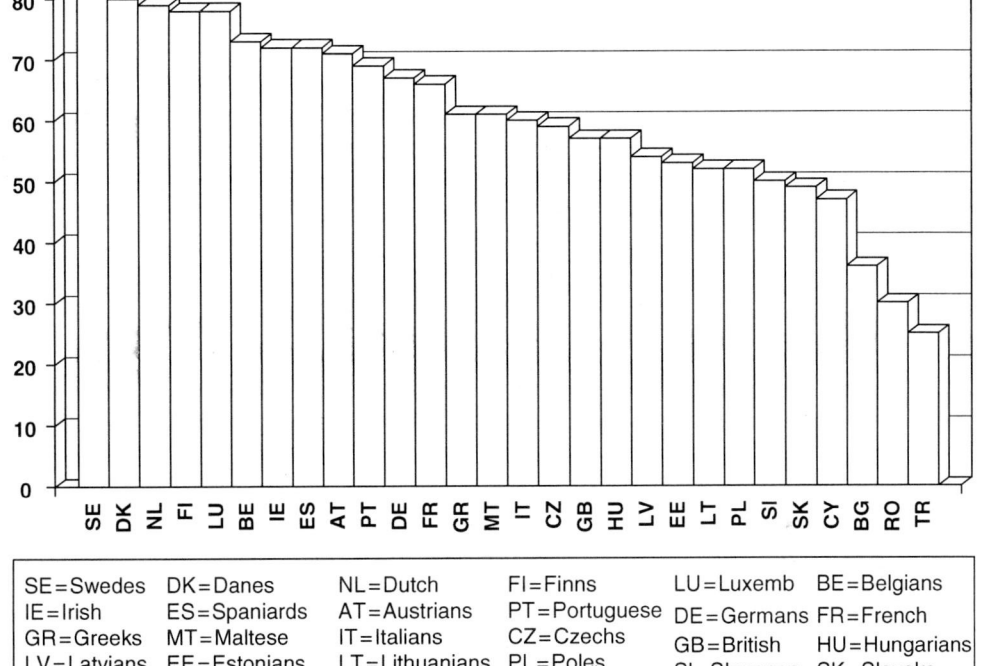

Figure 9.2. Trust in other peoples

didate member states in Central and Eastern Europe, let alone Turkey, were not. These countries were hardly, or not at all, part of the 'mental map of Europe' of the people of the, at that point, mostly West European Union (Scheuer 1995: 41). Therefore, we expect that the recent enlargement will have a negative effect on the sense of community in the EU as a whole.

In Figure 9.2 countries are ordered according to the level of trust people across Europe have in the people of these countries. The figure contains one very clear message. The further East we move in Europe, the less peoples are trusted by their fellow Europeans. The left part of the figure is occupied by West European countries. In particular, the people from the Nordic and BeNeLux countries are highly trusted. All of them are relatively small countries. Among the older member states the Italians and British are least trusted. With the exception of the Maltese, the people of all new member states are found in the right tail of the figure. But the very tail of the figure is occupied by the people from the then-candidate countries Bulgaria and Romania, and from Turkey. Trust in the people from these countries is very low. The figure clearly indicates that the 2004 enlargement had a negative impact on the level of integration of the Union by admitting countries whose people are far less trusted than the people from the older member states. Why this is the case is not immediately clear. Is it because these countries have only just entered the Union, because of their weak economy, or for the simple reason that from the perspective of Western Europe they are far(ther) away and unknown?

Our main research question is to what extent membership breeds trust. The answer to that question is highly relevant for the future development of European integration. If it does, the present low level of trust in the people from the new member states might be a temporary phenomenon that will gradually disappear. In Table 9.4, we show the level of trust among different member states, grouping the states according to length of membership. The table is asymmetric because people in EU countries were asked to what extent they trust the Bulgarians, the Romanians, and the Turks, but not the other way around as no survey was conducted in these three countries.

Apart from the clear difference between the newcomers and the older member states, the length of membership does not seem to explain very much. If social integration were an effect of EU membership, of the existence of a European polity, we should expect to find the highest levels of mutual trust among the people from the six founding member states. This, however, is not the case. Although trust among them is relatively high (80 per cent), it is somewhat lower than the trust people from these countries have in the people from Austria, Finland, and Sweden, countries that did not join the Union until the 1990s. Therefore, any attempt to explain these differences in trust in terms of a clear distinction between those who belong or do not belong to the political community of the EU is disputable.

The data in Table 9.4 are from a single point in time. Longitudinal data seem to suggest that membership does indeed breed community. Delhey (2005) observes that in the early 1970s mutual trust between the people from the then-six member states was at about the same level as the present trust in the people from the Eastern enlargement countries. Also, the mutual trust between the people of EU countries substantially increased during the 1970s and 1980s, but fell back somewhat in the early 1990s (Niedermayer 1995; Scheuer 1995). In particular, trust in the people from the countries of the second enlargement (Greece, Portugal and Spain) increased during this period. This again suggests that the establishment of common political institutions does indeed enhance a sense of commu-

European Citizenship and Identity after Enlargement

nity as was suggested by, among others, David Easton. But this does not necessarily mean that history will repeat itself. The figures in Table 9.4 clearly demonstrate that there is no linear relationship between length of membership and mutual trust. As the Nordic enlargement indicates, other factors like geographical and cultural proximity seem to be at least as important. And because the EU gradually spread over the European continent, it is difficult to disentangle the effects of membership from other factors like geographic proximity.

In Table 9.5 countries are classified according to their geographic location. The reason to do so is that insofar as mutual trust is mainly based on familiarity and a common culture, geographic vicinity is a proxy for familiarity and a certain commonality of cultural traditions. We have grouped together the original six minus Italy but including Austria, Britain, and Ireland (Western Europe); the Nordic countries (Denmark, Sweden, and Finland); the Southern European countries (Greece, Portugal, Italy, and Spain); the new member states in Central Europe; and the Baltic states.[8] These results show that geographic proximity seems to be related to trust.[9] In particular, the countries in the North-West form a community of countries where mutual trust is very high. Mutual trust between these countries and the Southern European countries is somewhat lower but still clearly on the positive side. But as we observed above, the relationship between the people of the 'old' EU and the people from the new member states is a totally different story.

Table 9.4. Levels of trust by admission year

	Original six	1973 Enlargement	1980s Enlargement	1990s Enlargement	2004 Enlargement	Bulgaria and Romania	Turkey
Original six[a]	77.74	72.46	75.89	83.56	51.73	29.28	24.02
1973[b] Enlargement	74.22	75.92	68.45	84.17	50.74	35.35	28.05
1980s Enlargement	65.54	56.71	64.47	66.94	45.27	33.97	22.2
1990s Enlargement[c]	74.74	77.57	70.45	85.92	57.24	30.8	28.7
2004[d] Enlargement	62.46	64.84	64.13	67.38	52.62	34.02	23.11

Note:
[a] Question not asked in Belgium.
[b] Question not asked in Great Britain.
[c] Question not asked in Sweden.
[d] Question not asked in Malta and Lithuania.

Table 9.5. Levels of trust by geographic location

	Western Europe	Nordic countries	Southern Europe	Central Europe[d]	Baltic States	Bulgaria and Romania	Turkey
Western Europe[a]	75.05	86.32	71.56	50.87	55.57	31.65	26.75
Nordic countries[b]	84.06	93.72	67.31	56.85	55.22	37.03	30.65
Southern Europe	62.95	71.81	64.57	43.87	40.42	29.16	19.6
Central Europe	65.88	75.25	65.38[d]	62.21	49.38	43.07	28.96
Baltic[c] States	63.37	73.56	43.55	46.38	73.75	35.12	18.2

Note:
[a] Question not asked in Belgium and Great Britain.
[b] Question not asked in Sweden.
[c] Question not asked in Lithuania.
[d] Hungarians did not rate the Portuguese.

As most possible explanatory factors of these varying levels of trust, such as length of membership, geographic vicinity, and cultural similarity, are highly correlated, it is difficult to disentangle their separate effects. Delhey (2005) found that trust between nations is not significantly related to either length of membership or spatial distance, if other determinants are controlled for, especially cultural similarity. The most important determinant of trust that comes out of his analysis is the degree of modernity of the rated nationality, followed by cultural affinity and perceived threat (as indicated by the size of the country: larger countries form a threat for their smaller neighbours). In order to fully test our main hypothesis, that common membership years breed trust, we replicate Delhey's analysis on data from the 2004 European Election Study. For his analysis of 1997 Eurobarometer data, Delhey constructed a dataset where a unit is each nationality's rating of the trustworthiness of each of the other nationalities, that is, a dataset where country-dyads are the units of analysis. Following the same approach, we constructed a dataset consisting of country-dyads where citizens of most of the EU25 states indicate how much trust they have in citizens of other member states.[10] The trust variable we use as dependent variable measures the proportion of individuals in the 2004 European Election Study stating that they have a lot of trust in the people from a specific country.

Our main independent variable describes how many years the rating and the rated nation have simultaneously been members of the EU. We also include a number of other variables describing the relationship between the rated and the rating nationality. More specifically, we measure the distance between the countries' capitals, whether the people of both countries belong to the same family of religions and the same family of languages, and whether the two countries were allies in World War II.

We also measure some features describing the economic and political situation of the rated and the rating nationality (GDP per capita, level of inequality, quality of government, e.g. corruption, and level of democracy). The idea is to control for as many features as possible that could account for a potential correlation between common membership years and mutual trust.[11]

In Models 1, 2, and 3 in Table 9.6, we present the results from a bivariate regression with common membership years as the independent variable, and two multivariate regressions controlling for features describing the relationship between the truster and the trusted nationality and features of the rated nationality. In all three models, the length of membership exerts a positive effect, giving support to the hypothesis that the longer countries have been members of the EU, the more likely they are to trust each other. Several other variables also exert significant effects on the level of interpersonal trust, for example, countries located far away from each other display a lower level of trust between their citizens, people belonging to the same language family trust each other more, and people from countries with a higher quality of government and higher levels of democracy are trusted more.

In Model 4 we also include a number of features of the rating nationality, such as the GDP per capita and quality of government. The reason for including these features in our model is that such characteristics of the rating country may influence the ratings indirectly through the general trust level among its citizens (Delhey and Newton 2005). Some people may simply be more trusting than others, and we need to control for this in order to be sure that the apparent effect of EU membership years is not a result of the fact that early EU members are more trusting in general. Another way to control for this is of course to gauge the general trust level in the rating country, which we do in Model 5 by including a measure of general trust based on a question in the World Values Survey asking respondents to state to what extent they believe that most people can be trusted.[12]

In both of these latter models, we find that a high number of common membership years positively affects the level of interpersonal trust.[13] But it is also clear that mutual trust does not only depend on the experience of common membership. Other factors like cultural distance, economic development, and the quality of democratic institutions are important as well. None of these factors is immune to change and all of them are probably positively affected by EU membership. Therefore, as much as the collective identity of the people across the EU, as measured by mutual

Table 9.6. Regression analysis with trust as dependent variable, 474 country-dyads

	Percentage having a lot of trust				
	(1)	(2)	(3)	(4)	(5)
Relationship features					
Common years of EU membership	0.667*** (0.054)	0.509*** (0.052)	0.355*** (0.053)	0.437*** (0.054)	0.322*** (0.054)
Distance between capitals (km)	—	−0.004*** (0.001)	−0.004*** (0.001)	−0.001 (0.001)	−0.004*** (0.001)
Same family of religions	—	10.457*** (1.662)	1.475*** (1.733)	−2.286 (1.618)	1.015 (1.731)
Same family of languages	—	7.817*** (1.977)	7.682*** (1.771)	7.523*** (1.539)	7.598*** (1.759)
Allies in WWII	—	1.775 (1.649)	0.456 (1.477)	2.680** (1.306)	0.707 (1.470)
Features of the rated nationality					
GDP/Capita ($1,000)	—	—	−0.091 (0.115)	−0.096 (0.101)	−0.000 (0.000)
Level of inequality (Gini)	—	—	0.278* (0.148)	0.031 (0.132)	0.293** (0.147)
Quality of government (ICRG)	—	—	4.603*** (0.691)	4.641*** (0.601)	4.663*** (0.687)
Level of democracy (Polity/FH)	—	—	5.160*** (1.506)	6.356*** (1.317)	5.358*** (1.498)
Features of the rating nationality					
GDP/Capita	—	—	—	0.416*** (0.090)	—
Level of inequality (Gini)	—	—	—	−1.446*** (0.145)	—
Quality of government (ICRG)	—	—	—	−0.425 (0.592)	—
Level of democracy (Polity/FH)	—	—	—	−5.025* (2.679)	—
General trust level (WVS)	—	—	—	—	11.349*** (4.242)
Number of dyads	474	474	474	474	474
Adjusted R2	0.247	0.374	0.502	0.628	0.508

Note: Significant at * the .10 level, ** the .05 level, *** the .01 level. Entries are unstandardized regression coefficients with standard errors in parentheses.
Abbreviations: GDP/capita = Gross Domestic Product per capita, USD = US dollars, Gini = Gini coefficient, measure of inequality of income distribution, ICRG = International Country Risk Guide, Polity/FH = Measure of the level of democracy created as an average of the Polity and Freedom House indexes, WVS = World Values Survey.

trust, was negatively affected by the 2004 enlargement, this effect will not necessarily last.

9.5. In conclusion

In this chapter we distinguished two rival theories on the relationship between European citizenship in the sense of a legal construct on the one hand, and a European collective identity on the other hand. According to the first theory, a collective identity is a necessary condition for the development of a legitimate European political community. The second theory claims that there is indeed an empirical relationship between these two concepts, but the causal sequence is not necessarily unidirectional. Once a political community is established it can breed a sense of community.

In order to test the relative empirical validity of these theories, we operationalized the concepts *sense of citizenship* and *sense of community*. Unfortunately, the data available makes it impossible to clearly establish the causal sequence between the development of a sense of community and a sense of citizenship. However, we were able to test the hypothesis that formal citizenship breeds both a sense of European citizenship and a sense of European community. Our analyses do not offer firm evidence in support of the hypothesis in either case. A superficial analysis of longitudinal data on the sense of citizenship suggests an increase of such feelings with the length of membership of a country. However, a more refined analysis reveals that it is the time of entry of the Union rather than the length of membership that explains differences in the sense of European citizenship. Since the 2004 enlargement brought in a number of countries with a low sense of citizenship, this might have a lasting effect on the development of citizenship in the Union.

The evidence with regard to a sense of European community is mixed. In a multivariate analysis, length of membership turned out to have a significant effect on the sense of European community, as measured by mutual trust. In Western Europe, mutual trust in general is high, but there is little evidence that this is due to EU membership as such. The 2004 enlargement effected a serious blow to the development of a European community. Among the citizens of the older member states, trust in the people of at least some of the accession countries, not to speak of (then) candidate countries like Bulgaria, Romania, and Turkey, is very low, whereas the low level of interpersonal trust in most of the new member states is reflected in low levels of trust in the people from other member states, in whichever part of Europe.

Our analyses of the causes of this lack of mutual trust suggest that it might be a temporary phenomenon. But this offers little comfort in the short run. The feasibility of the EU as a polity strongly depends on the consent of the people. The lesson to be learned from our analyses is that if the Union extends too fast beyond the borders within which its citizens feel more or less comfortable, this rapid expansion is bound to have a negative effect on people's support for the European project. This might be at least part of the explanation for the misgivings people across Europe apparently have with the development of the Union, as became so obvious in the 2005 referenda on the draft Constitutional Treaty in France and the Netherlands.

Notes

1. More or less because what Bruter defines as the cultural component of European identity still refers to the political community.
2. A possible explanation of the low correlations between these items and their poor scalability is that they are suppressed by the aggregation of different patterns at the national level. However, this does not seem to be the case. The analysis of these items for countries separately yields similar results.
3. Unfortunately the wording of this question was changed in 1992. Since 1992 the wording of the question is: 'In the near future do you see yourself as (nationality) only, (Nationality) and European, European and (Nationality), European only?' The figures in Figure 9.1 refer to the sum of the last three categories. Until 1992 the question asked was: 'Do you ever think of yourself not only as an [COUNTRY] citizen, but also as a citizen of the European Union?' (often, sometimes, never). The figures in Figure 9.1 refer to the sum of the first two categories.
4. Marsh and Mikhaylov in Chapter 7 argue for logging the membership years variable. We obtain similar results when we take the log of membership years (significant effect in a bivariate and multivariate analysis, but not significant when country dummies are included). We have, for simplicity, decided to keep the (unlogged) membership years specification.
5. The independent variables included in our models are: net transfers from the European Union, GDP per capita (logged), growth, inflation, unemployment, and the proportion of trade within the EU. All of the variables included in this analysis are described more thoroughly in the appendix of Chapter 7. We would like to thank Slava Mikhaylov for making these data available to us.
6. By adding a dummy for each country on the right-hand side of the regression we focus on the variation across time (within countries), that is, we are no

longer studying the variation across countries (see, e.g., Persson and Tabellini 2003).
7. We have also run a model including all the control variables and the lagged dependent variable (European identity measured at $t-1$). When we include the lagged dependent variable, the membership years variable fails to exert a significant effect. The effect of the lagged identity variable is positive (0.816) and significant at the .01 level, suggesting that if a country's citizens identify as European one year, they are likely to do so the next year also. There are several reasons for including the lagged dependent variable when working with time-series cross-section data, for example, it helps to control for serial correlation in the error terms (see, e.g. Beck and Katz 1996; 2004). We have also used another method for controlling for autocorrelation, using STATA:s,c(a) option, which means that we assume that there is a common serial correlation for all panels (AR(1)). When we use this method (applied to Models 1 and 2), the membership years variable exerts a positive and significant effect, whereas none of the control variables exert a significant effect in this model specification.
8. Cyprus and Malta were left out. They might be included in the group of South Western Europe, but given their size they would have a disproportionate effect on trust in these countries.
9. The reverse side of the proximity argument is of course that neighbouring countries often have a long history of wars. It is obvious indeed that the Irish hardly trust the British. In principle the same argument might be applied to the rest of Europe, in particular to Germany and its neighbouring countries. However, taking into account that bigger countries in general are less trusted, sixty years of peaceful cooperation in Western Europe apparently had a very positive effect on trust. As Figure 9.2 shows, Germans are pretty well trusted, in particular in Western Europe.
10. Countries included in the analysis as rating nations (nineteen countries) are: Germany, France, Italy, Luxembourg, Netherlands, Denmark, Ireland, Greece, Spain, Portugal, Austria, Finland, Czech Republic, Hungary, Poland, Slovakia, Estonia, Latvia, and Slovenia. Rated nations (twenty-six countries) are the rating countries plus Sweden, Belgium, United Kingdom, Lithuania, Turkey, Bulgaria, and Romania.
11. Most of the variables that we include have been proposed as explanations to generalized/interpersonal trust (see, e.g., Delhey 2005; Delhey and Newton 2005; Rothstein and Uslaner 2005). *Common years of EU membership* measures the number of shared years of EC/EU membership of each pair of countries, where 2006 is the year of reference, and with scores ranging from 0 (rated country not a member in 2006) to 55 (both countries founding members of the Community). *Distance between capitals* is taken from the data set provided by Kristian Skrede Gleditsch (http://privatewww.essex.ac.uk/~ksg/data-5.html) and is measured in kilometers. The dummy variables *Same family of religions* and *Same family of languages* were coded by the authors, with the following

classification of language families: Germanic (SE, DK, DE, NL, GB, IE, AS, LU), Romance (PT, SP, IT, FR, BE, RO), Slavic (PL, CZ, SL, BG, SLO), Finno-Ugric (FI, EST, HU), Baltic (Let, Lit), Greek (GR), Turkish (TK), and the following classification in religious families, based on the historically dominant religious tradition: Western-Christian (NL, DE, BE, UK, LU, SP, PT, DK, IE, SE, PL, Lit, Let, FI, CZ, AS, IT, SLO, HU), Orthodox-Christian (Ro, BG, EST), Greek-orthodox (GR), Islamic (TK). *Allies in WWII* is a dummy variable coded by the authors where countries were classified into Allies, Axis powers and Neutrals. *GDP per capita* (2006) is measured in purchasing power standards and is based on Eurostat data. *Level of inequality* is measured using the Gini index drawn from the World Bank (2003), which measures inequality over the entire distribution of income or consumption, and where a value of 0 represents perfect equality, and a value of 100 perfect inequality. The *Quality of government* variable is an index based on three indicators drawn from the International Country Risk Guide (ICRG) (2005) data: 'Bureaucracy Quality', 'Control of Corruption', and 'Law and Order'. Drawing on an assessment done by Hadenius and Teorell (2005), we measure *Level of democracy* as an average of the two indices most widely used: the one provided by Freedom House (only 'political rights'), and the one provided by Polity. *General trust level* is measured using data from the fourth wave of the World Values Survey (1999–2001). Here the share of individuals stating that 'most people can be trusted' are given (http://www.worldvaluessurvey.org/services/main.html).

12. The results in these two models (Models 4 and 5) are similar in most respects, but the R^2 is higher in Model 4, which may indicate that the features of the rating nationality do a better job at measuring a general trust level among the rating citizens than the WVS variable included in Model 5.
13. Jan Delhey (2005) does not find a significant effect of common membership years on the level of trust when controlling for a number of variables, e.g. the level of modernization of the rated nationality. There are four main differences in our specifications that could account for this difference in the results: (1) We do not measure trust exactly the same way as Delhey, who uses an index of trust ranging from $+100$, indicating that all people in a country tend to trust people from another country, to -100, indicating a complete lack of trust. We do not believe that this can explain the difference in the results, since the variation in trust levels across countries should still be the same, regardless of how the dependent variable is specified (both our variables are based on the same type of survey question). (2) Delhey uses the 1997 Eurobarometer data to measure trust, whereas we use the 2004 European Election Study. This could potentially explain the difference in the results, for example, since trust levels may have changed in some countries during the past years. (3) Delhey does not include exactly the same independent variables as we do. In order to control for this we have run a model including almost the same variables as Delhey, measuring the distance between capitals, common EU years, same family of

religions and same family of languages, variables measuring the level of modernization of the rated and the rating nationality (we have chosen to include separate measures of democracy, quality of government, e.g. corruption, and GDP per capita instead of creating a modernization index), the population size of the rated nationality and dummies specifying if the countries were allies or enemies in World War II. The result that common membership years has a positive and significant effect still holds in this model specification. (4) We do not have exactly the same sample as Delhey (we have more rating and rated countries). However, we have tried to replicate Delhey's analysis, by only including the countries also included in his sample, and the membership years variable still exerts a significant effect in this analysis.

10

Legitimacy and Electoral Abstention in European Parliament Elections

Cees van der Eijk and Hermann Schmitt

10.1. Introduction

Levels of abstention in European Parliament (EP) elections have been high ever since they were held for the first time in 1979. This was also clearly the case in 2004, the first year in which the ten new member states of the 2004 enlargement took part in these elections. The elections in 2004 showed unprecedented low turnout, particularly in some of the new member states. In five of the formerly communist countries of Central and Eastern Europe, less than 30 per cent of eligible citizens cast their votes, with Slovakia and Poland registering the lowest levels of turnout of all member states – 17.0 per cent and 20.9 per cent respectively (see Table 10.1, below, which presents turnout at EP elections since 1979, per country).

As had been the case when very low levels of turnout were registered at previous EP elections, these results generated widespread discussion on how to interpret abstentions. In view of the fact that turnout in EP elections everywhere was lower than customary in elections for national parliaments, it is hardly surprising that the root cause of high levels of abstention was often sought in the distinguishing characteristics of EP elections, of the EP itself, or even of the EU. Repeatedly, and in different guises, one interpretation of low turnout has proven to be popular and is of specific relevance to the core questions posed in this book, namely that it reflects a lack of support for European integration, or for the EU, or for its institutional arrangements. Stated differently: abstentions would be a manifestation of lack of legitimacy.

Legitimacy and Electoral Abstention in European Parliament Elections

This chapter investigates the empirical validity of such interpretations, an undertaking covering all EU countries. Moreover, and following the line of argument presented in Chapter 1, we also address the question of whether or not strong differences exist in this respect between the populations of the various countries. The smaller such between-country differences may be, the more likely it is that European elections can be effective as an instrument of representing political views of the European people at the level of the EP. The second question that this chapter thus addresses is whether the interpretation of abstentions in terms of low EU legitimacy would be more (or conceivably, less) relevant in the member states of the 2004 enlargement of the Union, and particularly in the former communist states of Eastern and Central Europe.

Our focus on legitimacy implies – as we will elaborate below – that we are interested in the motivations and orientations of citizens that contribute to non-voting. In other words, our aim is to understand differences between voters and non-voters at the individual level. Consequently, we do not aspire to analyse and model differences in EP turnout at the aggregate level, i.e., differences in turnout between member states. Such aggregate differences are known to be largely generated by contextual factors that cannot in any sensible manner be interpreted in terms of legitimacy, such as whether voting is compulsory or not, whether EP elections are held on the same day as other elections, or how soon EP elections are held after the previous national parliamentary elections.[1]

10.2. Previous research

When the first direct election of the EP was called in 1979, a broad non-partisan mobilization campaign was launched in all member countries of the Union (Blumler 1983). Those efforts have been repeated on a smaller scale in subsequent elections. In spite of this, turnout was widely considered disappointingly low in 1979. A superficial glance at the development of turnout since then seems to indicate a downward trend. EU-wide participation dropped steadily from a cross-country average of 66 per cent in 1979 to 48 per cent in 2004 (see Table 10.1). Franklin (2001, 2007*b*) argues that this apparent decline is somewhat of an artefact, largely being the consequence of successive enlargements of the Union by countries without compulsory voting, of the disappearance of a 'first election boost', and of coincidental variations in the salience of EP elections caused by their timing in the domestic electoral cycle. When these

The Legitimacy of the European Union after Enlargement

Table 10.1. Turnout at elections for the European Parliament, 1979–2004 (per cent)

Country	1979	1981	1984	1987	1989	1994	1995	1999	2004	Average
Austria							67.7	49.4	42.4	53.2
Belgium	90.4		92.2		90.7	90.7		91.0	90.8	91.0
Britain	32.2		32.6		36.2	36.1		24.0	38.8	33.3
Cyprus									71.2	71.2
Czech Republic									28.3	28.3
Denmark	47.8		52.4		46.2	52.9		50.5	47.9	49.6
Estonia									26.8	26.8
Finland							60.3	31.4	39.4	43.7
France	60.7		56.7		48.7	52.7		46.8	42.8	51.4
Germany	65.7		56.8		62.3	60.0		45.2	43.0	55.5
Greece		78.6	77.2		79.9	71.2		75.3	63.2	74.2
Hungary									38.5	38.5
Ireland	63.6		47.6		68.3	44.0		50.2	58.8	55.4
Italy	84.9		83.4		81.5	74.8		70.8	73.1	78.1
Latvia									41.3	41.3
Lithuania									48.4	48.4
Luxembourg	88.9		88.8		87.4	88.5		87.3	89.0	88.3
Malta									82.4	82.4
Netherlands	57.8		50.6		47.2	35.6		30.0	39.3	43.4
Poland									20.9	20.9
Portugal				72.4	51.2	35.5		40.0	38.6	47.5
Slovakia									17.0	17.0
Slovenia									28.3	28.3
Spain				68.9	54.6	59.1		63.0	45.1	58.1
Sweden							41.6	38.8	37.8	39.4
Country Average*	65.8	78.6	63.8	70.7	62.9	58.4	56.5	52.9	47.7 (52.6**)	50.6
N	9	1	10	2	12	12	3	15	25 (15)	89

* Average of cell entries per column.
** Only counting the 15 'old' member states.

effects of composition and timing are removed, participation in EP elections is relatively stable, at least for the 'old' member states (see also Wessels and Schmitt 2000), but low.

Past research is somewhat inconclusive with regard to the question whether abstentions can be regarded as reflecting lack of support for the EU. Schmitt and Mannheimer, in their 1991 analysis of the 1989 European Election Study data, find that participation in EP elections is virtually unrelated to attitudes about European integration. In 1989 at least, electoral participation was mostly a matter of habitual voting: 'People went to the polls because they are used to doing so on election day' (1991: 50). Later analyses based on the same 1989 European Election Study included, in addition to individual level factors, systemic and contextual characteristics and their interaction with individual-level variables (see Franklin, Van der Eijk, and Oppenhuis 1996). Attitudes about European integration and the (then) European Community were again found to be virtually unrelated to electoral participation. Subsequent analyses of data pertaining to the 1994 and 1999 EP elections came to the same conclusion (cf. Schmitt and Van der Eijk 2003, 2007, 2008).

This negative result seems to be quite unpalatable for people who seem emotionally attached to the conventional wisdom of politicians and journalists that non-participation must indicate lack of support for European integration. Smith, for example, is one of those who after correctly noticing that 'Franklin, Van der Eijk and Oppenhuis have challenged the sort of claims made in this section...' dismisses these results and contends without any empirical evidence or argument whatsoever that '...Despite their skepticism it seems that attitudes do have a part to play in explaining behavior in EP elections' (Smith 1999: 123, note 10).

Fortunately, other critiques of these previous findings are based on empirical evidence and analysis, rather than on preconceptions impervious to empirical argument. Blondel, Sinnott, and Svenson (1998) conducted an extensive empirical study of electoral participation in the 1994 elections to the EP. They found, in contrast to the conclusions about the 1989 elections referred to above, 'voluntary Euro-abstention to be significantly affected by attitudes to European integration, by attitudes to the EP, and by attitudes to the parties and candidates in the election' (Sinnott 2000: 70 summarizing Blondel, Sinnott, and Svenson 1998: 222–36).

While having an open mind to the possibility that the character of non-voting in EP elections may have changed after 1999, or that it may be caused by different factors in the 2004 enlargement countries than in the 'old' member states, we are nevertheless sceptical about the validity of the analyses on which the conclusions of Blondel et al. rest. Their claims have to be questioned on methodological grounds.

Blondel et al. define voluntary Euro-abstainers as those respondents who, in the course of the interview, gave one or more of the following reasons when asked (in an open-ended question) why they had abstained: 'Lack of interest, distrust of or dissatisfaction with politics and politicians, lack of knowledge and dissatisfaction with the EP electoral process' (1998: 50). Three objections can be made to their procedure.

Our first objection concerns the use of self-reported reasons or motivations for behaviour. Alvarez and Nagler (2000: 61) express in a related context severe doubts about the validity of such information: 'Researchers using these survey questions do not appear to have seriously considered the quality of the survey responses obtained for questions asking for justifications of reported political behavior.' They particularly doubt whether respondents are always able to cognize and verbalize the factors influencing their behaviour. One can equally doubt whether the context of a mass survey allows them to express all the reasons they may have in mind. A related, but somewhat different problem is whether we can assume that what people see as the reasons for their own behaviour can be equated with the reasons that a researcher would see. In the words of Kaplan (1964: 32): '(...) it is of crucial importance that we distinguish between the meaning of the act to the actor (...) and its meaning to us as scientists, taking the action as subject-matter. I call these, respectively, *act meaning* and *action meaning*.' He emphasizes that the two will in general be quite different. Open-ended questions about reasons for behaviour (in this particular case, for non-voting) may be useful for describing act meaning, although even that claim may be contested (see Alvarez and Nagler, above). By taking these responses as the reasons ('causes') for non-voting that would be satisfactory from a researcher's perspective, Blondel et al. naively assume that act meaning and action meaning coincide. In doing so they shrink away from their own responsibility to formulate falsifiable accounts for the respondents' behaviour: their approach leaves no room for falsifying the reasons for non-voting given by respondents.

This problem of non-falsifiability leads to our second major objection to the Blondel et al. approach, which is that it suffers from *selection-bias* (King, Keohane, and Verba 1994: 128–36). This often occurs 'when we, knowing what we want to see as the outcome of the research (the confirmation of the favourite hypothesis), subtly or not so subtly select observations on the basis of combinations of the independent and dependent variables that support the desired conclusion' (p.128). In the case of the approach of Blondel et al., the open-ended question about reasons for non-voting could only be asked to non-voters. Consequently, only non-voters could be found to be uninterested in or dissatisfied with European integration and the EP. Therefore, the attribution of non-voting to this lack of interest or dissatisfaction cannot be falsified: we simply do not know how (un)interested or (dis)satisfied those are who did turn out to cast their vote in the European elections. Thus, the analysis is implicitly restricted to only one category of the dependent variable (the non-voters). As a consequence 'nothing whatsoever can be learned about the causes of the dependent variable' (King, Keohane, and Verba, 1994: 129).

Our third objection to Blondel et al.'s approach is that (self-reported) motivations for non-voting that refer to European integration or the EU and its institutions are uncritically taken at face value. Van der Eijk (1984) demonstrated that responses to survey questions relating to 'European'

Legitimacy and Electoral Abstention in European Parliament Elections

stimuli are often generated by general, and sometimes by strictly domestic political orientations and attitudes, which spill over into the response to questions about less familiar political domains, such as the EU.

In our approach, we explicitly look at voters *and* non-voters, and our independent variables derive from questions that have been asked of *all* respondents, irrespective of their behaviour. Moreover, we will control for general and domestic political orientations and attitudes. Therefore, our findings are not tainted by selection bias, by problems of self-reported motivations, or by misattribution of causal effects. As stated above, it is quite possible that things have changed since we previously explored the causes of non-voting for the 1989, 1994, and 1999 EP elections, and it is equally possible that things are different in the 2004 enlargement countries. In the remainder of this chapter, we investigate whether or not this is the case.

10.3. Abstentions and orientations to the EU: A first look

In order for abstentions to be interpretable as manifestations of low legitimacy of the EU, we would expect at the very least that voters and non-voters differ significantly in terms of their orientations and attitudes to the EU. One of the survey questions tapping such orientations asks whether EU membership of one's country is a 'good' thing, a 'bad' thing, or neither. Scheuer's (2005) extensive analysis of legitimacy beliefs demonstrated that this item, used in Eurobarometers and other surveys since 1972, serves this purpose very well.

Table 10.2 reports the difference in the proportion of voters (as opposed to non-voters) between those who responded that membership of the EU is a 'good' thing and those who stated that it is a 'bad' thing.[2] In virtually all member states we see that abstentions are considerably higher amongst those who evaluate the EU negatively. Averaged over the countries the difference is more than 17 per cent. Only in one country (Belgium), we see a difference in the opposite direction, but that difference is not significant, while in Greece and Ireland the difference – although in the expected direction – is not significant either.

Our survey data contain additional items that can also be interpreted in terms of legitimacy beliefs, and some show in broad terms a similar difference in abstentions between people who are supportive of the EU and those who are not. Which of these items correlates most strongly with abstentions varies across countries, and the 'good'–'bad' item is not always

Table 10.2. Difference in the proportion of abstentions between those who consider the EU a 'bad' thing and those who consider it a 'good' thing (in percentage points)

Austria	22
Belgium	−2
Britain	8
Cyprus	29
Czech Republic	17
Denmark	8
Estonia	36
Finland	22
France	16
Germany	24
Greece	5
Hungary	23
Ireland	4
Italy	16
Latvia	28
Luxembourg	2
Netherlands	19
Poland	17
Portugal	10
Slovakia	35
Slovenia	19
Spain	18
Sweden	22
Average across countries	17

Source: EES 2004, unweighted data.

Reading example: in Austria, there are 22 per cent more abstainers amongst those who consider membership of the EU a 'bad' thing compared to those who think it is a 'good' thing.

the strongest in this respect. These differences reflect the particular ways in which political debate and public opinion on European integration have evolved in the member states and how they are intertwined with political contestation in the national political arena.

Which particular item best reflects EU legitimacy beliefs in a particular country is not of primary concern to us; rather we are interested in measuring the relevant set of such beliefs as adequately as possible in each country. Therefore, we selected a set of five items that all correlate with voting versus non-voting in most of the countries. We did not select items that – although conceivably interpretable in terms of legitimacy beliefs – were not or were very weakly correlated with abstentions. Obviously, this 'stacks the deck' somewhat in favour of the legitimacy interpretation of abstentions, but it avoids unnecessary clutter and compounding missing data problems. The items that we selected are[3]:

* Whether or not EU membership of one's country is a 'good' thing, a 'bad' thing, or neither.
* Whether one sees oneself not only as a citizen of one's own country, but also as a citizen of the EU.
* Whether or not one feels proud to be a citizen of the EU.
* Whether one feels that political decisions taken at EU level are in the interest of one's country.
* Whether one feels that political decisions taken at EU level are in one's own interest.

To assess the strength of the joint relationship between these five items and abstentions, we use logistic regression, and report in Table 10.3 to what extent they can account for the difference between voting and not-voting. The coefficients reported are R^2s, calculated along the lines proposed by Menard (2002: .23).[4] When looked at in terms of explained variances, the importance of legitimacy beliefs for explaining abstentions

Table 10.3. Explanatory power of EU legitimacy beliefs for analysing electoral abstention in 2004 EP election

	Adjusted R^{2*}
Austria	0.06
Belgium	0.00
Britain	0.01
Cyprus	0.08
Czech Republic	0.07
Denmark	0.02
Estonia	0.08
Finland	0.05
France	0.04
Germany	0.06
Greece	0.02
Hungary	0.05
Ireland	0.01
Italy	0.02
Latvia	0.07
Luxembourg	0.03
Netherlands	0.06
Poland	0.06
Portugal	0.03
Slovakia	0.07
Slovenia	0.09
Spain	0.05
Sweden	0.05**
Average across countries	0.05

* See endnote 4.
** See endnote 3.

is less dramatic, but this has to be seen in the context that the explanatory power of individual-level analyses of voting and not-voting is never very high (cf. Schmitt and Mannheimer 1991; Oppenhuis 1995; Franklin et al. 1996; Schmitt and Van der Eijk 2007), and rarely exceeds 0.20. Table 10.3 shows that in most countries there is a non-negligible association between EU legitimacy beliefs on the one hand and abstentions on the other. Moreover, it also shows that this association is stronger in the Eastern and Central European (formerly communist) countries than in the 'older' member states: in all these Eastern and Central European countries, the R^2 is at or above the overall country average.

If the results presented in Tables 10.2 and 10.3 could be interpreted in causal terms, they would lend considerable support to the interpretation that low turnout in EP elections reflects – at least in part – low legitimacy of the EU and its institutions. The question is, however, to what extent these associations reflect causal relationships, or, alternatively, whether they are spurious effects of other factors. In order to assess that, we have to broaden our approach and include variables that represent other causal factors.

10.4. EU legitimacy beliefs amidst other factors

In order to avoid misattribution of causal effects we cannot limit the analysis to variables relating to the legitimacy of the EU only, as that would risk interpreting spurious correlations as causal effects. We have to control for antecedent variables, which raises the question what those could be? When thinking in terms of causal antecedence, two groups of variables come to mind: (1) social structural and demographic variables, and (2) political orientations and attitudes belonging to the domestic political realm.

Social structural and demographic variables include gender, year of birth, education, occupation, religion, class, urbanization of domicile, etc. The origin of these variables is obviously antecedent to the development of people's orientations and attitudes with respect to European integration and the EU. Moreover, these variables change very rarely (if at all), making it impossible to see them as consequences of EU legitimacy beliefs. In spite of this, they do not qualify as suitable control variables when analysing the effects of legitimacy beliefs.[5] The causal mechanism that would generate any association between these variables and abstentions would largely involve other factors, which are not measured and for which demographic and social structural variables would be proxies.

Whether those factors would be antecedent to legitimacy beliefs – and would thus have to be used as controls – is uncertain, however. To the extent that they are not, controlling for these variables would risk underestimating effects that could be attributed to legitimacy beliefs.[6]

The second group of variables that is antecedent to EU legitimacy beliefs consists of political orientations and attitudes belonging to the domestic political sphere. Here we find factors such as political interest,[7] affective,[8] and instrumental[9] orientations towards political parties, and evaluations of democracy in the country[10] and of the performance of the incumbent government.[11] These variables can plausibly be regarded as causally antecedent to whatever EU legitimacy beliefs respondents hold, mainly because of the overwhelming dominance of the domestic political sphere in citizens' everyday lives and in the political communication to which they are exposed. Moreover, political interest and closeness to parties are stable characteristics that have roots in early socialization, which makes it even less likely that they themselves are influenced by evolving experiences with and orientations towards the EU. This last argument does not hold for instrumental orientations towards political parties, but we know from previous research that these are mostly determined by domestic political factors and hardly (if at all) by EU-related matters. Finally, satisfaction with democracy and approval of the national government are, like the other variables in this group, predominantly determined by the dominance of domestic political stimuli and the simultaneous paucity of EU-related ones. In view of this, it is much more plausible that spill over in evaluations runs from the domestic to the European political sphere rather than the other way around (which implies that we have to control for these domestic evaluations). These various considerations about causal antecedence allow us to use this group of variables safely as controls when assessing the influence of EU legitimacy beliefs on abstentions.

Having specified which antecedent variables to control for, the subsequent assessment of the effect of EU legitimacy beliefs on abstentions is straightforward. Using logistic regression with voting versus non-voting as the dependent variable, we establish in a block-recursive fashion the improvement of the model when adding the set of EU legitimacy beliefs to the set of domestic political control variables. If these improvements are large, then these legitimacy beliefs can sensibly be regarded as a factor that helps to account for abstentions. If they are negligible or small, abstentions in EP elections cannot be interpreted in terms of low legitimacy of the EU in the eyes of the citizens. For the purposes of this chapter, we are not interested in which, if any, of the legitimacy beliefs has any

Table 10.4. Proportion correct predictions of electoral participation versus abstention

	Model including only control variables	Increase from also including EU legitimacy beliefs
Austria	0.73	0.01
Britain	0.67	0.00
Cyprus	0.90	0.00
Czech Republic	0.70	0.01
Denmark	0.75	0.01
Estonia	0.63	0.04
Finland	0.76	0.01
France	0.70	0.01
Germany	0.76	0.00
Greece	0.85	0.01
Hungary	0.72	0.02
Ireland	0.87	0.00
Italy	0.95	0.00
Latvia	0.75	0.01
Netherlands	0.76	0.02
Poland	0.71	0.03
Portugal	0.64	0.01
Slovakia	0.63	0.02
Slovenia	0.75	0.07
Spain	0.75	0.00
Average across all countries	0.75	0.01

impact. This may be different between countries for reasons explained earlier (see Section 10.3). Therefore, we are not interested in the coefficients of the independent variables, but only in the extent to which they jointly strengthen the explanatory model.

Table 10.4 reports the relevant results of our analyses.[12] The first column reports the proportion of respondents whose electoral participation or abstention was correctly predicted by the model in which only the control variables (relating to the domestic political environment) are included. The second column gives the increase in this proportion generated by the additional inclusion of the EU legitimacy beliefs as explanatory variables.[13]

Inspection of Table 10.4 shows, first, that on average EU legitimacy beliefs add hardly any explanatory power to the model once control variables are included. Evidently, the association between these beliefs and abstentions is largely spurious, and cannot be interpreted in causal terms. This reflects the considerable spill over from general and domestic political orientations and attitudes into responses on questions about less salient political stimuli. In spite of the overall weakness of EU legitimacy beliefs for explaining electoral abstentions, there are one or two countries where these beliefs do help to account for abstentions: Slovenia and perhaps Estonia. Low turnout in these two countries seems to be interpretable, at least to a limited degree, in terms of low legitimacy of the EU. Here, it is impossible for us to determine what it is about these countries that makes them stand apart. It would be incorrect, we think, to attribute this to a heritage from their former communist regimes, as the other five formerly communist countries (Czech Republic, Hungary, Latvia, Poland, and Slovakia) do not show any signs that EU legitimacy plays a role in electoral abstentions.

10.5. If not legitimacy beliefs, what then causes low turnout in EP elections?

EP elections resemble elections to national parliaments, yet are different in ways that necessarily lead to more abstentions. The resemblance concerns particularly the set of parties from which voters can choose. Typically these are the same as those that compete for seats in the national parliament, which gives EP elections a strong domestic flavour, reinforced by national issues and national politicians dominating their campaigns. Indeed, it is mainly national politics that political actors are dealing with in these elections. EP elections have therefore been described as second-order national elections (cf. Reif and Schmitt 1980). They are second-order because, unlike elections for national parliament, national executive power is not at stake, although their results usually affect the standing of the national government indirectly. As such, they are similar to mid-term elections in the US; *Landtagswahlen* in Germany; by-elections in Britain; and so on.[14] Moreover, at the level of the EU, executive power is not at stake either; no European government is formed (or, for that matter, removed from power) as a consequence of the strengths of political groups in the newly elected EP.

One of the major consequences of the second-order character of EP elections is low turnout.[15] The absence of direct consequences of EP elections for executive power (at the level of the EU as well as at the national level) entails that there is politically 'less at stake' than in national parliament elections. And this affects the behaviour of political parties, the media, and voters alike. Political parties are found to 'fight' their campaigns half-heartedly (Reif 1985; De Vreese et al. 2007), and on small budgets.[16] As a consequence, mass-media interest in and coverage of such non-events is usually extremely low (Blumler and Fox 1982; Blumler 1983; De Vreese and Schmitt 2007). Voters are thus poorly mobilized: the half-hearted ways in which parties, politicians, and media operate during EP election campaigns impress upon voters the message that there is not much at stake. In such circumstances stronger individual motivation is required to go out and vote than when the political consequences of an election seem to be clearer, more direct, and of greater significance. In national parliamentary elections, participation requires a certain degree of interest, some positive level of affective and instrumental orientations towards parties, and so on. In EP elections these same factors are required, but in higher doses. Voters' legitimacy beliefs with respect to the EU do not figure in all of this.

The 'less at stake' factor also helps explain why – *ceteris paribus* – turnout in EP elections rises with increasing intervals since the last national parliament elections (cf. Franklin 2007a). The longer the time span since the previous first-order election (i.e. one where executive power is at stake), the more political parties are in need of updates about where they stand in terms of electoral support. They need such updates to adapt, where necessary, their policy stances or their communications with voters in order to be best positioned for the next first-order election. Second-order national elections are real-life updates, and as the need for them increases, so does the interest of political parties (and as a derivative, the interest of the media) in EP elections. This strong empirical regularity cannot in any way be explained in terms of voters' legitimacy beliefs regarding the EU, but it can easily be done in terms of the 'less at stake' perspective.[17]

10.6. Conclusions and reflections

We set out to answer two questions: first, to what extent abstentions in EP elections can be interpreted in terms of low legitimacy of the EU, and second, whether the 2004 enlargement of the EU has made any difference in this respect. The answers to these questions are straightforward. Not-voting is not a manifestation of the EU lacking legitimacy in the eyes of the voters – with the exception of Slovenia and possibly also Estonia, where legitimacy beliefs do play a minor role in generating low turnout.[18] Moreover, in view of the almost uniform applicability of this finding across EU member states, the 2004 enlargement – and particularly the membership of formerly communist countries of Eastern and Central Europe – did not make a difference in this respect. Although these answers to our questions are very straightforward – and consistent with many earlier studies – we are well aware that they may seem surprising or even implausible to many people. The reason for such incredulity is not only some a priori plausibility of the idea of abstentions being generated by legitimacy beliefs (i.e. by Euro-scepticism, Euro-hostility, or Euro-phobia) but, more importantly, that there is a real and sometimes strong association between such beliefs and abstentions (see, e.g., Table 10.2). Our conclusions do not deny this.

Nevertheless, not all correlation reflects causation, and distinguishing between the two requires theoretical explication in terms of causal antecedence, and statistical control for antecedent factors. Unfortunately, this is rarely done in journalistic and political (and sometimes not even in academic) discourse. Voter responses that seem at first instance to pertain to European integration or the EU, often reflect nothing other than general political attitudes and beliefs that are generated predominantly by the domestic political environment. Although we focused in this chapter on differences between voters, not on differences between countries, this insight may nevertheless help to understand the generally lower levels of turnout in the formerly communist member states. Democratic political processes – domestically as well as at the level of the EU – are generally regarded with greater scepticism in formerly communist countries than in more consolidated European systems (e.g. Fuchs and Klingemann 2002), thus depressing turnout.

The considerably lower turnout in the East in the 2004 EP election may, additionally, be related to the more limited mobilization capacity of political parties in new democracies under the particular circumstance of a second-order election. The linkages between voters and parties are also weakening in many of the older member states as a result of the declining political importance of social cleavages (cf. Dalton et al. 1984; Franklin et al. 1992) and concomitant ideological de-polarization (cf. Schmitt and Wüst 2006; Wessels and Schmitt 2008; Schmitt and Freire forthcoming). However, these linkages are weaker still in the formerly communist new democracies of Eastern Europe (Tavits 2008).

Our findings indicate the absence of any systematic differences between different kinds of EU countries with respect to the interpretation of electoral abstentions. As elaborated in Chapter 1, this is good news for the potential of an EU-wide system of political representation. The dominant motivations behind abstentionism are an important (although unspoken and unwritten) element of the public sphere, and the finding that in this respect the public spheres in the member states are mutually compatible is reassuring.

Yet, the generally high levels of abstentions in EP elections are problematic for other reasons. Lijphart (1997) reminds us that because of socio-economic differences between voters and non-voters, the electoral process is '...systematically biased in favour of more privileged citizens – those with higher incomes, greater wealth, and better education – and against less advantaged citizens'. The groups that are most reliant on support from the state are therefore not sufficiently heard through the democratic vote. This is particularly troublesome when realising that the core business of EP decision making is about substantive policy areas that impinge on socio-economic inequality, not on constitutional issues. This problem of bias does, of course, also plague political representation at the national level (except in the few countries where turnout is almost universal), but its nefarious consequences are, owing to much lower turnout, potentially larger in the context of the EP.

Not least, high levels of abstentions in EP elections are discomforting because they contribute to the habituation of abstention in elections as such. Franklin (2004) demonstrated convincingly that not-voting lowers the probability of voting in (any kind of) subsequent elections, and that repeated not-voting results in habitual behaviour from which it is difficult to escape. As such habituation is particularly formed when voters are young, this 'infectious' effect of low turnout in EP elections will be small amongst voter cohorts that were socialised before the first elections of the EP in 1979. But that group gradually diminishes in size because of generational replacement, and will have disappeared by 2040, some 60 years after 1979. Until then, however, we can expect the habit-forming effects of abstentions in European elections to affect an increasing segment of the electorates in EU member states. As a consequence, abstentions in other elections will – *ceteris paribus* – rise. Comforting as our findings may be for the potential of an EU-wide system of political representation, all is not well when looking at electoral abstentions in EP elections.

Notes

1. Turnout is boosted, *ceteris paribus*, by compulsory voting, by concurrent elections, and by increasing length of time since the most recent national elections (cf. Franklin et al. 1996; Franklin 2001).
2. Our analyses do not cover Malta and Lithuania, owing to absence of relevant survey data.
3. Of these items, the second, fourth, and fifth were not asked in Sweden. We substituted two other items for them, namely whether European integration has 'gone too far' or 'should be pushed further', and whether when jobs are scarce,

priority should be given to people from one's own country over citizens from other EU member countries. We tested for each of the countries separately whether the explanatory power of the logistic regression could be increased significantly by adding additional independent variables (i.e. other attitude variables on the EU that can conceivably be interpreted in legitimacy terms). This was not the case.

4. One of the problems in logistic regression is the absence of a sensible equivalent to the R^2 (explained variance) for OLS regressions. A series of so-called pseudo-R^2 coefficients exists, none of which is very satisfactory, and each of which is prone to yield wildly misleading values under various multivariate circumstances. Menard (2002) proposed as an alternative to pseudo-R^2 coefficients a direct analogon to the OLS R^2, which is obtained by saving the predicted probabilities from a multivariate logistic regression, and regressing these with OLS on the observed dichotomous variable (which is thus in this second regression used as independent variable). The R^2 from this OLS regression is a valid measure of the explanatory power of the set of independent variables that was used in the multivariate logistic regression. Moreover, it has all the advantages of ease of interpretation that OLS-based R^2 coefficients have.

5. Obviously, these variables should be included in any model that tries to account as comprehensibly as possible for the difference between voting and non-voting. But that is not our aim in this chapter, as we limit ourselves to the question to what extent EU legitimacy beliefs can account for the difference between voting and non-voting.

6. Obviously, *not* controlling for demographic and social structural variables is not without risk either, as some of the factors that might generate associations between these variables and abstentions could very well be antecedent to EU legitimacy beliefs, in which case they should be controlled for. In view of the findings of our previous research, and our critique on the approach (and interpretations) by Blondel et al. (see Section 10.2), we prefer the risk of undercontrolling (which might overestimate the effect of legitimacy beliefs) to overcontrolling (which might underestimate it).

7. This is measured by the question 'To what extent would you say you are interested in politics? Very, somewhat, a little, or not at all?' and by questions about usage of television and newspapers as sources of political information.

8. Measured by the combination of two questions: 'Do you consider yourself to be close to any particular party?' and 'Do you feel yourself to be very close to this party, fairly close, or merely a sympathiser?'

9. Measured by two variables. First, the propensity to vote for the most preferred of the national political parties. These propensities are derived from responses to the question 'How probable is it that you will ever vote for the following parties?' The logic of these variables in the context of analyses of non-voting is elaborated extensively in Franklin et al. (1996); see also Van der Eijk et al. (2006). Second, as an indicator of the extent to which the party system offers ideologically compatible parties, the smallest distance to any of the available parties in left/right terms.

10. Indicator: 'On the whole, how satisfied are you with the way democracy works in [your country]?'
11. Indicator: 'Do you approve or disapprove of the government's record to date?'
12. Because some of the most powerful control variables were not included in the questionnaires used in Belgium, Luxembourg, and Sweden, we could not conduct these analyses for these three countries.
13. Model improvement can, of course, also be assessed in terms of explanatory power of the model (e.g. R^2 according to the procedure explained in footnote 5), or in yet other ways, such as via the application of ROC curves. Those alternative ways of presentation lead to the same substantive conclusions as Table 10.4 does.
14. Anderson and Ward (1997) when analysing German *Landtagswahlen* and British by-elections have used the term 'barometer elections' to describe second-order national elections.
15. There are other consequences, relating to the tendency for government parties to do poorly, and for small and new parties to do relatively well. The discussion of those effects falls outside the remit of this chapter, which focuses on the causes of electoral abstentions.
16. In a country like Germany, where the state is refunding campaign costs on a flat rate basis, a considerable part of the money granted to the parties is often saved for more important political events to come.
17. The relevance of the 'less at stake' factor, and its consequences in terms of voter motivation is enhanced by its ability to help explain variations in turnout in other elections as well. The closeness of an election race and the degree of policy differences (i.e. polarization) between the major contenders for government office are both related to differences in turnout (cf. Van Egmond 2003, Wessels and Schmitt 2008). The so-called 'golden formula' in Switzerland, which stipulated that the same coalition would rule irrespective of the outcome of national elections, implied that after its introduction there was less 'at stake' in an election, which in turn had a dramatic effect on the development of turnout (cf. Franklin 2004). In all these instances, the 'what is at stake' aspect impinges directly on voter motivations, without legitimacy beliefs of one kind or another playing a role.
18. Unfortunately absence of relevant data made it impossible to include some EU member states in our analyses: Belgium, Luxembourg, Lithuania, Malta, and Sweden (see also footnote 13). Therefore, we cannot draw with certainty any conclusions about the relevance of legitimacy beliefs for abstentions in those countries. However, in view of the extremely high turnout in Belgium, Luxembourg, and Malta (see Table 10.1) there is hardly any room for such beliefs to play a role in terms of voter turnout, and, moreover, our previous research in this area (see Section 10.2) failed to find even the slightest shred of evidence for this in Belgium and Luxembourg. For Sweden, earlier analyses on the 1999 EP election did suggest some effects of legitimacy beliefs, but the verdict remains open as to whether this was still the case in 2004.

11

In Conclusion: The Legitimacy of the European Union after Enlargement

Jacques Thomassen

11.1. Introduction

In this volume we have tried to assess the legitimacy of the European Union (EU) after enlargement using two different methods. The first method involves evaluating the functioning of the political system of the EU against a set of criteria deduced from the normative theory of democracy and more specifically from the model of party government. This model has the major advantage in that it can be formulated as a number of requirements that can be used as benchmarks to assess the quality of a system of political representation. In the first part of the book (Chapters 2 through 5) we systematically evaluated to what extent the system of political representation of the EU meets the requirements of the party government model. In the next section we summarize our findings with regard to each of these requirements.

The second method of evaluating the legitimacy of the political system of the EU entails assessing to what extent the system is legitimate in the eyes of the beholders, the European people. In applying this method, we followed the conceptual framework originally developed by David Easton by making a distinction between three objects of political support: the (performance of the) authorities, the political regime, and the political community. In the second part of the book (Chapters 6 through 9) we reported our findings from this perspective. These findings are summarized in Section 11.3. We also analysed the relationship between turnout and legitimacy in Chapter 10.

In Section 11.4, we summarize what our findings allow us to say regarding the effects of the 2004 enlargement on the legitimacy of the EU. In Section

11.5, we reflect on the quality of the system of representative democracy in the EU. Finally, in Section 11.6, we discuss whether politicization could improve the quality of the system of representative democracy both at the European and the national level.

11.2. The European Union and representative democracy

In order to evaluate the system of political representation at the level of the European Union we derived the following criteria from the model of party government:

1. Voters do have a choice, that is, they can choose between at least two parties with different policy proposals.
2. Voters do vote according to their policy preferences, that is, they choose the party that represents their policy preferences best.
3. The internal cohesion of parliamentary parties is sufficient to enable them to implement their policies.
4. The party or coalition of parties winning the elections takes over the government.
5. Both the policy programmes of political parties and the policy preferences of voters are constrained by a single ideological dimension.

A preliminary question we had to answer first is whether this model, which was developed in the context of the national state, can be applied to the EU at all. We argued that there are good reasons to do so. Even though one might still qualify the EU as a union of sovereign states, successive treaties have enlarged the possibility to take decisions according to a supranational rather than an intergovernmental regime of decision making.

If one accepts the argument we made that the process of political representation should be at the same level of government where decisions are taken, there should be a system of political representation at the European level in addition to the national systems. This principle was recognized in the Constitutional Treaty and maintained in the Lisbon Treaty. In these treaties it is recognized that 'the functioning of the Union shall be founded on representative democracy', that 'citizens are directly represented at Union level in the European parliament' and that 'political parties at European level contribute to forming European political awareness and to expressing the will of citizens of the Union'. These clauses are consistent with the requirements specified in the party government model with one noticeable exception: The requirement that the

In Conclusion: The Legitimacy of the European Union after Enlargement

outcome of elections should be reflected in the composition of the 'government' or the European Commission is missing. This absence of a formal link between the outcome of European elections and the composition of the Commission is often seen as an important element of the alleged democratic deficit of the EU.

We decided to focus on the remaining requirements of the party government model. But even then our story could have been a short one. It hardly needs to be argued that the first two requirements of the model are not met at the level of the EU either. There are no European political parties competing for the votes of a European electorate; European elections are still fought by national political parties and mainly on national issues. Also, voters make their choices on the basis of their opinions on national rather than European issues and their perception of the position of national political parties on these issues. As a consequence, European elections fail as an instrument of democracy at the European level, that is, they fail to express the will of the European people on European issues.

As we explained in the introductory chapter we do not quarrel with this traditional verdict on the European system of political representation, but rather with its conclusion. Even though there is no truly European system of political representation, European elections can still be an effective instrument of linkage if the national systems of political representation are compatible with regard to each of the remaining requirements of the party government model, that is, if:

a. Political parties of the same party family across member states develop similar policy programmes for their election campaigns.
b. Their voters across Europe vote according to similar considerations.
c. Being a member of a particular party group rather than national background defines the policy views and the roll-call behaviour of members of the European Parliament.
d. The policy programmes of political parties, the policy preferences of voters across member states, and the behaviour of Members of the European Parliament are constrained by the same ideological dimension.
e. The public spheres across member states are compatible.

These requirements are directly related to the requirements of the party government model, except the last one, which we added in the introductory chapter. In the first part of the book we tried to assess to what degree these requirements are met.

From previous studies of the European Election Studies group (Van der Eijk and Franklin 1996; Schmitt and Thomassen 1999; Katz and Wessels 1999; Van der Brug and Van der Eijk 2007) we already knew that these requirements were amazingly well met until the 2004 enlargement. However, it was still to be seen whether the political parties and their voters in the new post-communist member states were sufficiently similar to their West European counterparts to fit into the existing party system.

Our findings suggest that they fit much better in the existing structure than often anticipated. In Chapter 2, we assessed the effect of enlargement on the characteristics of the European party system, in particular its competitiveness and cohesiveness. Surprisingly enough, the EU party system has hardly changed as a result of Eastern enlargement. The EPP-ED has gained additional strength, both PES and the Far Left became relatively weaker, and the proportion of unaffiliated members at first increased due to the fact that a good number of Eastern members did not join one of the traditional party groups. Moreover, enlargement had hardly an effect on the characteristics of the party system. The party space is still dominated by two dimensions, the left–right dimension and the pro-/anti-European integration dimension. Party competition in the EU on these two dimensions can still be characterized by a horseshoe pattern, with centre-left and centre-right groups more in favour of further integration than far-left and far-right groups. The competitiveness and cohesiveness of the party system were hardly affected by enlargement. The party groups by and large still are as competitive and cohesive as they were before enlargement.

An important element in our assessment of the compatibility of national systems of political representation is the compatibility of national public spheres. Most political information reaching the people is filtered and interpreted by the media. Therefore, in the communication between political parties and voters, the media are at least as important as the formal documents and statements of political parties. For this reason the compatibility of national public spheres is important for our purposes as well. In Chapter 3, we found a substantial degree of Europeanization of national debates, which suggests that a European public sphere 'light' in the form of Europeanized national debates is gaining ground. Compared to 1999, the 2004 elections were more visible. The new EU members are as Europeanized or not, as their older counterparts, depending on whether one wants to see the glass as half full or half empty.

The inclusion of the post-communist countries into the EU did not produce a fundamental change in the left–right structuring of voting behaviour (Chapter 4). Just like in the older member states, left–right is

In Conclusion: The Legitimacy of the European Union after Enlargement

by far the most important factor structuring the voting behaviour of the electorate in the new member states. Therefore, the idea of a single European electorate, primarily motivated by the same left–right dimension, can still be maintained.

However, this is not to say that there are no differences. The effect of left–right orientations on party choice is significantly weaker in the new member states in Central and Eastern Europe than in the older member states. Also, citizens in Central and Eastern Europe in general tend to differ greatly from the citizens of the established European democracies on a number of issues: they are more egalitarian, anti-immigrant and socially conservative than Western Europeans. In general, they tend to be less libertarian. Hence, even though the differences between the voters of different parties follow the same pattern in new and old member states, at the electoral level the East-West differences *within* the party groups with regard to these issues are in a few cases even larger than the differences *between* them. This means that although the left–right dimension still is a suitable vehicle for mass-elite communication across the EU, the issue space that needs to be represented by a single European party group is further stretched.

A similar conclusion can be drawn with regard to the development of the party groups in the European Parliament (Chapter 5). With or without the new members, the party groups in the European Parliament look very much the same. An analysis of roll-calls in the European Parliament since 2004 proves that the left–right divide is by far the most important dimension explaining roll-call behaviour, just like it was before enlargement. Nevertheless, there are indications of an increase of latent tensions within the major party groups. Just like the voters from Central and Eastern European countries, MEPs representing them tend to be less libertarian and more traditional or authoritarian than their colleagues from Western Europe. In particular the PES, the socialist party group, has become less cohesive in this respect. But as a general conclusion we can maintain that the 2004 enlargement had less effect on the effectiveness of the European system of political representation than often expected.

11.3. The legitimacy of the European Union: The support of the people

In the second part of the book we applied our second method of evaluating the legitimacy of the EU by assessing to what extent the Union is supported by the people of Europe. We assessed people's support for the performance of the authorities (Chapter 7), their trust in the political regime (Chapter 8), and their support for the political community (Chapter 9). Finally, we explored to what extent the low turnout figures in European elections can be explained by a lack of legitimacy (Chapter 10).

But first (in Chapter 6), we explored how much 'Europe' citizens across Europe really want, that is, in which policy fields they want the Union to take responsibility. Our findings show that people's support for the EU as the most appropriate level of government for solving the most important problems they see has considerably declined in the older member states since 1999. In the new member states, the support for the European Union as the preferred level of government is lower on average than in the older member states. Therefore, the joint effect of the development in the older states and the 2004 enlargement is a considerable decline of the support for the EU as the preferred level of government to deal with the most important problems people perceive.

Chapter 7 mapped the development of people's support for the performance of the EU. People's perceptions of how much their country has benefited from being a member of the EU have followed a cyclical pattern. They grew steadily more positive until 1991, only to fall equally steadily for the next five years, after which they have again risen fairly steadily, without regaining the heights of 1991, when an average of 66 per cent of the population in each country saw the EU as beneficial for their country. This cyclical pattern is not due to the changing composition of EU membership over the years. A similar pattern over time can be observed in each of the country groups that joined the Union in successive waves of enlargement. The 2004 enlargement did not have a strong effect on the average level of perceptions of benefits from the Union, although the average perceived benefit in most of the accession countries was below the EU average in the year they entered the Union.

Variations in people's perceptions of benefits can to a large extent be explained by economic factors affecting their country, such as transfer payments via the EU budget and the extent to which trade is intra-EU. Also, people seem to respond to domestic economic considerations and are inclined to give the EU credit for 'good times'. Socialization is also important, with the accumulation of years of membership associated with more positive feelings. Clear exceptions here though are the six founding member states. In these countries the perception of benefits has gradually decreased over time.

Chapter 8 assessed to what extent people's perceptions of policy performance spill over to trust in the political institutions of the EU, as the

In Conclusion: The Legitimacy of the European Union after Enlargement

theory of political support suggests. In light of all pessimistic observations about the development of the legitimacy of the EU and its institutions, some of the findings in this chapter are remarkable. First, trust in European institutions in the early years of the twenty-first century is higher than in the 1990s. In particular, trust in the European Parliament increased continuously. Second, trust in European as well as national political institutions decreased dramatically between May and November 2004. This drop coincided with the Eastern enlargement and the signing of the Constitutional Treaty in Rome, although it is hard to prove a causal relationship between these events and the drop of trust in institutions. Third, throughout the 1990s until 2006, trust in the European Parliament on average was higher than trust in national parliaments. From 1993 until May 2004, this was the case in eleven of the fifteen member states. A few months later, at the time of the European Elections, this situation had dramatically changed. Suddenly, the trust in European institutions was higher than in national ones in only three of the older member states. Again, these findings suggest a relationship with the events in 2004, that is, enlargement and the discussion about the Constitutional Treaty.

The new member states on average differed from the older ones in two respects. First, their trust in European institutions was higher than in the older member states. Second, in contrast to the older member states (at least at that moment in time), their trust in European institutions was higher than in their own national institutions, which they trusted considerably less than citizens in the older member states. The comparison of trust in national and European institutions yields a rather clear pattern. Where trust in national institutions is rather low, trust in EU institutions is higher.

These findings strongly support the hypothesis that positive evaluations of policy performances spill over to trust in political institutions. The development of trust in political institutions follows a more or less similar path as the development of perceived benefits (see Chapter 7). Also, developments in trust are related to objective economic indicators: high inflation leads to a decline of trust, whereas high growth rates lead to an increase of trust.

In Chapter 9, the effect of the 2004 enlargement on people's support for the Union as a political community was assessed. We started our analysis by distinguishing two different views on the meaning of a European demos and European identity as a prerequisite for the development of the EU as a democratic political system. According to the first view, the establishment of a legitimate democracy requires the pre-existence of a collective identity. As long as there is no European collective identity there can be no European demos, and therefore every attempt to establish a democratic Europe is bound to fail. According to a rival theory, a demos is a legal construct in the sense of all people who are subject to the jurisdiction of a particular polity. It does not deny the relevance of a collective identity but assumes that it can develop as consequence of the establishment of a political community rather than being a prerequisite of it. Therefore, in both views a causal relationship between the development of a political community and a collective identity is recognized, but the causal direction is different.

We tested the hypothesis that membership breeds both a sense of citizenship and a sense of collective identity. Our analyses do not offer firm evidence in support of the hypothesis in either case. The sense of citizenship at the time of entry of the Union – rather than the length of membership – seems to explain differences in the sense of European citizenship. Since the 2004 enlargement brought in a number of countries with a low sense of citizenship, this might have a lasting effect on the development of citizenship in the Union. The evidence with regard to a sense of European community is mixed. Length of membership turned out to have a significant effect on the sense of European community, as measured by mutual trust. In Western Europe, mutual trust in general is high, but there is little evidence that this is due to European Union membership as such. The 2004 enlargement meant a serious blow to the development of a European community. Among the citizens of the older member states, trust in the people of at least some of the accession countries, not to mention (then) candidate countries like Bulgaria, Romania, and Turkey, is very low, whereas the low level of interpersonal trust in most of the new member states is reflected in equally low levels of trust in the people from other member states, in whichever part of Europe.

11.4. The effects of enlargement on the legitimacy of the European Union

Let us shortly summarize our findings relating to the effects of the 2004 enlargement on the legitimacy of the Union. The effects on political support seem to be much stronger than on the quality of the system of political representation and can be distinguished in two kinds. First, enlargement had an effect on the political support in the older member states. The support for the EU as the appropriate level of government has declined since 1999. Also, trust in European political institutions declined at the time of enlargement. However, although these changes coincided

In Conclusion: The Legitimacy of the European Union after Enlargement

with enlargement, we cannot be entirely sure that they are really due to enlargement. Second, in some respects the level of support in the new member states is lower than in the older member states. Here we can simply conclude that enlargement had a negative effect on the level of support in the Union as a whole. This was the case with the preferred level of government, support for EU performance, and the sense of European citizenship. However, the level of trust in EU political institutions immediately after enlargement was higher in the new than in the older member states. This seems to be a reflection of the low trust people in Central and Eastern Europe have in their own national political institutions. The functioning of the national rather than the European political system seems to explain the dramatically low turnout in most of the accession countries as well.

The strongest and most negative effect of enlargement we found is on mutual trust between the people across Europe. The trust people from the older member states have in the people from the new member states in Central and particularly in Eastern Europe is dramatically low compared to the mutual trust among the people from the older member states. This lack of trust is related to the same factors that seem to entice people from the new member states to put their trust in the institutions of the Union: a low level of economic development and poor democratic performance, including corruption.

If these are indeed the factors behind these low levels of mutual trust, they might be resolved in the future. But this offers little comfort in the short run. The feasibility of the EU as a polity strongly depends on the consent of the people. The lesson to be learned from our analyses is that if the Union extends too fast beyond the borders within which its citizens feel more or less comfortable, this is bound to have a negative effect on people's support for the European project. An ever-wider Union is clearly at odds with an ever-closer Union. This might be at least part of the explanation for the misgivings people across Europe apparently have with the development of the Union, as became so obvious in the 2005 referenda on the draft Constitutional Treaty in France and the Netherlands, and in the 2008 referendum on the Lisbon Treaty in Ireland.

With regard to the quality of political representation, we found that the requirements we derived from the party government model are amazingly well met, although the 2004 enlargement did have a slightly negative effect on the extent to which they are. Both before and after enlargement, political contestation in the EU is strongly constrained by a single ideological dimension, the left–right dimension. The party groups are distinct and cohesive on this main dimension, both in the way they communicate with their voters and in the way they behave in the European Parliament. Voters across the European Union, both before and after enlargement, can be considered as a single electorate in the sense that their considerations to vote for a party belonging to a particular party group are very similar.

11.5. The quality of political representation in the European Union

Do these latter findings prove that the system of political representation in the EU is functioning effectively? They do, in the sense that the left–right dimension proved to be a strong ideological device able to link the policy preferences of the people to the decision-making process in the European Parliament, at least as far as these policy preferences are related to the left–right dimension.

However, it would be naive to conclude from these findings that representative democracy in the EU is functioning perfectly well. First, we derived our criteria for testing the quality of political representation in the EU from the party government model. As noticed above, the system of political representation at the European level obviously fails to meet one essential requirement of this model: European elections have no visible consequences for the composition of the European Commission, that is, there is no electoral authorization of the Executive. Therefore, in this respect, the EU system of political representation is clearly failing.

Second, we should keep in mind that the research question in the first part of this book referred to the *feasibility* of a truly European system of political representation, since we recognized from the outset that at present such a system does not really exist: there are no European political parties competing for the votes of a European electorate on the basis of European issues, just like there is no European electorate voting for European political parties on the basis of European issues. However, we argued that the absence of a truly European system of political representation does not necessarily mean that elections for the European Parliament fail as an instrument of linkage, that is, in connecting the will of the European people to the decision-making process in the European Parliament. European elections can still serve that function if the national systems of political representation are compatible to the extent that they can be aggregated to the European level without losing any of their essential characteristics. More precisely, if European party groups are still distinct and

In Conclusion: The Legitimacy of the European Union after Enlargement

cohesive and voters do vote for similar reasons for parties belonging to the same party groups. We found that even after the 2004 enlargement the systems of political representation across the member states are still remarkably compatible. Therefore, when it comes to issues related to the main dimension of contestation, the left–right dimension, elections for the European Parliament can still be remarkably successful in linking the will of the European people to the decision-making process in the European Parliament.

However, we should not misinterpret these findings. As far as the process of linkage is successful, it is so *in spite of* the absence of a truly European system of political representation rather than *because of* it. A system of political representation in which a successful linkage is the by-product of the actions of the main actors in the process – political parties and voters – rather than the product of their deliberate action, can hardly be called a successful process of political representation. According to many authors, if representation is not wilful or intentional, it does not count as popular representation at all. At best one could speak of representation 'malgré lui' (Converse and Pierce 1986: 502), 'lui' in this case referring both to the individual voter, voting for a national candidate on the basis of national political issues, and to the individual candidate running for office on behalf of a national political party on the basis of a nationally oriented political programme.

What we proved is that a truly European system of political representation is feasible as far as it depends on the compatibility of national systems of political representation. For the possible development of a truly European system of political representation, this finding is important enough. But being feasible does not mean of course that it exists or is likely to develop in the near future. European elections still are what they used to be, that is, second-order national elections (Reif and Schmitt 1980; Van der Brug et al. 2007). Our findings do not provide a single piece of evidence to quarrel with that more or less classical characterization of European elections.

Third, there seems to be an obvious discrepancy between our findings in the two parts of the book. Our findings on the support for European political institutions and the lack of trust people from the older member states have in their new fellow European citizens seem to suggest that people in the older member states had misgivings about the 2004 enlargement. At the same time we concluded that the effectiveness of the system of political representation was hardly affected by enlargement. One might wonder whether these conclusions are not incompatible. In itself, they are not necessarily. The quality of political representation depends on whether the system of political representation is responsive to these misgivings. But how responsive to these feelings can a system of representation be that is dominated by the left–right dimension (as we repeatedly found), if this dimension does not function as an instrument of linkage for people's attitudes on European integration (as we also found)?

11.6. Party government as a cure for the democratic deficit of the EU?

The major democratic deficits in the European Union we discussed in the previous section, that is, the lack of consequences of the outcome of European elections for the composition of the Commission, the absence of a truly European system of political representation, and the possible lack of responsiveness with regard to the pro-/anti-European integration dimension, can easily be expressed in terms of the party government model. Since we also came to the conclusion that a system of party government at the European level is at least feasible, the introduction of a system of party government at the level of the EU seems to be the obvious solution for the democratic deficit.

There is an ongoing debate on whether or not this indeed might be the cure for the legitimacy problems of the EU.[1] According to an optimistic view the introduction of a model of party government would politicize the relationship between the European Parliament and the Commission and create a pattern of government and opposition within Parliament. It would allow voters to reward or punish political parties for supporting or opposing the Commission. As a consequence it would increase the accountability of European decision making to the European people. This in turn would increase the stakes in European elections, transforming them more into truly European elections instead of second-order national elections. Also, it might increase the interest of the European people in European politics and increase turnout. An open political battle might better link EU politics to citizens' interests and preferences. As a consequence politicization might even reduce the existing euroscepticism insofar as this is based on people's dissatisfaction with the failing democratic processes in the EU (Hix 2006, 2008).

However, the hesitations about this optimistic view are legion. As much as political contestation or competition is recognized as one of the most essential characteristics of modern democracy (Dahl 1971; Powell 1983), it is generally recognized that unrestrained political contestation in a heterogeneous society might undermine the stability of the political system, in particular when the dimensions of conflict are mutually reinforcing rather than cross-cutting (Lipset 1966). Therefore, as we argued elsewhere (Thomassen, Noury, and Voeten 2004), a competitive party system at the European level will only be a positive factor of European integration when the major cleavage dimensions are cross-cutting, in particular when they cut across national borders. The more political differences coincide with national borders, the more disruptive politicization of these differences will be. Therefore, politicization of policy differences on the pro-/anti-European integration dimension would be highly disruptive. It would articulate national differences rather than cross-national political cleavages. In that case the remedy might be worse than the disease (Thomassen, Noury, and Voeten 2004: 164). There can only be a European demos and a European polity if the national demoi are willing to consent to the idea of a European demos and a European polity. Therefore, the acceptance of a European political order is a condition for the development of a European democratic polity in which majoritarian decision making would be considered legitimate. But enforcing a European political system by majoritarian decision making is bound to be considered illegitimate. As Bartolini (2005: 355) argues, 'One cannot have at the same time a system of representation that concerns the territorial and functional boundaries of a polity and its internal differentiation of opinions/interests. The two alignments delegitimize and destructure each other'.

These objections do not apply to the left–right dimension. Left–right positions are hardly related to national background. There might be different majorities in different countries but not as a permanent state of affairs. People are used to a regular 'changing of the guard' by the left and the right at the national level and would have little reason to see themselves as a member of a permanent minority when the same system would be introduced at the European level. Also, the left–right dimension refers to the 'internal differentiation of opinions' rather than the territorial boundaries of the polity. Therefore, there is no reason to assume that politicization would undermine the stability of the Union as long as it is limited to the left–right dimension. This seems to be well recognized by the advocates of politicization who explicitly argue for politicization on the left–right dimension (e.g. Hix 2006). Also, the left–right dimension could develop into the dominant dimension of political contestation at the European level because constitutional issues are deliberately kept from the agenda of supranational decision making and are mostly subject to the intergovernmental regime that meets all essential characteristics of consociational rather than adversarial politics.

However, it is still to be seen whether politicization at the European level can be limited to the left–right dimension once the ghost is out of the bottle. According to Bartolini there is a serious risk that the politicization process will spill over from 'benign left–right issues' to 'threatening constitutive issues' (Bartolini 2006: 35). Bartolini also disputes two further claims of the politicization thesis. First, a crucial expectation of the 'politicization' thesis is that if contentious EU issues were more openly politicized, this might provide a stronger link between citizen's interests and preferences and the internal EU political debate. Referring to our (Schmitt and Thomassen 1999) earlier work indicating that voters and their representatives live in two different worlds with regard to constitutive issues, Bartolini argues that politicization on the left–right dimension does not provide a stronger link because constitutive issues are not related to this dimension. Therefore, it is equally unlikely that politicization will eventually generate more support for the EU – another claim of the politicization thesis (Bartolini 2006: 41–2).

In the remaining part of this section we discuss three issues in this debate: First, the lack of representation on what Bartolini calls constitutive issues; second, the possible spill over from politicization on the left–right dimension to politicization on constitutive issues, and finally, the claim that politicization will lead to less euroscepticism.

It is hardly a matter of dispute that the process of political representation in the EU fails with regard to constitutive issues. There is a big gap between a large majority of the people and most of the political elite on these issues. This gap can persist because the process of representation as we described it throughout this volume is based on the left–right dimension. Since views on constitutive issues are orthogonal to positions on the left–right dimension, politicization on the left–right dimension will not help to solve this problem.

In the introductory chapter we argued that the problem of connecting the preferences of the people on constitutive issues, that is, on (quasi-) constitutional issues including enlargement, is mostly a problem of the national rather than the European channel of political representation. But this, of course, is a normative rather than an empirical statement and, more importantly, it does not solve the problem. National systems of political representation are equally failing as an instrument of linkage with regard to constitutive issues and for the same reason. Like at the European level, views on these issues are not correlated with positions on the left–right dimension at the level of political parties or at the level of the voters. This means that if people vote according to their left–right

In Conclusion: The Legitimacy of the European Union after Enlargement

position, as they do in large numbers (see Chapter 4), they might end up with a party that does not represent their feelings on the dimension of European integration. The only solution[2] to this problem[3] is that for a large number of people the European dimension will replace the left–right dimension as the main dimension determining their party choice.

There are speculations that the European dimension is indeed becoming more important in national elections. Van der Eijk and Franklin (2004) coined the metaphor of a 'sleeping giant' in this connection. In their view the pro-/anti-European integration dimension already appears much riper for politicization (in terms of the number of voters who hold opinions and the extremity of these positions) than does the left–right dimension. This being the case, it is surely only a matter of time before policy entrepreneurs in some countries seize the opportunity presented to their parties by these quite polarized opinions to differentiate themselves from other parties in EU terms. Indeed, as Van der Eijk and Franklin argue, this already appears to have happened in some countries where small parties of the far left or far right have taken up distinctly pro- or (more often) anti-EU stances. In some countries these stances even appear to have paid electoral dividends by attracting voters who would not otherwise have voted for a party at the extreme of the left/right spectrum (Van der Eijk and Franklin 2004). If they are right, elections might indeed become a better instrument of linkage for European issues.

But how likely is it that the European dimension will replace the left–right dimension as the main dimension of contestation in national elections, or even seriously compete with it? In order for an issue dimension to have an effect on electoral behaviour, people should not only have an opinion on it and be aware of the position of political parties, but the issue should also be salient, that is, it should be important to the voters. If it is not, why would they waste their vote on it? There is hardly an indication that 'Europe' is becoming a salient issue in a single member state. At least it pales in comparison with a number of other issues. In the European Election Study 2004, people were asked what in their perception was the most important problem in their country. European unification was hardly mentioned as an important issue at all. Therefore, for the foreseeable future it is very unlikely that many voters will make their party choice in national parliamentary elections dependent on the issue of European unification.

Follesdal and Hix (2005) rightly claim that this lack of salience is at least partly endogenous, a consequence of a lack of political contestation. This 'apathy is likely to change if media and political parties start to claim that EU decisions impact on high-salience issues such as health care provision,

239

education, law and order, pensions and social security policy, and taxation' (Follesdal and Hix 2005: 18). However valid this argument may be, it only gets us into a vicious circle. Political parties have all sorts of reasons for not politicizing the issue of Europeanization. If we consider political parties as rational actors, it is hard to think of a reason why they would want to. Even Schumpeter, the early champion of elitist democracy, argued that if an issue is really important to the people, politicians and political parties will include it in their platform for no other reason than their own interest, that is, maximizing their vote. But for the same reason, less salient issues simply will be neglected (Schumpeter 1976). Up to now the European issue seems to fit in that category. Furthermore, the major political parties at election time will try to emphasize the issues on which they differ from each other, not the issues on which they agree. Finally, the major political parties in favour of European integration, the major political parties have nothing to win by politicizing the issue. Being well aware that a large part of their potential electorate is not with them on this issue, they have nothing to win and much to lose by politicizing it. Therefore, as both at the elite and the mass level the incentives for politicizing the issue dimension of European integration are missing, national elections will not easily develop into an effective mechanism of linkage for issues related to the European dimension.

However, there is an alternative and perhaps more likely scenario that might make national elections into a more effective instrument of linkage on European issues after all, but in a more indirect way. As we discussed in Chapter 2, the monopoly of the left–right dimension as the single most important dimension constraining the attitudes and behaviour of both voters and political parties might be challenged by the growing importance of the libertarian-authoritarian or, more particularly, the globalization/anti-globalization dimension. The rise of populist parties on both sides of the left–right dimension in several countries is the most visible evidence of this phenomenon. In contrast to the left–right dimension, attitudes toward European integration are constrained by this dimension. Opponents of globalization will be inclined to oppose European unification as well. Therefore, the globalization dimension might serve as an information cost-saving device (Downs 1957) or a shortcut (Converse 1964) just like the left–right dimension does. By voting for a particular party because of its general position on globalization, people might end up with the party where they 'belong' on the issue of Europeanization without even being aware of it. Therefore, to the extent that this dimension is becoming more important in the communication between

In Conclusion: The Legitimacy of the European Union after Enlargement

parties and voters, national parliamentary elections indirectly might evolve into a more effective instrument of linkage on European issues.

If European elections are indeed second-order national elections, the salience of the globalization/anti-globalization dimension will probably spill over from the national to the European level. So the interesting paradox of European elections being secondary national elections is that the dimension of European unification – be it indirectly – will only become a salient dimension of conflict in these elections if it has evolved as such at the national level first. Should this happen the dimension of European unification as a specification of the globalization/anti-globalization dimension might be politicized more in European than in national elections. This is a different but perhaps more likely spill over effect than the one Bartolini fears: not a spill over from the politicization of the left–right dimension to the dimension of European integration, but from the national to the European level on the latter dimension. However, it is equally unlikely that such a spill over will be benign to the process of European integration. As argued above, the major established political parties, which tend to be on the pro-globalization and pro-European side of this dimension, have nothing to win by politicizing constitutive issues. Therefore, as could be observed in campaigns for referenda on European treaties, they are inclined to leave the battlefield to the – so far mostly small – parties on the anti-globalization/anti-European integration pole of the dimension. As a consequence this one-sided politicization will not contribute to increasing people's support for the European project. Given the big gap between the major political parties and a large part of the mass public on the issue of European integration, politicization can only lead to a mobilization of euroscepticism. Therefore, in this scenario the expectation that politicization might strengthen the support for the European project seems to be no more than wishful thinking.[4]

Also, politicization of the dimension of European integration might have a disastrous effect on the European party system, the very basis of an effective European system of party government. The European party groups are internally divided on constitutive issues, 'and there is no chance whatsoever that they may organize and compete by structuring opinions on the integration dimension' (Bartolini 2005: 348).

11.7. In conclusion

The two methods we used in this book for evaluating the legitimacy of the EU led to different conclusions, in particular with regard to the effects of

The Legitimacy of the European Union after Enlargement

the 2004 enlargement. We started our evaluation of the system of political representation of the EU from the perspective of the party government model with the observation that this system clearly fails for the simple reason that a system of party government at the European level does not exist. Therefore, we focussed on the question whether such a system would be desirable from a normative point of view and feasible from an empirical point of view. We argued that it is desirable because the process of political representation should take place at the same level as that where decisions are taken. Since at least part of the decisions on EU policy making are subject to the supranational regime, there should be a system of political representation at the European level as well. And since party government is the model of political representation people in most member states are used to, this model is an obvious candidate for such a system at the European level as well.[5]

Furthermore, we argued that from an empirical point of view such a system would be feasible when the national systems of party government were similar enough to be aggregated to the European level without losing any of their essential characteristics as an effective instrument of linkage. We found that the similarity of these national systems is surprisingly high, even after enlargement. This is because the main dimension of contestation across Europe is the left–right dimension. Therefore, aggregating these national systems to the European level would yield a European system of party government hardly less effective as an instrument of linkage than these national systems.

If a European system of party government is both desirable and feasible, the only logical conclusion is that it should be implemented. According to Hix and other proponents of a further democratization of the EU, a development towards a European model of party government is already underway. As far as this is the case, we can only see this as a positive development. However, we also argued that both from a normative and an empirical point of view a European system of party government can and should be based on the left–right dimension and *not* on the dimension of pro-/anti-European integration. The normative reason is that decisions on issues related to this dimension, that is, on constitutive issues, are not subject to the supranational regime. Also, there are good political-philosophical reasons why they should not. There are no 'people of the European Union' in the sense of a European demos who – like in the preamble of the American constitution – can 'ordain and establish this Constitution for [the United States of] Europe'. Since the European Union consists of sovereign states, only the European demoi or the member states representing

In Conclusion: The Legitimacy of the European Union after Enlargement

them can do so. From an empirical point of view we made the argument that the European party system cannot handle constitutive issues and would fall apart if it would have to.

However, this leaves us, or rather the European people, with a problem. Our second method of evaluating the legitimacy of the EU, by assessing the extent to which the European polity is supported by the European people, led to more mixed findings. The legitimacy of the Union from this perspective is limited and was negatively affected by the 2004 enlargement. Therefore, it would be hard to maintain that a European system of political representation is effective if people's feelings with regard to the Union itself are not effectively represented. The argument we made that such issues are basically national rather than European is not very helpful in this context because at the national level exactly the same problem occurs. Because the dimension of pro-/anti-European integration is orthogonal to the left–right dimension, national elections are not an effective instrument of linkage with regard to issues related to this dimension either. National elections can only evolve into an effective instrument of linkage with regard to such issues if the pro-/anti-European integration dimension replaces the left–right dimension as the main dimension of contestation. This is neither desirable nor likely to happen. It is not desirable because it would only reverse the problem and probably make it even worse. It would mean that national elections would no longer be an effective instrument of linkage with regard to issues related to the left–right dimension. Such a consequence seems to be a bit out of proportion. It is unlikely to happen because both the major political parties and a great majority of the electorate seem to share this view.

A more realistic scenario sketched above is the possibility that the globalization/anti-globalization dimension might replace or at least compete with the left–right dimension as the major dimension of contestation. Such a development would have two effects. First, it would make national elections a better instrument of linkage for issues related to this rather new dimension of conflict, including 'European' issues. Second, as we argued above, the increasing importance of this dimension would most likely spill over to the European level, mobilizing euroscepticism and disrupting the incipient European system of party government in the process.

Apparently, there is a tension between a more democratic and an ever-closer and wider Union. This will probably be the case as long as the functional and, in particular, the territorial boundaries of the Union are not clearly defined but are a permanent issue of debate. Strengthening governing *by* the European people will almost certainly slow down and probably even set back the process of European integration. Yet, as long as political elites both at the European and the national level will not accept that it is not only to them to decide what is good *for* the European people, the EU will never become a Union *of* the people.

Notes

1. Even though this debate is not necessarily conducted in terms of the conceptual framework of the party government model.
2. Apart from a referendum, in which issue dimensions do not have to compete with each other.
3. But only for this problem because it would immediately create the same problem of linkage on issues related to the left–right dimension.
4. Of course, the argument that politicization might increase political support referred to politicization on the left–right dimension. But this argument is based on the assumption that people's lack of support for European unification is based on dissatisfaction with the performance of European democracy. However, there are no signs that this is really the case. Euroscepticism seems to be based more on general fears of the consequences of globalization and Europeanization than on dissatisfaction with procedural democracy.
5. But considering all problems related to this model even at the national level it most certainly is not the only model of representative democracy that might come to mind (Mair and Thomassen 2010).

References

Alesina, A., Angeloni, I., and Schuknecht, L. (2005). 'What Does the European Union Do?' *Public Choice*, 12 (3): 275–319.

Almond, G., and Verba, S. (1963). *The Civic Culture: political attitudes and democracy in five nations*, Boston: Little, Brown.

Alter, K. J. (2004). 'The European Parliament and Supranational Party System: A Study in institutional development'. *Comparative Political Studies*, 37 (1): 121–4.

Alvarez, R. M., and Nagler, J. (2000). 'A New Approach for Modelling Strategic Voting in Multiparty Elections'. *British Journal of Political Science*, 30: 57–75.

Anderson, C. J. (1995*a*). 'Economic Uncertainty and European Solidarity Revisited: Trends in Public Support for European Integration'. *The State of The European Union Building a European Polity*: 111–33.

Anderson, C. (1995*b*). *Blaming the Government. Citizens and the Economy in Five European Democracies*, Armonk, NY: M. E. Sharpe.

Anderson, C. J. (1998). 'When in Doubt, Use Proxies: Attitudes toward Domestic Politics and Support for European Integration'. *Comparative Political Studies*, 31 (5): 569.

——and Kaltenthaler, K. C. (1996). 'The Dynamics of Public Opinion toward European Integration, 1973–93'. *European Journal of International Relations*, 2 (2): 175.

——and Reichert, M. S. (1996). 'Economic Benefits and Support for Membership in the European Union: A Cross-National Analysis'. *Journal of Public Policy*, 15 (3): 231–49.

——and Ward, D. S. (1997). 'Barometer Elections in Comparative Perspective'. *Electoral Studies*, 15: 447–60.

Andeweg, R. (1995). 'The Reshaping of National Party Systems'. *West European Politics*, 18: 58–78.

Anselin, L. (2001). 'Spatial Econometrics', in B. H. Baltagi (ed.), *A companion to theoretical econometrics*. Malden, Mass.: Blackwell.

Arellano, M., and Bond, S. (1991). 'Some Tests of Specification for Panel Data'. *Review of Economic Studies*, 58 (2): 277–97.

Aspinwall, M. (2002). 'Preferring Europe. Ideology and National Preferences on European Integration'. *European Union Politics*, 3 (1): 81–111.

Attina, F. (1990). 'The Voting-Behavior of the European Parliament Members and the Problem of the Europarties'. *European Journal of Political Research*, 18 (5): 557–79.

References

Baltagi, B. H. (2005). *Econometric analysis of panel data*, 3rd ed, Chichester; Hoboken, NJ: J. Wiley & Sons.

Banting, K., and Kymlickz, W. (2003). *Do Multiculturalism Policies Erode the Welfare State?* Luxembourg: Luxembourg Income Study Working Paper No. 366.

Bartolini, S. (2005). *Restructuring Europe. Centre formation, system building, and political structuring between the nation state and the European Union*, Oxford: Oxford University Press.

—— (2006). 'Should the Union be 'Politicised'? Prospects and Risks', in *Politics: The Right or the Wrong Sort of Medicine for the EU?* Brussels: Notre Europe.

—— and Mair, P. (1990). *Identity, Competition, and Electoral Availability. The Stabilisation of European Electorates 1885–1985*, Cambridge: Cambridge University Press.

Beck, N. (2007). 'From Statistical Nuisances to Serious Modeling: Changing How We Think About the Analysis of Time-Series Cross-Section Data'. *Political Analysis*, 15 (2): 97–100.

—— and Katz, J. N. (1995). 'What to do (and not to do) with Time-Series Cross-Section Data'. *The American Political Science Review*, 89 (3): 634–47.

—— and Katz, J. (1996). 'Nuisance vs. Substance: Specifying and Estimating Time-Series Cross-Section Models'. *Political Analysis*, 6: 1–36.

—— —— (2004). 'Time-Series–Cross-Section Issues: Dynamics, 2004'. Working Paper, *The Society of Political Methodology*.

—— —— (2004). *Time-Series-Cross-Section Issues: Dynamics, 2004*, Draft of July 24: 2004.

Bednar, J., Ferejohn, J., and Garrett, G. (1996). 'The Politics of European Federalism'. *International Review of Law and Economics*, 16 (3): 279–94.

Beetham, D., and Lord, C. (1998a). *Legitimacy and the EU*, London: Longman.

—— —— (1998b). 'Legitimacy and the European Union', in A. Weale and M. Nentwioch (eds), *Political Theory and the European Union*. London: Routledge, 15–33.

Beichelt, T. (2004). 'Euro-Skepticism in the EU accession Countries'. *Comparative European Politics*, 2: 29–50.

Berg, L. (2007). *Multi-level Europeans. The Influence of Territorial Attachments on Political Trust and Welfare Attitudes*, Göteborg: Göteborg University.

Beyers, J., and Dierickx, G. (1997). 'Nationality and European Negotiations: the working Groups of the Council of Ministers'. *European Journal of International Relations*, 3 (4): 435–71.

Bielasiak, J. (2004). *Party Systems and EU Accession: Euroscepticism in East Europe*, Conference on Public Opinion about the EU in Post-Communist Eastern Europe, Indiana University, Bloomington, April 2–3.

Birch, S. (2001). *Electoral Systems and Party System Stability in Post-Communist Europe*, 97th Annual Meeting of the American Political Science Association, San Francisco, August 30–September 2.

Blondel, J., Sinnot, R., and Svenson, P. (1998). *People and Parliament in the European Union*, Oxford: Clarendon Press.

References

Blumler, J. G. (1983). 'Communication and Turnout', in J. G. Blumler (ed.), *Communicating to Voters: Television in the First European Parliament Elections*. London/Beverly Hills: Sage.

—— and Fox, A. D. (1982). *The European Voter: Popular Responses to the First European Community Elections*, London: Policy Studies Institute.

Bogdanor, V. (1989). 'Direct Elections, Representative Democracy and European Integration'. *Electoral Studies*, 8: 205–16.

Borre, O., and Goldsmith, M. (1995). 'The Scope of Government', in O. Borre, and E. Scarborough (eds.), *The Scope of Government*. Oxford: Oxford University Press.

Börzel, T. (2005). 'Mind the gap! European integration between level and scope'. *Journal of European Public Policy*, 12 (2): 217–36.

Brinegar, A., Jolly, S., and Kitschelt, H. (2004). 'Varieties of Capitalism and Political Divides over European Integration', in G. Marks and M. R. Steenbergen (eds.), *European Integration and Political Conflict*. Cambridge/New York: Cambridge University Press.

Bruter, M. (2003). 'Winning Hearts and Minds for Europe. The Impact of News and Symbols on Civic and Cultural European Identity'. *Comparative Political Studies*, 36 (10): 1148–79.

—— (2005). *Citizens of Europe? The emergence of a mass European identity*, Basingstoke: Palgrave Macmillan.

Budge, I., Klingemann, H.-D., Volkens, A., Bara, J., Tanenbaum, E., with R. Fording, D. Hearl, H. Kim, M. McDonald and S. Mendez (2001) *Mapping Policy Preferences. Estimates for Parties, Electors, and Governments 1945–1998*, Oxford: Oxford University Press (including CD-ROM with MRG/CMP data for 25 countries 1945–1998).

Burgess, M. (2006). *Comparative Federalism: Theory And Practice*, London: Routledge.

Carey, S. (2002). 'Undivided Loyalties: Is National Identity an Obstacle to European Integration?' *European Union Politics*, 3 (4): 387–413.

Carrubba, C. J., Gabel, M., Murrah, L., Clough, R., Montgomery, E., and Schambagh, R. (2006). 'Off the Record: Unrecorded Legislative Votes, Selection Bias and Roll-Call Vote Analysis'. *British Journal of Political Science*, 36: 691–704.

Christin, T., and Hug, S. (2002). 'Referendums and Citizen Support for European Integration'. *Comparative Political Studies*, 35 (5): 586–617.

—— and Trechsel, A. H. (2002). 'Joining the EU? Explaining Public Opinion in Switzerland'. *European Union Politics*, 3 (4): 415–43.

Citrin, J., and Sides, J. (2004). 'Can There Be Europe without Europeans? Problems of Identity in a Multinational Community', in R. K. Herrmann, M. B. Brewer and T. Risse-Kappen (eds.), *Transnational Identities: Becoming European in the EU*. Lanham: MD: Rowman & Littlefield.

Commisso, E. (1997). 'Is the Glass Half Full or Half Empty? Reflections on Five Years of Competitive Parties in Eastern Europe'. *Communist-Post-Communist Politics*, 30 (1): 1–21.

Converse, P. E. (1964). 'The Nature of Belief Systems in Mass Publics', in D. Apter (ed.), *Ideology and Discontent*. New York: The Free Press.

References

Converse, P. E., and Pierce, R. (1986). *Political Representation in France*, Cambridge MA: Belknap Press.

Dahl, R. A. (1956). *A Preface to Democratic Theory*, Chicago: University of Chicago Press.

Dahl, R. A. (1971). *Polyarchy: Participation and Opposition*, New Haven: Yale University Press.

Dahl, R. (1989). *Democracy and its critics*, New Haven: Yale University Press.

Dahl, R., and Tufte, E. (1974). *Size and democracy*, Stanford: Stanford University Press.

Dalton, R. J., Flanagan, S., and Beck, P. A. (eds.) (1984). *Electoral Change in Advanced Industrial Democracies: Realignment or Dealignment?* Princeton: Princeton University Press.

De Hoyos, R. E., and Sarafidis, V. (2006). 'XTCSD: Stata module to test for cross-sectional dependence in panel data models'. *Statistical Software Components S456736*.

Delanty, G. (1995). *Inventing Europe: Idea, Identity, Reality*, New York: Wiley.

Delhey, J. (2005). 'A Trade-off between Enlargement and Integration? An Analysis of Trust between EU Nationalities', in *WZB Discussion Papers*, Berlin: Social Science Research Center Berlin (WZB).

——and Newton, K. (2005). 'Predicting Cross-National Levels of Social Trust: Global Pattern of Nordic Exceptionalism'. *European Sociological Review*, 21 (4): 311–27.

Deutsch, K. W., Burrell, S. A., Kann, R. A., Lee Jr., M., Lichtermann, M., Loewenheim, F. L., and Van Wagenen, R. W. (1957). *Political Community and the North Atlantic Area*, Princeton: Princeton University Press.

De Vreese, C. H. (2002). *Framing Europe: Television news and European integration*, Amsterdam: Aksant Academic Publishers.

——(2003). *Communicating Europe*, London: The Foreign Policy Centre.

——(2007). *A European public sphere?* Mannheim: Living Review, Connex.

——and Boomgaarden, H. G. (2006). 'Media Effects on Public Opinion about the Enlargement of the European Union'. *Journal of Common Market Studies*, 44 (2): 419–36.

——Banducci, S., Semetko, H. A., and Boomgaarden, H. G. (2006). 'The news coverage of the 2004 European Parliamentary election campaign in 25 countries'. *European Union Politics*, 7 (4): 477–504.

——Lauf, E., and Peter, J. (2007). 'The media and European Parliament elections: Second-rate coverage of a second-order event?', in W. van der Brug and C. van der Eijk (eds.), *European elections and domestic politics. Lessons from the past and scenarios for the future*. Notre Dame: University of Notre Dame Press.

——Peter, J., and Semetko, H. A. (2001). 'Framing Politics at the Launch of the Euro: A cross-national Comparative Study of Frames in the News'. *Political Communication*, 18 (2): 107–22.

——and Schmitt, H. (eds.) (2007). *A European Public Sphere: How much of it do we have and how much do we need?* [CONNEX Report Series No. 02] Mannheim: MZES.

References

—— and Semetko, H. A. (2002). 'Cynical and engaged: strategic campaign coverage, public opinion and mobilization in a referendum'. *Communication Research*, 29 (6): 615–41.

—— —— (2004). 'News Matters: Influences on the Vote in the Danish 2000 Euro Referendum Campaign'. *European Journal of Political Research*, 43 (5): 699–722.

De Winter, L. (2008). 'La recherche sur les identités ethno-territoriales en Belgique'. *Revue Internationale de Politique Comparée*, 14 (1): 575–95.

—— Swyngedouw, M. (1999) 'The Scope of EU Government', in H. Schmitt and J. J. A. Thomassen (eds.), *Political Representation and Legitimacy in the European Union*. Oxford: Oxford University Press.

Dickey, D. A., and Fuller, W. A. (1979). 'Distribution of the Estimators for Autoregressive Time Series With a Unit Root'. *Journal of the American Statistical Association*, 74 (366): 427–31.

Dobson, A. (2000). *Green Political Thought*, London: Routledge.

Downs, A. (1957). *An Economic Theory of Democracy*, New York: Harper and Row.

Driscoll, J. C., and Kraay, A. C. (1998). 'Consistent Covariance Matrix Estimation with Spatially Dependent Panel Data'. *The Review of Economics and Statistics*, 80 (4): 549–60.

Duch, R., and Taylor, M. (1997). 'Economics and the Vulnerability of the Pan-European Institutions'. *Political Behavior*, 19 (1): 65–80.

Easton, D. (1965a). *A Systems Analysis of Political Life*, New York: John Wiley.

—— (1965b). *A Framework for Political Analysis*, Englewood Cliffs, NJ: Prentice Hall.

—— (1975). 'A Re-Assessment of the Concept of Political Support'. *British Journal of Political Science*, 5: 435–57.

—— (1979). *A Systems Analysis of Political Life*, Chicago: University of Chicago Press.

Eder, K. (2000). 'Zur Transformation nationalstaatlicher Öffentlichkeit in Europa'. *Berliner Journal für Soziologie*, 2: 167–84.

—— and Kantner, C. (2002). 'Interdiskursivität in der europäischen Öffentlichkeit'. *Berliner Debatte Initial*, 13 (5/6): 78–88.

Egeberg, M. (1999). 'Transcending intergovernmentalism? Identity and role perceptions of national officials in EU decision-making'. *Journal of European Public Policy*, 6 (3): 456–74.

Eichenberg, R. C. (1999). *Measurement Matters: Cumulation in the Study of Citizen Support for European Integration*, Medford: Tufts University.

—— and Dalton, R. J. (1993). 'Europeans and the European Community: The Dynamics of Public Support for European Integration'. *International Organization*, 47: 507–34.

—— —— (2007). 'Post-Maastricht Blues: The Transformation of Citizen Support for European Integration, 1973–2004'. *Acta Politica*, 42 (2/3): 128–52.

Enyedi, Z. (2005). 'The role of agency in cleavage formation'. *European Journal of Political Research*, 44: 697–720.

Erbe, J. (2005). " 'What Do the Papers Say?' How Press Reviews Link National Media Arenas in Europe". *Javnost - The Public*, 12 (2): 75–92.

References

Estella de Noriega, A. (1997). *The principle of subsidiarity and its critique. A 'Contextual' Analysis of the Principle of Subsidiarity*, Unpublished PhD. Thesis. Florence: European University Institute.

Eulau, H., and Lewis-Beck, M. S. (eds.). (1985). *Economic Conditions and Electoral Outcomes*, New York: Agathon Press.

Evans, G. (1996a). 'The Social Bases of Democratization and Marketization in Eastern Europe', in L. Whitehead (ed.), *Political and Economic Liberalization*. Oxford: Oxford University Press, 225–44.

—— (1996b). 'Social Class and Interest Formation in Post-Communist Societies', in D. J. Lee and B. S. Turner (eds.), *Conflicts About Class: Debating Inequality in late Industrialism*. London: Longman, 225–44.

—— and Whitefield, S. (1993). 'Identifying the bases of party competition in Eastern Europe'. *British Journal of Political Science*, 23: 521–48.

—— —— (2000). 'Explaining the formation of electoral cleavages in post-communist democracies', in H.-D. Klingemann, E. Mochmann, and K. Newton (eds.), *Elections in Central and Eastern Europe: The First Wave*. Berlin: Edition Sigma, 36–70.

Fligstein, N. (2008). *Euroclash: The EU, European Identity, and the Future of the EU*, Oxford: Oxford University Press.

Follesdal, A., and Hix, S. (2005). 'Why there is a Democratic Deficit in the EU; a Response to Majone and Moravcsik'. *European Governance Papers*.

Franklin, M. N. (2001). 'How Structural Factors cause Turnout in European Parliament Elections'. *European Union Politics*, 2: 309–28.

—— (2004). *Voter Turnout and the Dynamics of Electoral Competition in Established Democracies since 1945*, New York: Cambridge University Press.

—— (2007a). 'Effects of Space and Time on Turnout in European Parliament Elections', in W. van der Brug and C. van der Eijk (eds.), *European Elections and Domestic Politics: Lessons from the Past and Scenarios for the Future*. Notre Dame, IN: University of Notre Dame Press.

—— (2007b). 'Turning out or turning off? How the EP elections of 2004 shed light on turnout dynamics', in M. Marsh, S. Mikhaylov and H. Schmitt (eds.), *European Elections after Eastern Enlargement* [CONNEX Report Series No. 01] Mannheim: MZES.

—— Mackie, T., and Valen, H. (1992). *Electoral Change. Responses to Evolving Social and Attitudinal Structures in Western Countries*, Cambridge: Cambridge University Press.

—— Marsh, M., and McLaren, L. (1994). 'Uncorking the Bottle: Popular Opposition to European Unification in the Wake of Maastricht'. *Journal of Common Market Studies*, 32 (4): 455–72.

—— Van der Eijk, C., and Marsh, M. (1995). 'Referendum Outcomes and Trust in Government: Public Support for Europe in the Wake of Maastricht', in J. E. S. Hayward (ed.), *The Crisis of Representation in Europe*. London/Portland, OR: Frank Cass.

References

—— and Oppenhuis, E. (1996). 'The Institutional Context: Turnout', in C. van der Eijk and M. Franklin (eds.), *Choosing Europe? The European Electorate and National Politics in the Face of Union*. Ann Arbor: The University of Michigan Press.

Fuchs, D. (1989). *Die Unterstützung des politischen Systems der Bundesrepublik Deutschland*, Opladen: Westdeutscher Verlag.

—— (1993). 'A Metatheory of the Democratic Process'. *WZB Discussion paper FS III*: 93–203.

—— (2000). 'Demos und Nation in der Europaeischen Union', in H.-D. Klingemann and F. Neidhardt (eds.), *Zur Zukunft der Demokratie – Herausforderungen im Zeitalter der Globalisierung*. Berlin: Sigma.

—— and Klingemann, H.- D. (1990). 'The Left-Right Schema', in M. K. Jennings and J. Van Deth (eds.), *Continuities in Political Action*. Berlin: de Gruyter.

—— —— (2002). 'Eastward Enlargement of the European Union and the Identity of Europe'. *West European Politics*, 25: 19–54.

Gabel, M. J. (1998a). 'Economic Integration and Mass Politics: Market Liberalization and Public Attitudes in the European Union'. *American Journal of Political Science*, 42 (3): 936–53.

—— (1998b). *Interests and Integration: Market Liberalization, Public Opinion and European Union*, Ann Arbor: University of Michigan Press.

—— and Palmer, H. D. (1995). 'Understanding Variation in Public Support for European Integration'. *European Journal of Political Research*, 27 (1): 3–19.

—— and Whitten, G. D. (1997). 'Economic Conditions, Economic Perceptions, and Public Support for European Integration'. *Political Behavior*, 19 (1): 81–96.

Gamson, W. A. (1968). *Power and Discontent*, Homewood, IL: Dorsey Press.

Giscard d'Estaing, V. (1990). *Rapport de la Commission institutionnelle sur le principe de subsidiarité*. Parlement Européen, A3–267/90, Luxembourg: OPOCE.

Gijsberts, M., and Nieuwbeerta, P. (2000). 'Class Cleavages in Party Preferences in the New Democracies in Eastern Europe: A Comparison with Western Democracies'. *European Societies*, 2: 397–430.

Goetz, K., and Hix, S. (eds.) (2001). *Europeanised politics? European Integration and national political systems*, London: Frank Cass.

Grimm, D. (2004). 'Treaty or constitution? The legal basis of the European Union after Maastricht', in E. O. Eriksen, J. E. Fossum and A. J. Menéndez (eds.), *Developing a Constitution for Europe*. London: Routledge, 69–87.

Habermas, J. (1962). *Strukturwandel der Öffentlichkeit: Untersuchungen zu einer Kategorie der bürgerlichen Gesellschaft (The Structural Transformation of the Public Sphere. An Inquiry into a Category of Bourgeois Society)*, Neuwied: Hermann Luchterhand Verlag.

—— (1994). 'Citizenship and National Identity', in B. van Steenbergen (ed.), *The Condition of Citizenship*. London: Sage.

—— (1996). *Between Facts and Norms: Contributions to a Discourse Theory of Law and Democracy*, Cambridge: MA: MIT Press.

References

Habermas, J. (2001). 'Warum braucht Europa eine Verfassung?' *Deutschland*, 6: 62–5.

Hadenius, A., and Teorell, J. (2005). 'Assessing Alternative Indices of Democracy'. *C&M. Working Papers*, IPSA.

Haesly, R. (2001). 'Euroskeptics, Europhiles and Instrumental Europeans: European Attachment in Scotland and Wales'. *European Union Politics*, 2 (1): 81–102.

Handley, D. (1981). 'Public opinion and European integration: The crisis of the 1970s'. *European Journal of Political Research*, 9 (4): 335–64.

Henig, S. (ed.) (1979). *Political Parties in the European Community*, London: George Allan & Unwin.

Hix, S. (1999). 'Dimensions and Alignments in European Union Politics: Cognitive Constraints and Partisan Responses'. *European Journal of Political Research*, 35 (1): 69–106.

—— (2001). 'Legislative behaviour and party competition in the European Parliament: An application of nominate to the EU'. *Journal of Common Market Studies*, 39 (4): 663–88.

—— (2006). 'Why the EU needs (Left-Right) Politics? Policy Reform and Accountability are impossible without it', in *Politics: The Right or the Wrong Sort of Medicine for the EU?* Brussels: Notre Europe.

—— (2008). *What's Wrong with the European Union & How to Fix it*, Cambridge: Polity Press.

—— and Lord, C. (1997). *Political Parties in the European Union*, Houndsmills and London: Macmillan.

—— and Noury, A. (2006). *After enlargement: Voting patterns in the sixth European Parliament*. Typescript, available at <http://personal.lse.ac.uk/HIX/Working_Papers/> (Accessed May 31st 2006.

—— —— and Roland, G. (2005). 'Power to the parties: Cohesion and competition in the European Parliament, 1979–2001'. *British Journal of Political Science*, 35: 209–34.

—— —— —— (2006a). *Democratic Politics in the European Parliament*, Cambridge: Cambridge University Press.

—— —— —— (2006b). 'Dimensions of politics in the European Parliament'. *American Journal of Political Science*, 50 (2): 494–511.

Hooghe, L. (2003). 'Europe Divided? Elites vs. Public Opinion on European Integration'. *European Union Politics*, 4 (3): 281–305.

—— and Marks, G. (2001). *European Integration and Multi-Level Governance*, Lanham: Rowman and Littlefield.

—— —— (2004). 'Does Identity or Economic Rationality Drive Public Opinion on European Integration?' *PS: Political Science and Politics*, 37 (3): 415–20.

—— —— (2005). 'Calculation, Community and Cues: Public Opinion on European Integration'. *European Union Politics*, 6 (4): 419.

—— —— (2008). 'European Union?' *West European Politics*, 32 (1/2): 108–29.

—— —— and Wilson, C. (2002). 'Does Left/Right Structure Party Positions on European Integration?' *Comparative Political Studies*, 35: 965–89.

References

—————(2004). 'Does Left/Right Structure Party Positions on European Integration?', in G. Marks and M. R. Steenbergen (eds.), *European Integration and Political Conflict*. Cambridge: Cambridge University Press, 120–40.

Huber, J., and Inglehart, R. (1995). 'Expert Interpretations of Party Space and Party Locations in 42 Societies'. *Party Politics*, 1 (1): 73–111.

Hug, S., and König, T. (2002). 'In View of Ratification. Governmental Preferences, and Domestic Constraints at the Amsterdam Intergovernmental Conference'. *International Organization*, 56 (2): 447–76.

Inglehart, R., (1970). 'The New Europeans: Inward or Outward Looking?' *International Organization*, 24 (1): 129–39.

—— (1977). *The Silent Revolution: Changing Values and Political Styles among Western Publics*, Princeton: NJ: Princeton University Press.

—— and Norris, P. (2004). *Scared and Secular. Religion and Politics Worldwide*, Cambridge: Cambridge University Press.

—— and Rabier, J. R. (1978). 'Economic Uncertainty and European Solidarity: Public Opinion Trends'. *The ANNALS of the American Academy of Political and Social Science*, 440 (1): 66.

Jones, E. (2004). 'The politics of Europe 2003: differences and disagreements'. *Industrial Relations Journal*, 35 (6): 483–99.

Kaase, M. (1979). 'Legitimitätskrise in westlichen demokratischen Industriegesellschaften: Mythos oder Realität?', in H. Klages and P. Kmieciak (eds.), *Wertewandel und gesellschaftlicher Wandel*. Frankfurt a.M.: Campus.

Kaplan, A. (1964). *The Conduct of Inquiry*, Scranton, PA: Chandler Publishing Company.

Katz, R. S., and Wessels, B. (1999). *The European Parliament, the National Parliaments and European Integration*, Oxford: Oxford University Press.

Keating, M. (2008). 'Thirty Years of Territorial Politics'. *West European Politics*, 32 (1/2): 60–81.

—— and Hughes, J. (eds.) (2003). *The regional challenge in Central and Eastern Europe: territorial restructuring and European integration*, Brussels: Peter Lang.

Kielmansegg, P. Graf (1993). 'Vereinigung ohne Legitimität'. *Merkur: Deutsche Zeitschrift für europäisches Denken*, 47 (7): 561–75.

—— (1996). 'Integration und Demokratie', in M. Jachtenfuchs and B. Kohler-Koch (eds.), *Europäische Integration*. Opladen: Leske & Budrich, 47–71.

King, G., Keohane, R. D., and Verba, S. (1994). *Designing Social Inquiry*, Princeton: Princeton University Press.

Kitschelt, H. (1988). 'Left-libertarian parties'. *World Politics*, 40: 194–234.

—— (1992). 'The Formation of Party Systens in East Central Europe'. *Politics and Society*, 20: 7–50.

—— Mansfeldova, Z., Markowski, R., and Tóka, G. (1999). *Post-Communist Party Systems: Competition, Representation, and Inter-Party Cooperation*, Cambridge: Cambridge University Press.

Kleinsteuber, H. J. (2001). 'Habermas and the Public Sphere: From a German to a European Perspective'. *Javnost - the public*, 9 (1): 95–108.

References

Klingemann, H.-D., Hofferbert, R. I., and Budge, I. (1994). *Parties, Policies, and Democracy*, Boulder: CO: Westview Press.

——and Wattenberg, M. P. (1992). 'Decaying Versus Developing Party Systems: A Comparison of Party Images in the United States and West Germany'. *British Journal of Political Science*, 22: 131–49.

Koopmans, R. (2004). *Analysis of Political Claims in European Print Media*. Europub.com Integrated Report: Cross-national, cross-issue, cross-time. WP2.

——(2007). 'Who Inhabits the European Public Sphere? Winners and Losers, Supporters and Opponents in Europeanised Political Debates'. *European Journal of Political Research*, 46 (2): 183–210.

——and Erbe, J. (2004). 'Towards a European Public Sphere? Vertical and Horizontal Dimensions of Europeanised Political Communication'. *Innovation*, 17: 97–118.

Kreppel, A. (2002). *The European Parliament and the Supranational Party System*, New York: Cambridge University Press.

——and Hix, S. (2003). 'From "grand coalition" to left-right confrontation - Explaining the shifting structure of party competition in the European Parliament'. *Comparative Political Studies*, 36 (1/2): 75–96.

Kriesi, H., Grande, E., Lachat, R., Dolezal, M., Bornschier, S., and Frey, T. (2006). 'Globalization and The Transformation of the National Political Space: Six European Countries Compared'. *European Journal of Political Research*, 45: 921–56.

Lawson, K., Rommele, A., and Karasimeonov, G. (eds.) (1999). *Cleavages, Parties and Voters: Studies from Bulgaria, the Czech Republic, Poland and Romania*, London: Praeger.

Lijphart, A. (1997). 'Unequal Participation: Democracy's Unresolved Dilemma. (Presidential Address, American Political Science Association 1996)'. *The American Political Science Review*, 91: 1–14.

Lindberg, L. N., and Scheingold, S. A. (eds.) (1970). *Europe's Would-Be Policy: Patterns of Change in the European Community*, Englewood Cliffs: Prentice-Hall.

Lindström, U. (1991). 'East European Social Democracy: Reborn to be Rejected', in L. Karvanen and J. Sundberg (eds.), *Social Democracy in Transition. Northern, Southern, and Eastern Europe*. Aldershot: Dartmouth, 269–301.

Lipset, S. M. (1966). *Political Man*, London: Mercury Books.

——and Rokkan, S. (1967). 'Cleavage Structures, Party Systems, and Voter Alignments: An Introduction', in S. M. Lipset and S. Rokkan (eds.), *Party Systems and Voter Alignments: Cross-National Perspectives*. New York: Free Press.

————(1967). 'Cleavage Structures, Party Systems and Voter Alignments: Cross-National Perspectives', in S. M. Lipset and S. Rokkan (eds.), *Party Systems and Voter Alignments: Cross-National Perspectives*. New York: Free Press, 1–64.

————(1967). *Party Systems and Voter Alignments: Cross-National Perspectives*, New York: Free Press.

Lodge, J. (1996). *Political Union in Europe*. Cheltenham: Edward Elgar Publishers.

References

Lord, C. (2004). *A Democratic Audit of the European Union*, Houndmills: Palgrave Macmillan.

Luhmann, N. (1968). *Vertrauen. Mechanismus der Reduktion sozialer Komplexität*, Stuttgart: Enke Verlag.

Mair, P., and Mudde, C. (1998). 'The Party Family and its Study'. *Annual Review of Political Science*, 1: 211–29.

—— Thomassen, J. (2010). 'Electoral democracy and political representation in the European Union. *Journal of European Public Policy*, (Spring).

Majone, G. (1993). 'The European Community: Between social policy and social regulation'. *Journal of Common Market Studies*, 31: 153–69.

—— (1994). 'The Rise of the Regulatory State in Europe'. *West European Politics*, 17 (3): 78–102.

—— (1996). *Regulating Europe*, London: Routledge.

Marks, G. (1998). 'Territorial Identities in the European Union', in J. J. Anderson (ed.), *Regional Integration and Democracy: Expanding on the European Experience*. Lanham, MD: Rowman & Littlefield.

—— Hooghe, L., Nelson, M., and Edwards, E. (2006). 'Party Competition and European Integration in East and West: Different Structure, Same Causality'. *Comparative Political Studies*, 39 (2): 1–21.

—— and I. Llamazares (2007). 'Multi-level Governance in Southern Europe: Euorpean Integration and Regional Mobilization', in P. Nikiforos Diamandouros, R. Gunther and G. Pasquino (eds.), *The Changing Functions of the State in the New Southern Europe*. Baltimore: Johns Hopkins University Press.

—— and Steenbergen, M. (2002). 'Understanding Political Contestation in the European Union'. *Comparative Political Studies*, 35 (8): 879–92.

Marsh, M. (1999). 'Policy Performance', in H. Schmitt and J. Thomassen (eds.), *Political Representation, and Legitimacy in the European Union*. Oxford: Oxford University Press, 90–107.

Marshall, T. H. (1950). 'Citizenship and Social Class', in T. Bottomore (ed.), *Citzenship and Social Class*. London: Pluto Press.

Mateju, P., and Reháková, B. (1996). 'Turning Left or Class Realignment? Analysis of the Changing Relationship between Class and Party in the Czech Republic, 1992–96'. *East European Politics and Societies*, 11: 507–47.

McCrone, D., and Kiely, R. (2000). 'Nationalism and Citizenship'. *Sociology*, 34 (1): 1934.

McElroy, G., and Benoit, K. (2007). 'Party Groups and Policy Positions in the European Parliament'. *Party Politics*, 13: 5–28.

McGarry, J., and Keating, M. (eds.) (2006). *European integration and the nationalities question*, London/New York: Routledge.

McLaren, L. M. (2002). 'Public Support for the European Union: Cost/Benefit Analysis or Perceived Cultural Threat?' *The Journal of Politics*, 64 (2): 551–66.

—— (2006). *Identity, interests and attitudes to European integration*, Basingstoke: Palgrave Macmillan.

References

Medrano, D. (2003). *Framing Europe: Attitudes to European Integration in Germany, Spain, and the United Kingdom*, Princeton: Princeton University Press.

Medrano, J. D., and Gutiérrez, P. (2001). 'Nested Identities: National and European Identity in Spain'. *Ethnic and Racial Studies*, 24 (5): 753–78.

Menard, S. (2002). *Applied logistic regression analysis*, 2nd Edition. Thousand Oaks, CA: Sage Publications.

Mershon, C., and Pasquino, G. (eds.) (1995). *Italian Politics – Ending the First Republic*, Boulder, CO: Westview.

Meulemann, H. (2004). 'Enforced Secularization - Spontaneous Revival? Religious Belief, Unbelief, Uncertainty and Indifference in East and West European Countries 1991–1998'. *European Sociological Review*, 20: 47–61.

Miller, A. H., and Klobucar, T. (2000). 'The Development of Party Identification in Post-Soviet States'. *American Journal of Political Science*, 44: 667–86.

Moravscik, A. (1998). *The Choice for Europe: Social Purpose and State Power from Messina to Maastricht*, New York: Cornell University Press.

—— (2002). 'In Defense of the "Democratic Deficit": Reassessing the Legitimacy of the European Union'. *Journal of Common Market Studies*, 40 (4): 603–34.

Müller-Rommel, F. (1989). *New Politics in Western Europe: The Rise and Success of Green Parties*, Boulder, CO: Westview.

Neidhardt, F. (1994). 'Offentlichkeit, offentliche Meining, soziale Bewegungen'. *Sonderheft Kolner Zeitschrift fur Soziologie und Sozialpsychologie*, Opladen: Westdeutscher, 7–41.

Netjes, C. E., and Edwards, E. (2005). 'Taking Europe to Its Extremes. Examining Cueing Effects of Right-Wing Populist Parties on Public Opinion Regarding European Integration'. *WZB discussion paper SP IV 2005-202*.

Niedermayer, O. (1995). 'Trust and Sense of Community', in O. Niedermayer and R. Sinnott (eds.), *Public Opinion and International Governance*. Oxford: Oxford University Press.

Norris, P. (1999*a*). 'The political regime', in N. H. Schmitt and J. Thomassen (eds.), *Political Representation and Legitimacy in the European Union*. Oxford: Oxford University Press.

—— (1999*b*). *Critical Citizens: Global Support for Democratic Government*, Oxford: Oxford University Press.

Noury, A. G. (2002). 'Ideology, Nationality, and Euro-Parliamentarians'. *European Union Politics*, 3 (2): 33–58.

Novy, L. (2003). *Reporting the Future of Europe: Identity, Mass Media and the Public Sphere in the European Union*, paper presented at the Annual MAGES Graduate Student Conference, Georgetown University.

Nye, J., Zelikow, P., and King, D. (1997). *Why People Don't Trust Government. Cambridge*, MA: Harvard University Press.

Oates, W. E. (1972). *Fiscal Federalism*, New York: Harcourt Brace Jovanovich.

O'Leary, S. (1996). *The Evolving Concept of Community Citizenship*, The Hague: Kluwer Law International.

References

Oppenhuis, E. (1995). *Voting Behaviour in Europe*, Amsterdam: Spinhuis.

Ostrogorski, M. (1902). *Democracy and the American Party System*, New York: MacMillan.

Palmer, H., and Gabel, M. (1999). *National Interest, Public Opinion, and European Integration: A Political Economy Model of National-Level Public Support*. Working paper presented at the 1998 Meeting of the Public Choice Society, New Orleans, LA.

Persson, T., and Tabellini, G. (2003). *The Economic Effects of Constitutions*, Cambridge: The MIT Press.

Peter, J., and De Vreese, C. H. (2004). 'In Search of Europe – A Cross-national Comparative Study of the European Union in National Television News'. *Harvard Journal of Press/Politics*, 9 (4): 3–24.

Peters, B., Wessler, H., Sifft, S., Bruggemann, M., and Kleinen-von Koningslow, K. (2007). *The Transnationalization of Public Spheres*, Basingstoke: Palgrave Macmillan.

Peterson, P. E. (1995). *The Price of Federalism*, New York: Twentieth Century Fund Book.

Poole, K. T. (2000). 'Non-Parametric Unfolding of Binary Choice Data'. *Political Analysis*, 8: 211–37.

——(2005). *Spatial models of parliamentary voting*, New York: Cambridge University Press.

——and Rosenthal, H. (1985). 'A Spatial Model for Legislative Roll Call Analysis'. *American Journal of Political Science*, 29: 357–84.

————(1997). *Congress: A Political-Economic History of Roll Call Voting*, New York: Oxford University Press.

Powell, B. (1983). *Contemporary Democracies*, Cambridge: Harvard University Press.

Preisendörfer, P. (1995). 'Vertrauen als soziologische Kategorie. Möglichkeiten und Grenzen einer entscheidungstheoretischen Fundierung des Vertrauenskonzepts'. *Zeitschrift für Soziologie*, 24: 263–72.

Rae, D. W., and Daudt, H. (1976). 'The Ostrogorski Paradox: a Peculiarity of Compound Majority Decision'. *European Journal of Political Research*, 4: 391–8.

Raunio, T. (2002). 'The European Parliament and supranational party system: A study in institutional development'. *West European Politics*, 25 (4): 242–3.

Ray, L. (2003). 'Reconsidering the Link between Incumbent Support and Pro-EU Opinion'. *European Union Politics*, 4 (3): 259–79.

Reif, K. (ed.) (1985). *Ten European Elections: Campaigns and Results of the 1979/1981 First Direct Elections to the European Parliament*, Aldershot: Gower.

——and Schmitt, H. (1980). 'Nine Second-Order National Elections. A Conceptual Framework for the Analysis of European Election Results'. *European Journal of Political Research*, 8: 3–44.

Renwick, A., and Tóka, G. (1998). 'East Meets West', in R. Jowell et al., *International Social Attitudes: The 15th British Social Attitudes Report*, Dartmouth: Aldershot, 149–71.

Riker, W. H. (1982). *Liberalism versus Populism: A Confrontation between the Theory of Democracy and the Theory of Social Choice*, San Francisco: W. H. Freeman.

References

Risse, T. (2002). 'Nationalism and Collective Identities. Europe Versus the Nation-State?', in P. Heywood, E. Jones and M. Rhodes (eds.), *Developments in West European Politics 2*. Houndmills: Palgrave.

Risse, T. (2005). 'Neofunctionalism, European Identity, and the Puzzles of European Integration'. *Journal of European Public Policy*, 12 (2): 291–309.

——and Van de Steeg, M. (2003). *An emerging European public sphere? Empirical Evidence and Theoretical Clarifications*. Paper presented at the International conference: Europeanisation of Public Spheres, Political Mobilisation, Public Communication and the European Union, Berlin.

Rohrschneider, R. (2002). 'The Democracy Deficit and Mass Support for an EU-Wide Government'. *American Journal of Political Science*, 46 (2): 463–75.

——and Whitefield, S. (2006). 'Political Parties, Public Opinion and European Integration in Post-Communist Countries: The State of the Art'. *European Union Politics*, 7 (1): 141.

——— (2008). *Understanding Cleavages in Party Systems: Issue Position and Issue Salience in 13 Post-Communist Democracies*. Paper presented at the conference on Representation, Immigration and the 2009 Election to the European Parliament. Bloomington.

Rose, R. (1995). 'Mobilizing Demobilized Voters in Post-Communist Societies'. *Party Politics*, 1 (4): 549–63.

——and Mishler, W. (1998). 'Negative and Positive Party Identification in Post-communist Countries'. *Electoral Studies*, 17: 217–34.

Rosenthal, H., and Voeten, E. (2004). 'Analyzing Roll Calls with Perfect Spatial Voting'. *The American Journal of Political Science*, 48 (3): 620–32.

Rothstein, B., and Uslaner, E. (2005). 'All for All: Equality, Corruption and Social Trust'. *World Politics*, 58: 41–72.

Sánchez-Cuenca, I. (2000). 'The Political Basis of Support for European Integration'. *European Union Politics*, 1 (2): 147–71.

Sani, G., and Sartori, G. (1983). 'Polarisation, Fragmentation and Competition in Western Democracies', in H. Daalder and P. Mair (eds.), *Western European Party Systems: Continuity and Change*. Beverly Hills/London: Sage.

Scharpf, F. W. (1996). 'Economic Integration, Democracy and the Welfare State'. *MPIfG Working Paper 96/2*.

—— (1999). *Governing Europe: Effective and Democratic?* Oxford: Oxford University Press.

—— (2003). 'Legitimate Diversity: The New Challenge of European Integration'. *Zeitschrift für Staats- und Europawissenschaften*, 1 (1): 32–60.

Scheuer, A. (1995). 'A Political Community?', in H. Schmitt and J. J. A. Thomassen (eds.), *Political Representation and Legitimacy in the European Union*. Oxford: Oxford University Press.

—— (2005). *How Europeans See Europe. Structure and Dynamics of European Legitimacy Beliefs*, Amsterdam: Amsterdam University Press.

References

Schlesinger, P. (1999). 'Changing Spaces of Political Communication: The Case of the European Union'. *Political Communication*, 16 (3): 263–79.

Schmidt, V. (2008). 'European Political Economy: Labour Out, State Back in, Firm to the Fore'. *West European Politics*, 32 (1/2): 302–20.

Schmitt, H. (Forthcoming). *Causes and consequences of ideological polarisation*, Mannheim: MZES (Ms).

—— and Mannheimer, R. (1991). 'About Voting and Non-voting in the European Parliament Elections of June 1989'. *European Journal of Political Research*, 19: 31–54.

—— Sanz, A. and Brann D. (2008). 'Micro-foundations of 2nd-order elections theory. A theoretical reconstruction and empirical test'. Paper prepared for presentation at the Fourth ECPR general Conference, Potsdam.

—— and Thomassen, J. J. A. (eds.). (1999). *Political Representation and Legitimacy in the European Union*, Oxford: Oxford University Press.

———— (2000). 'Dynamic representation: The Case of European Integration'. *European Union Politics*, 3 (1): 318–39.

Schmitt, H., and Van der Eijk, C. (2003). 'Die politische Bedeutung niedriger Beteiligungsraten bei Europawahlen: Eine empirische Studie über die Motive der Nichtwahl', in Hrsg. E. Roller, F. Brettschneider and J. van Deth, *Die Europäisierung der öffentlichen Meinung*. Opladen: Leske und Budrich.

———— (2007). 'Non-voting in European Parliament elections and support for European integration', in W. van der Brug and C. van der Eijk (eds.), *European Elections and Domestic Politics – Lessons from the Past and Scenarios for the Future*. Notre Dame: University of Notre Dame Press.

———— (2008). 'There is not much Euro-sceptic non-voting in European Parliament elections', in A. Sczcerbiak and P. Taggart (eds.), *Opposing Europe*, Vol. 2. Oxford: Oxford University Press.

—— and Wüst, A. M. (2006). 'The Bundestag election of 2005: The interplay of long-term trends and short-term factors'. *German Politics and Society*, 24: 27–46.

Schmitter, P. C. (2005). 'Ernst B. Haas and the Legacy of Neofunctionalism'. *Journal of European Public Policy*, 12 (2): 255–72.

Schulz-Forberg, H. (2007). 'The EU and the European public sphere: A historical reflection on a current issue', in H. A. Persson and B. Straath (eds.), *Reflections on Europe*. Brussels: Peter Lang, 183–200.

Schumpeter, J. (1976). *Capitalism, Socialism and Democracy*, London: George Allen & Unwin.

Semetko, H. A., Van der Brug, W., and Valkenburg, P. M. (2003). 'The Influence of Political Events on Attitudes Towards the European Union'. *British Journal of Political Science*, 33 (4): 621–34.

Shaw, J. (1997). 'Citizenship of the union: towards post-national membership?', *Jean Monnet Working Paper*, No.6/97, documented at: <http://www.jeanmonnet-program.org/papers/01/011401.html>

References

Sinnott, R. (1995). 'Policy, Subsidiarity and Legitimacy', in O. Niedermayer, and R. Sinnott (eds.), *Public Opinion and International Governance*, 2. Oxford: Oxford University Press, 246–76.

—— (2000). 'European Parliament Elections: Institutions, Attitudes, and Participation', in H. Agné, C. van der Eijk, B. Laffan, B. Lejon, P. Norris, H. Schmitt, and R. Sinnot (eds.), *Citizen Participation in European Politics* (Demokrati Utredningens skrift nr. 32). Stockholm: Statens Offentliga Utredningar.

Sitter, N. (2002). 'Cleavages, Party Strategy and Party System Change in Europe, East and West'. *Perspectives on European Politics and Society*, 3: 425–51.

Siune, K. (1983). 'The campaign on television: What was said and who said it?', in J. Blumler (ed.), *Communicating to voters. Television in the first European parliamentary elections*. London: Sage, 223–40.

Smith, J. (1999). *Europe's Elected Parliament*, Sheffield: Sheffield Academic Press.

Steenbergen, M., and Marks, G. (2004). 'Introduction: Models of political conflict in the European Union', in G. Marks and M. Steenbergen (eds.), *European Integration and Political Conflict*. Cambridge: Cambridge University Press.

Swenden, W. (2006). *Federalism and Regionalism in Western Europe: a comparative and thematic approach*, Basingstoke: Palgrave.

Szelényi, I., Fodor, É., and Hanley, E. (1997). 'Left Turn in Postcommunist Politics: Bringing Class Back In?' *East European Politics and Societies*, 11 (1): 190–224.

Tavits, M. (2008). 'On the linkage between electoral volatility and party system instability in Central and Eastern Europe'. *European Journal of Political Research*, 47: 537–55.

Thomassen, J. J. A. (1994). 'Empirical Research into Political Representation: Failing Democracy or Failing Models?', in W. E. Miller, M. K. Jennings and T. E. Mann (eds.), *Elections at Home and Abroad; Essays in Honor of Warren Miller*. Ann Arbor: University of Michigan Press.

—— Noury, A. G., and Voeten, E. (2004). 'Political Competition in the European Parliament: Evidence from Roll Call and Survey Analysis', in G. Marks and M. R. Steenbergen (eds.), *European Integration and Political Conflict*. Cambridge: Cambridge University Press, 141–64.

—— and Schmitt, H. (1997). 'Policy representation'. *European Journal of Political Research*, 32 (2): 165–84.

—— —— (1999a). 'Introduction: Political Representation and Legitimacy in the European Union', in H. Schmitt, and J. Thomassen (eds.), *Political Representation and Legitimacy in the European Union*. Oxford: Oxford University Press.

—— —— (1999b). 'In Conclusion', in H. Schmitt and J. J. A. Thomassen (eds.), *Political Representation and Legitimacy in the European Union*. Oxford: Oxford University Press.

—— —— (1999c). 'Partisan Structures in the European Parliament', in R. M. Katz and B. Wessels (eds.), *The European Parliament, the National Parliaments, and European Integration*. Oxford: Oxford University Press.

—— —— (2004). 'Democracy and Legitimacy in the European Union'. *Tidsskrift for Samfunnforskning*, 45 (2): 375–408.

Tillie, J. (1995). *Party Utility and Voting Behavior*, Amsterdam: Het Spinhuis.

Tóka, G. (1992). 'The Impact of the Religion Issue on Electoral Preferences in Hungary 1990–1991', in O. W. Gabriel and K. G. Troitzsch (eds.), *Wahlen in Zeiten des Umbruchs*. Frankfurt a.M.: Peter Lang, 331–77.

Tomka, M., and Zulehner, P. (1999). *Religion in den Reformlaendern Ost(Mittel) Europas. Gott nach dem Kommunismus*, Ostfildern: Schwabenverlag.

Trenz, H.- J. (2004). 'Media Coverage on European Governance Exploring the European Public Sphere in National Quality Newspapers'. *European Journal of Communication*, 19: 291–320.

—— and Eder, K. (2004). 'The Democratizing Dynamics of a European Public Sphere Towards a Theory of Democratic Functionalism'. *European Journal of Social Theory*, 7 (1): 5.

Valentino, N. A., Beckmann, M. N., and Buhr, T. A. (2001). 'A spiral of cynicism for some: The contingent effects of campaign news frames on participation and confidence in government'. *Political Communication*, 18 (4): 347–67.

Van der Brug, W. (2004). 'Issue Ownership and Party Choice'. *Electoral Studies*, 23 (2): 209–33.

—— Fennema, M., and Tillie, J. (2000). 'Anti-immigrant Parties in Europe: Ideological or Protest Vote'. *European Journal of Political Research*, 37: 77–102.

—— and Van der Eijk, C. (1999). 'The Cognitive Basis of Voting', in H. Schmitt and J. Thomassen (eds.), *Political Representation and Legitimacy in the European Union*. Oxford: Oxford University Press.

—— —— (eds.) (2007). *European Elections and Domestic Politics. Lessons from the Past and Scenarios for the Future*, Notre Dame: University of Notre Dame Press.

—— —— and Franklin, M. (2007). *The Economy and the Vote: Economic Conditions and Elections in 15 Countries*, Cambridge: Cambridge University Press.

—— Schmitt, H., Marsh, M., Franklin, M., Thomassen, J., Semetko, H., and Bartolini, S. (2007). 'European Elections, Domestic Politics, and European Integration', in W. van der Brug and C. van der Eijk (eds.), *European Elections and Domestic Politics. Lessons from the Past and Scenarios for the Future*. Notre Dame: University of Notre Dame Press.

Van der Eijk, C. (1984). 'Dutch voters and European elections in 1979 and 1984', in K. Reif (ed.), *European elections 1979/81 and 1984*. Berlin: Quorum Verlag.

—— (2002). 'Design Issues in Electoral Research: Taking Care of (Core) Business'. *Electoral Studies*, 21: 189–206.

—— and Franklin, M. N. (1996). *Choosing Europe? The European Electorate and National Politics in the Face of Union*, Ann Arbor: The University of Michigan Press.

—— —— (2004). 'Potential for Contestation on European Matters at National Elections in Europe', in G. Marks and M. R. Steenbergen (eds.), *European Integration and Political Conflict*. Cambridge: Cambridge University Press.

References

Van der Eijk, C. and Van der Brug, W. (1999). 'Policy Preferences and Party Choice', in H. Schmitt and J. Thomassen (eds.), *Political Representation and Legitimacy in the European Union*. Oxford: Oxford University Press.

—— Van der Brug, W., Kroh, M., and Franklin, M. (2006). 'Rethinking the Dependent Variable in Electoral Behavior — On the Measurement and Analysis of Utilities'. *Electoral Studies*, 25: 423–46.

Van Egmond, M. (2003). *Rain falls on all of us – but some manage to get more wet than others – Political context and electoral participation*. PhD dissertation. Amsterdam: University of Amsterdam.

Van Kersbergen, K. (2000). 'Political Allegiance and European Integration'. *European Journal of Political Research*, 37 (1): 1–17.

Voeten, E. (2005). *Legislator Preferences, Ideal Points and the Spatial Model in the European Parliament*. Working paper No. 6, Center on institutions and Governance. Berkeley: University of California.

Volkens, A. (2002). Manifesto Coding Instructions. Discussion Paper FS III 02-201, Berlin: WZB.

Weiler, J. H. H., Haltern, U. R., and Mayer, F. C. (1995). 'European Democracy and its Critique'. *West European Politics*, 18 (3): 4–39.

Wessels, B., and Kielhorn, A. (1999). 'Which Political Competencies for Which Political Level?', in R. Katz, and B. Wessels (eds.), *The European Parliament, National Parliaments, and European Integration*. Oxford: Oxford University Press, 174–97.

—— and Schmitt, H. (2000). 'Europawahlen, Europäisches Parlament und nationalstaatliche Demokratie: Formen und Folgen der Demokratisierung der Europäischen Union', in Hrsg. F. Neidhardt und H. - D. Klingemann, *Die Zukunft der Demokratie* (WZB-Jahrbuch 2000). Berlin: Sigma.

—— —— (2008). 'Meaningful Choices, Political Supply, and Institutional Effectiveness'. *Electoral Studies*, 27: 19–30.

White, S., Miller, B., Grødeland, Å., and Oates, S. (2000). 'Religion and Political Action in Postcommunist Europe'. *Political Studies*, 48: 681–705.

Whitten, G., Gabel, M., and Palmer, H. (1996). 'Euro-Pork': How EU Fiscal Policy Influences Public Support for European Integration'. *Presentation at the annual conference of the International Studies Association*: 18–22.

Wüst, A. M. and Volkens, A. (2003). *Euromanifesto Coding Instructions*, working papers. Mannheimer Zentrum für Europäische Sozialforschung, Vol. 64 Mannheim: MZES.

—— Schmitt, H. (2007). 'Comparing the views of parties and voters in the 1999 election to the European Parliament', in W. van der Brug and C. van der Eijk (eds.), *European Elections & Domestic Politics*. Notre Dame: University of Notre Dame Press.

Zielinski, J. (2002). 'Translating Social Cleavages into Party Systems: The Significance of New Democracies'. *World Politics*, 54: 184–211.

Index

Alesina, A. 130, 140
Almond, G. 132
Alter, K. J. 93
Althusius 118
Alvarez, R. M. 213, 214
Amsterdam Treaty 120
Anderson, C. J. 143, 144, 145, 154, 176, 188, 224
Andeweg, R. 12
Anselin 164
Arellano 163
Aristotle 118
Aspinwall, M. 138
Attina, F. 93

Bäck, H. E. 132
Baltagi 163
Banting, K. 134
Bartolini, S. 27, 237, 238, 241
Beck, N. 162, 163, 164, 205
Bednar, J. 144
Beetham, D. 2, 6, 7, 8, 44
Beichelt, T. 28
Benedict 188
Benoit, K. 30
Berg, L. 132
Beyers, J. 138
Bielasiak, J. 34
Birch, S. 27
Blondel, J. 211, 212, 223
Blumler, J. G. 209, 219
Bogdanor, V. 12
Bond 163
Boomgaarden, H. G. 50
Borre, O. 138
Börzel, T. 140
Brinegar, A. 144
Bruter, M. 132, 185, 188, 204
Budge, I. 42
Burgess, M. 118
Butler, D. M. 162, 163, 164

Carey, S. 145
Carrubba, C. J. 98
Christin, T. 145, 168
Citizenship, sense of 184, 187, 188, 190, 194, 203, 232
Citrin, J. 145
Cleavage dimensions 237
Cleavage structure 23, 26, 95, 221
Cohesion index 112
Collective identity 5, 185, 186
Collective identity, European 203
Collective identity, sense of 232
Commisso, E. 95
Community, sense of 186, 187, 188, 189, 190, 196, 197, 203
CONNEX 20
Constitutional Treaty 170, 204, 226, 233
Converse, Ph. E. 240

Dahl, R. A. 6, 10, 121, 132, 236
Dalton, R. J. 144, 145, 146, 151, 157, 158, 160, 166, 167, 168, 176, 221
Daudt, H. 10
De Hoyos 162
Delanty, G. 186
Delhey, J. 196, 198, 200, 201, 205, 206
Delors 119
Democracy, Madisonian theory of 6
Democracy, populist theory of 6
De-polarization 221
Deutsch, K. W. 19, 188, 189, 196
De Vreese, C. H. 45, 47, 48, 50, 52, 53, 59, 63, 219
De Winter, L. 139
Dickey 162
Dierickx, G. 138
Democratic legitimacy, dimensions of 3
Dobson, A. 118
Downs, A. 240
Driscoll, J. C. 155, 164
Duch, R. 144

263

Index

Easton, D. 3, 17, 44, 132, 142, 143, 147, 167, 168, 170, 186, 199, 225
Eder, K. 48, 50
Edwards, E. 166, 167
Egeberg, M. 138
Eichenberg, R. C. 144, 145, 146, 151, 157, 158, 160, 166, 167, 168, 176
Electoral democracy 4
Enyedi, Z. 40
Erbe, J. 47
Estella de Noriega 119
EU Constitution 120, 121
Eulau, H. 176, 178
Euromanifestos 35, 42
European citizenship 19, 186, 187, 188, 190, 203
European citizenship, sense of 195, 232
European community, sense of 19, 196, 203, 232
European demos 4, 8, 184, 186, 231, 237
European Election Studies 19
European identity 187, 188, 190, 231
European integration dimension, pro-/anti- 29, 31, 32, 34, 37, 107, 228, 236, 237, 239, 242, 243
European issues 12
European Parliament elections, visibility of 53, 54
European party groups, distinctiveness of 24, 28
European party groups/ party system, cohesion of 24, 28, 36, 39, 101, 228
European party system, competitiveness of the 36, 39, 228
European public sphere 15, 45, 46, 47, 49, 185, 228
European social capital 189
European Values Study 70, 89
Europe of the Regions 119
EU-sceptical parties 28
Euro-scepticism 108, 221, 236, 238
Euro-scepticism, mobilization of 241, 243
Evans, G. 27, 68, 95, 96
Expert survey 35

Federalism, theories of 118
Ferejohn, J. 144
Fichte 185
Fligstein, N. 135
Fodor, É. 68
Follesdal, A. 7, 239, 240
Fox, A. D. 219

Franklin, M. N. 19, 45, 65, 69, 78, 80, 85, 86, 145, 209, 210, 211, 216, 220, 221, 222, 223, 224, 228, 239
Freire 221
Fuchs, D. 65, 167, 168, 186, 187, 221
Fuller 162

Gabel, M. J. 143, 144, 154, 168, 178
Gamson, W. A. 168
Garrett, G. 144
Giscard d'Estaing, V. 139
Gijsberts, M. 68
Globalization/anti-globalization dimension 240, 241, 243
Goetz, K. 133
Goldsmith, M. 138
Granger 162
Greene 162
Grimm, D. 47
Gutiérrez, P. 145

Habermas, J. 15, 45, 46, 47, 187
Haesly, R. 145
Haltern, U. R. 4, 5
Handley, D. 168
Hanley, E. 68
Hegel 118
Henig, S. 39
Herder 185
Hix, S. 7, 30, 31, 39, 65, 93, 94, 95, 97, 98, 101, 102, 103, 106, 111, 112, 113, 133, 236, 237, 239, 240, 242
Hix–Lord model 29, 31, 35
Hoechle 164
Hooghe, L. 32, 40, 96, 119, 121, 134, 138, 142, 144, 145
Huber, J. 133
Hug, S. 138, 168
Hughes, J. 125

Inglehart, R. 96, 133, 135, 145, 190
Institutions, non-majoritarian 7
International relations model 29

Jolly, S. 144
Jones, E. 97

Kaase, M. 165
Kaltenthaler, K. C. 144
Kant 118
Kantner, C. 50
Kaplan, A. 212
Karasimeonov, G. 95
Katz, R. S. 19, 161, 162, 163, 205, 228

Index

Keating, M. 118, 125, 140
Keohane, R. D. 212
Kielhorn, A. 140
Kielmansegg, Graf P. 47, 185
Kiely, R. 188
King, G. 212
Kitschelt, H. 27, 68, 69, 96, 111, 144
Kittel 163
Kleinsteuber, H. J. 46
Klingemann, H.-D. 65, 68, 221
Klobucar, T. 68
König, T. 138
Koopmans, R. 48, 49
Kraay, A. C. 155, 164
Kreppel, A. 93
Kriesi, H. 31, 32, 121
Kymlickz, W. 134

Laeken declaration 18
Lawson, K. 95
Left-right dimension 16, 24, 29, 31, 32, 34, 37, 65, 66, 69, 85, 87, 107, 228, 229, 233, 234, 235, 236, 237, 238, 239, 240, 242, 243
Legitimacy, input oriented 4, 185
Legitimacy, method of assessing 1
Legitimacy of level of government/decision making 117, 121
Legitimacy, output-oriented 4
Lewis-Beck, M. S. 176, 178
Liberal democracy, principles of 2
Libertarian-authoritarian dimension 240
Lijphart, A. 221
Lincoln, Abraham 2, 4
Lindberg, L. N. 121
Lindström, U. 68
Lipset, S. M. 24, 95, 96, 135, 237
Lisbon Treaty 120, 226, 233
Llamazares, I. 145
Lodge, J. 119
Lord, C. 2, 3, 6, 7, 8, 31, 39, 44
Luhmann, N. 165

Maastricht Treaty 119, 121, 157, 158, 186, 187
Maddala 162
Mair, P. 27, 40
Majone, G. 6, 7, 44
Mannheimer, R. 210, 216
Marks, G. 29, 32, 93, 96, 107, 108, 110, 119, 121, 134, 142, 144, 145
Marsh, M. 132, 142, 143, 144, 145, 154, 169
Marshall, T. H. 188
Mateju, P. 68
Mayer, F. C. 4, 5

McCrone, D. 188
McElroy, G. 30
McGarry, J. 118
McLaren, L. M. 132, 145
Medrano, D. 143, 145
Menard, S. 215, 223
Mental map of Europe 197
Mershon, C. 40
Meulemann, H. 68
Mikhaylov, S. 132
Mill 118
Miller, A. H. 68
Mishler, W. 68, 83
Montesquieu 118
Moravcsik, A. 7, 8, 44
Mudde, C. 40
Müller-Rommel, F. 40
Mutual trust 189, 196, 198, 199, 201, 203, 232, 233

Nagler, J. 211, 212
Neidhardt, F. 47
Neo-functionalist approach 143
Netjes, C. E. 166, 167
Newbold, 162
Newey 164
New-politics dimension 32, 107
Newton, K. 201, 205
Niedermayer, O. 189, 198
Nieuwbeerta, P. 68
Norris, P. 121, 132, 133, 135, 167
Noury, A. G. 30, 93, 94, 95, 96, 97, 98, 101, 102, 103, 106, 111, 237
Novy, L. 48

Oates, W. E. 118
O'Leary, S. 187
Oppenhuis, E. 210, 211, 216
Ostrogorski paradox 10

Palmer, H. D. 143, 144, 168
Party competition, dimensions of 33
Party competition, structure of 103
Party democracy 9
Party government 9
Party government model 225, 226, 233, 234, 236, 242
Pasquino, G. 40
Permissive consensus 167
Peter, J. 50
Peters, B. 49, 50
Peterson, P. E. 117, 118
Polarization 224
Political community, sense of 186

Index

Political support, objects of 3, 44, 142, 165, 225
Poole, K. T. 103, 106
Post-Maastricht blues 166, 170, 182
Powell, B. 4, 236
Preisendörfer, P. 165
Proudhon 118
Public sphere 46

Rabier, J. R. 145
Rae, D. W. 10
Raunio, T. 93
Ray, L. 145
Regulated capitalism model 29
Regulatory state 6, 7
Reháková, B. 68
Reichert, M. S. 143, 144, 145, 154
Reif, K. 219, 235
Renwick, A. 87
Riker, W. H. 6
Risse, T. 48, 132, 145
Rohrschneider, R. 34, 145, 146
Rokkan, S. 24, 95, 96, 135
Roland, G. 93, 95, 97, 98, 101, 103, 106, 111
Roll-call behaviour 30, 229
Roll-call voting 94, 98, 99, 108
Rommele, A. 95
Rose, R. 68, 83
Rosenthal, H. 103, 106
Rothstein, B. 205

Saint-Simon 118
Sánchez-Cuenca, I. 145
Sani, G. 24
Sarafidis 163
Sartori, G. 24
Scharpf, F. W. 4, 5, 6, 121, 174, 175, 182, 185
Scheingold, S. A. 121
Scheuer, A. 147, 189, 197, 198, 215
Schlesinger, P. 47
Schmidt, V. 135
Schmitt, H. 6, 9, 12, 19, 23, 30, 31, 34, 93, 117, 134, 138, 210, 211, 216, 219, 221, 224, 228, 235, 238
Schmitter, P. C. 121
Schulz-Forberg, H. 46
Schumpeter, J. 4, 6, 240
Scope of EU government 121
Second-order national elections 219, 220, 235, 241
Semetko, H. A. 45, 50
Shaw, J. 188
Sides, J. 145
Sinnot, R. 121, 189, 211

Sitter, N. 40
Siune, K. 52
Smith, J. 213
Social community, sense of 186
Spinelli report 119
Steenbergen, M. 29, 93
Subsidiarity 118, 119, 120, 121, 125
Svenson, P. 211
Swenden, W. 118
Szelényi, I. 68

Taylor, M. 144
Tavits, M. 27, 221
Thomas Aquinas 118
Thomassen, J. J. A. 6, 9, 12, 19, 23, 30, 31, 65, 93, 96, 117, 132, 134, 138, 228, 237, 238
Tillie, J. 79
Tindemans report 119
Tocqueville 118
Tóka, G. 68, 87
Tomka, M. 68
Treaty establishing a Constitution for Europe 8
Treaty on European Union 9
Trechsel, A. H. 145
Trenz, H.-J. 49, 50
Trust in institutions, utilitarian explanation of 183
Trust in political institutions 165, 167, 170, 231, 232, 233
Tufte, E. 121

Uslaner, E. 207
Utilitarian explanation 178
Utilitarian perspective 144

Valentino, N. A. 45
Value orientations 69, 70
Van de Steeg, M. 49
Van der Brug, W. 19, 40, 65, 78, 80, 228, 235
Van der Eijk, C. 19, 40, 45, 65, 69, 78, 79, 80, 85, 86, 145, 210, 211, 212, 216, 223, 228, 239
Van Egmond, M. 224
Van Kersbergen, K. 145
Verba, S. 132, 212
Voeten, E. 30, 96, 98, 103, 237
Volkens, A. 42

Ward, D. S. 224
Wattenberg, M. P. 68
Wessels, B. 19, 132, 140, 210, 224, 228
Weiler, J. H. H. 4, 5

Index

Keating, M. 118, 125, 140
Keohane, R. D. 212
Kielhorn, A. 140
Kielmansegg, Graf P. 47, 185
Kiely, R. 188
King, G. 212
Kitschelt, H. 27, 68, 69, 96, 111, 144
Kittel 163
Kleinsteuber, H. J. 46
Klingemann, H.-D. 65, 68, 221
Klobucar, T. 68
König, T. 138
Koopmans, R. 48, 49
Kraay, A. C. 155, 164
Kreppel, A. 93
Kriesi, H. 31, 32, 121
Kymlickz, W. 134

Laeken declaration 18
Lawson, K. 95
Left-right dimension 16, 24, 29, 31, 32, 34, 37, 65, 66, 69, 85, 87, 107, 228, 229, 233, 234, 235, 236, 237, 238, 239, 240, 242, 243
Legitimacy, input oriented 4, 185
Legitimacy, method of assessing 1
Legitimacy of level of government/decision making 117, 121
Legitimacy, output-oriented 4
Lewis-Beck, M. S. 176, 178
Liberal democracy, principles of 2
Libertarian-authoritarian dimension 240
Lijphart, A. 221
Lincoln, Abraham 2, 4
Lindberg, L. N. 121
Lindström, U. 68
Lipset, S. M. 24, 95, 96, 135, 237
Lisbon Treaty 120, 226, 233
Llamazares, I. 145
Lodge, J. 119
Lord, C. 2, 3, 6, 7, 8, 31, 39, 44
Luhmann, N. 165

Maastricht Treaty 119, 121, 157, 158, 186, 187
Maddala 162
Mair, P. 27, 40
Majone, G. 6, 7, 44
Mannheimer, R. 210, 216
Marks, G. 29, 32, 93, 96, 107, 108, 110, 119, 121, 134, 142, 144, 145
Marsh, M. 132, 142, 143, 144, 145, 154, 169
Marshall, T. H. 188
Mateju, P. 68
Mayer, F. C. 4, 5

McCrone, D. 188
McElroy, G. 30
McGarry, J. 118
McLaren, L. M. 132, 145
Medrano, D. 143, 145
Menard, S. 215, 223
Mental map of Europe 197
Mershon, C. 40
Meulemann, H. 68
Mikhaylov, S. 132
Mill 118
Miller, A. H. 68
Mishler, W. 68, 83
Montesquieu 118
Moravcsik, A. 7, 8, 44
Mudde, C. 40
Müller-Rommel, F. 40
Mutual trust 189, 196, 198, 199, 201, 203, 232, 233

Nagler, J. 211, 212
Neidhardt, F. 47
Neo-functionalist approach 143
Netjes, C. E. 166, 167
Newbold, 162
Newey 164
New-politics dimension 32, 107
Newton, K. 201, 205
Niedermayer, O. 189, 198
Nieuwbeerta, P. 68
Norris, P. 121, 132, 133, 135, 167
Noury, A. G. 30, 93, 94, 95, 96, 97, 98, 101, 102, 103, 106, 111, 237
Novy, L. 48

Oates, W. E. 118
O'Leary, S. 187
Oppenhuis, E. 210, 211, 216
Ostrogorski paradox 10

Palmer, H. D. 143, 144, 168
Party competition, dimensions of 33
Party competition, structure of 103
Party democracy 9
Party government 9
Party government model 225, 226, 233, 234, 236, 242
Pasquino, G. 40
Permissive consensus 167
Peter, J. 50
Peters, B. 49, 50
Peterson, P. E. 117, 118
Polarization 224
Political community, sense of 186

265

Index

Political support, objects of 3, 44, 142, 165, 225
Poole, K. T. 103, 106
Post-Maastricht blues 166, 170, 182
Powell, B. 4, 236
Preisendörfer, P. 165
Proudhon 118
Public sphere 46

Rabier, J. R. 145
Rae, D. W. 10
Raunio, T. 93
Ray, L. 145
Regulated capitalism model 29
Regulatory state 6, 7
Reháková, B. 68
Reichert, M. S. 143, 144, 145, 154
Reif, K. 219, 235
Renwick, A. 87
Riker, W. H. 6
Risse, T. 48, 132, 145
Rohrschneider, R. 34, 145, 146
Rokkan, S. 24, 95, 96, 135
Roland, G. 93, 95, 97, 98, 101, 103, 106, 111
Roll-call behaviour 30, 229
Roll-call voting 94, 98, 99, 108
Rommele, A. 95
Rose, R. 68, 83
Rosenthal, H. 103, 106
Rothstein, B. 205

Saint-Simon 118
Sánchez-Cuenca, I. 145
Sani, G. 24
Sarafidis 163
Sartori, G. 24
Scharpf, F. W. 4, 5, 6, 121, 174, 175, 182, 185
Scheingold, S. A. 121
Scheuer, A. 147, 189, 197, 198, 215
Schlesinger, P. 47
Schmidt, V. 135
Schmitt, H. 6, 9, 12, 19, 23, 30, 31, 34, 93, 117, 134, 138, 210, 211, 216, 219, 221, 224, 228, 235, 238
Schmitter, P. C. 121
Schulz-Forberg, H. 46
Schumpeter, J. 4, 6, 240
Scope of EU government 121
Second-order national elections 219, 220, 235, 241
Semetko, H. A. 45, 50
Shaw, J. 188
Sides, J. 145
Sinnot, R. 121, 189, 211

Sitter, N. 40
Siune, K. 52
Smith, J. 213
Social community, sense of 186
Spinelli report 119
Steenbergen, M. 29, 93
Subsidiarity 118, 119, 120, 121, 125
Svenson, P. 211
Swenden, W. 118
Szelényi, I. 68

Taylor, M. 144
Tavits, M. 27, 221
Thomas Aquinas 118
Thomassen, J. J. A. 6, 9, 12, 19, 23, 30, 31, 65, 93, 96, 117, 132, 134, 138, 228, 237, 238
Tillie, J. 79
Tindemans report 119
Tocqueville 118
Tóka, G. 68, 87
Tomka, M. 68
Treaty establishing a Constitution for Europe 8
Treaty on European Union 9
Trechsel, A. H. 145
Trenz, H.-J. 49, 50
Trust in institutions, utilitarian explanation of 183
Trust in political institutions 165, 167, 170, 231, 232, 233
Tufte, E. 121

Uslaner, E. 207
Utilitarian explanation 178
Utilitarian perspective 144

Valentino, N. A. 45
Value orientations 69, 70
Van de Steeg, M. 49
Van der Brug, W. 19, 40, 65, 78, 80, 228, 235
Van der Eijk, C. 19, 40, 45, 65, 69, 78, 79, 80, 85, 86, 145, 210, 211, 212, 216, 223, 228, 239
Van Egmond, M. 224
Van Kersbergen, K. 145
Verba, S. 132, 212
Voeten, E. 30, 96, 98, 103, 237
Volkens, A. 42

Ward, D. S. 224
Wattenberg, M. P. 68
Wessels, B. 19, 132, 140, 210, 224, 228
Weiler, J. H. H. 4, 5

Index

West 164
White, S. 68
Whitefield, S. 27, 34, 95, 96, 146
Whitten, G. 143, 144, 178
Wilson, C. 32, 134
Wilson, S. E. 162, 163, 164
Winner 163
Wooldridge 163
World Values Survey 201
Wu 162, 163
Wüst, A. M. 31, 42, 221

Zielinski, J. 96
Zulehner, P. 68